Alternative Energy Strategies

John Hagel, III

The Praeger Special Studies program—utilizing the most modern and efficient book production techniques and a selective worldwide distribution network—makes available to the academic, government, and business communities significant, timely research in U.S. and international economic, social, and political development.

Alternative Energy Strategies

Constraints and Opportunities

PRAEGER SPECIAL STUDIES IN INTERNATIONAL ECONOMICS AND DEVELOPMENT

Praeger Publishers   New York   Washington   London

Library of Congress Cataloging in Publication Data

Hagel, John.
    Alternative energy strategies.

    (Praeger special studies in international economics
and development)
    Bibliography: p.
    Includes index.
    1. Energy policy—United States—Collected works.
2. Energy policy—Collected works.   3. Power resources—
United States—Collected works.   4. Power resources—
Collected works.   I. Title.
HD9502.U52H332   1976   333.7'0973   75-23968
ISBN 0-275-56090-2

PRAEGER PUBLISHERS
111 Fourth Avenue, New York, N.Y. 10003, U.S.A.

Published in the United States of America in 1976
by Praeger Publishers, Inc.

Printed in the United States of America

for my family

This book represents a revised and updated version of a study initially prepared under the auspices of the Petroleum Information Foundation in New York and privately distributed by the foundation throughout the international petroleum industry. This book summarizes the current status and future direction of energy research and development and investment strategies in the context of several possible scenarios regarding the availability and cost of crude oil imports. While it focuses on trends in the United States, consideration is also given to the two other primary energy-consuming areas of the non-Communist world—Western Europe and Japan—in order to evaluate the variations in policy that may arise in these areas as a result of differing conditions and to anticipate the impact of these policies on the world energy market.

The first chapter summarizes recent trends in the world energy market in order to provide a framework for the analysis that follows. Following chapters review the status of current development programs in alternative energy sources and suggest energy strategies that might be implemented using three different sets of assumptions regarding the availability and cost of crude oil imports.

My hope was to provide the layman with a comprehensive survey of the opportunities and constraints that will influence the formulation of alternative energy strategies. In practice, this has presented a persistent dilemma as to the degree of technical complexity to adopt in explaining the issues involved, particularly in the area of alternative energy research and development. I have generally sought to minimize the amount of technical knowledge the reader must bring with him in order to follow recent developments in this field while providing detailed footnotes for those who are interested in pursuing this work in greater detail. I hope I have succeeded in providing a general introduction to the subject while not sacrificing a sense of the complexity underlying every dimension of the field.

I am indebted to countless individuals, both in the petroleum industry and in various academic institutions, for the invaluable assistance they provided in the preparation of this book. While my debts are broadly distributed, there are several individuals to whom I am particularly grateful. Were it not for Jack Hayes at Mobil Oil Corporation and Jack Whittlesey at the Petroleum Information Foundation, this study would never have been launched. It was their confidence that gave me the initial opportunity to undertake this research. My greatest debt, however, remains to my family and close friends, without whose moral support this book would never have reached completion.

It is necessary to add that any deficiencies of this study are exclusively my own responsibility and that the views expressed herein are not necessarily shared by those who assisted me in its preparation.

LIST OF TABLES

LIST OF FIGURES

LIST OF ABBREVIATIONS

AEC	Atomic Energy Commission
AECL	Atomic Energy of Canada, Ltd.
AGR	advanced gas-cooled reactor
ATR	advanced thermal reactor
BHP	biological hazard potential
Btu	British thermal unit
BWR	boiling water reactor
CANDU	Canadian Deuterium Uranian (reactor)
CEGB	Central Electricity Generating Board
ECCS	emergency core cooling system
EEC	European Economic Community
EIA	Energy Independence Authority
EPA	Environmental Protection Agency
ERDA	Energy Research and Development Association
FBR	fast breeder reactor
FEA	Federal Energy Administration
f.o.b.	free on board
FPC	Federal Power Commission
GCFR	gas-cooled fast breeder reactor
GCOS	Great Canadian Oil Sands, Ltd.
HTGR	high-temperature gas-cooled reactor
HTR	high-temperature reactor
IEA	International Energy Agency
LMFBR	liquid metal fast breeder reactor
LNG	liquefied natural gas
LOCA	loss of coolant accident
LWR	light water reactor
MHD	magnetohydrodynamic
MIT	Massachusetts Institute of Technology
NASA	National Aeronautics and Space Administration
NPC	National Petroleum Council
NPE	net propulsion efficiency
NURE	National Uranium Resource Evaluation
OECD	Organization for Economic Cooperation and Development
OPEC	Organization of Petroleum Exporting Countries
OTA	Office of Technology Assessment
PWR	pressurized water reactor
RANN	Research Applied to National Needs
SGHWR	steam generating heavy water reactor
SWU	separative work units
TVA	Tennessee Valley Authority

Alternative Energy Strategies

RECENT TRENDS IN THE WORLD ENERGY MARKET

GENERAL TRENDS

Over the past century, one of the most salient features of the evolution of energy consumption throughout the world has been the emergence of fossil fuels—coal, crude oil, and natural gas as the primary source of energy. In the United States, wood accounted for more than 90 percent of all fuel sources as recently as 1850, while fossil fuels (coal) represented less than 10 percent. By 1925, fossil fuels had replaced wood as the source of 90 percent of U.S. energy supplies, and coal, crude oil, and natural gas have preserved this dominant role up to the present day.[1]

Several trends have characterized the world energy market since World War II: (1) high growth rates in aggregate energy demand accompanied by ample reserves of energy resources, (2) a progressive shift from coal to crude oil as the primary fossil fuel, (3) the rapid emergence of natural gas in overall energy consumption during the period 1955-70, and (4) unanticipated delays in the commercial development of the major short-term alternative to fossil fuels—nuclear energy. According to the British Petroleum Company's *Statistical Review of the World Oil Industry: 1974*, world consumption of energy reached approximately 6.1 billion tons of oil equivalent in 1974, and the United States alone consumed the equivalent of approximately 1.8 billion tons of oil in total energy.[2]

CRUDE OIL

Oil has supplied the major share of world energy demand growth since 1950—about 60 percent overall. This is due to a variety of factors—primarily the flexibility and economic advantage of oil in serving a broad spectrum of energy needs. Furthermore, with the rapid increase in aggregate energy demand, policies adopted by major consuming governments have placed constraints on the production and consumption of coal and have inhibited expansion of natural gas supplies. Prolonged delays in the introduction of commercial nuclear energy have shifted more of the burden of satisfying energy demand to oil.

It is particularly hazardous to anticipate future energy trends in view of the recent dramatic transformations in international petroleum markets. Even so, world consumption of energy will probably grow at a faster rate than U.S. consumption. Various estimates of growth in world energy demand suggest that it will be in the range of roughly 3.5 to 5 percent per year, while the U.S. annual growth has been estimated at between 2 and 3.5 percent.* In attempting to project the outlook for world energy demand, it is especially difficult to assess the participation of various energy resources in the overall market. This has been further complicated by two significant developments in the geography of crude oil during the past decade.

First, the Middle East has gradually emerged as the world's major producing region for crude oil, but even more importantly, it also possesses the largest share of worldwide "published proved" reserves.† At the end of 1974, its "published

---

*These estimates of growth in energy demand were revised downward significantly in the period following the dramatic price rises in Organization of Petroleum Exporting Countries (OPEC) crude oil which occurred in 1971-74. For example, pre-1972 projections anticipated an annual growth in world energy demand in the range of 4 to 6 percent. Revised estimates issued by the Organization for Economic Cooperation and Development (OECD) for annual growth in world energy demand are now in the range of 3.8 percent, compared with earlier estimates of 4.9 percent (*Nuclear News* 18 [February 1975]: 32). Similarly, estimates made in 1972 by the National Petroleum Council (NPC) of annual growth of U.S. energy demand were in the range of 3.4 to 4.4 percent, while more recent estimates suggest that annual growth will continue at much lower rates of 2 to 3.5 percent per year (National Petroleum Council, Committee on U.S. Energy Outlook, *U.S. Energy Outlook* [Washington, D.C., 1972], p. 36). For more recent estimates, see *Petroleum Intelligence Weekly*, May 26, 1974, p. 6; and *Petroleum Economist* 16 (October 1974): 404-05.

†A recent study suggests that "published proved" reserves statistics may seriously understate the ultimate recoverable reserves located in the Middle East, and if this is true, the Middle Eastern share of world crude oil reserves may prove to be even larger than is currently believed (Z.R. Beydoun and H.V. Dunnington, *The Petroleum Geology and Resources of the Middle East* [Beaconfield, England: Scientific Press, 1975]).

proved" reserves were estimated to represent 56 percent of the world total, while one country alone—Saudi Arabia—possessed almost one-fourth of the world reserves.[3] A survey of world "published proved" oil reserves at the end of 1974 is provided in Table 1.1, while Figure 1.1 summarizes world oil production patterns in 1973 and 1974.

These statistics should not be overemphasized, however, since the 1973 Arab oil boycott and recent price increases will intensify non-Middle Eastern exploration investment and may result in the discovery of important new reserves in other areas. The *Petroleum Economist* has estimated that by 1980, several new crude oil-producing regions outside the existing OPEC countries could contribute 9 million barrels per day of crude oil to world supplies, or approximately 25 percent of current shipments of crude oil from exporting nations to importing nations.[4] Nevertheless, experience in such diverse areas as the North Sea, the North Slope in Alaska, and the Amazon basin suggests that these additional reserves will constitute significantly higher cost sources of production.* Excluding major unanticipated new discoveries, the Middle East will fulfill progressively larger shares of petroleum product demand in the primary consuming regions over at least the next decade.

The second development has been the growth of the position of the United States as a substantial net importer of both crude oil and refined products. Imports (on a net basis) supplied about 9 percent of U.S. domestic consumption in 1950, compared with about 36 percent in 1975.[5] U.S. oil imports reached a high of 6.2 million barrels per day in 1973 and then declined slightly to 6.1 million barrels per day in 1974. Federal Energy Administration (FEA) estimates indicated that 1975 oil imports would rise to 6.3 million barrels and that oil imports would rise to 6.3 million barrels and that oil imports in 1977 will range between 6.3 and 7.6 million barrels per day, depending on measures adopted by the U.S. government in the interim. Domestic crude oil production has declined from a peak of 11.7 million barrels per day in 1972 to an estimated 10.4 million barrels per day in 1975. Although recent price increases have stimulated new exploratory drilling and intensified the development of existing fields, additional crude oil as a result of these activities will probably not come on stream for several years.[6]

---

*An OECD report estimated that the cost of the production of crude oil from offshore fields in the North Sea would range between $1.25 and $8 per barrel (in 1973 dollars) depending on the depth of the water (Organization for Economic Cooperation and Development, *Energy Research and Development: Problems and Perspectives* [Paris, 1975], cited in *Petroleum Intelligence Weekly*, March 10, 1975, pp. 2-3). Another study stated that increments of crude oil production capacity in the Middle East, Nigeria, and Libya can currently be added at costs ranging from $300 to $2,000 for each barrel per day of capacity, depending on the location of the field, in contrast with comparable costs of $2,800 to $3,200 for North Sea fields and $5,000 to $8,000 for offshore fields in the United States (Robert E. Geiger and John D. Moody, "Petroleum Resources: How Much Oil and Where?" *Technology Review* 77 [March-April 1975] : 39-45).

TABLE 1.1

World "Published Proved" Oil Reserves at End of 1974

Country/Area	Thousand Million Tons	Thousand Million Barrels	Share of Total (percentage)
United States	5.3	40.6	5.4
Canada	1.1	8.8	1.2
Caribbean	2.6	2.7	18.4
Other Western Hemisphere	3.1	22.2	3.1
Total Western Hemisphere	12.1	90.0	12.4
Western Europe	3.5	26.3	3.6
Middle East	55.0	403.4	56.3
Africa	9.1	68.3	9.3
Soviet Union	11.4	83.4	11.6
Eastern Europe	0.4	3.0	0.4
China	3.4	25.0	3.5
Other Eastern Hemisphere	2.8	21.0	2.9
Total Eastern Hemisphere	85.6	630.4	87.6
World (excluding Soviet Union, Eastern Europe, and China)	82.5	609.0	84.5
World	97.7	720.4	100.0

Note: Proved reserves are generally taken to be the volume of oil remaining in the ground which geological and engineering information indicates with reasonable certainty to be recoverable from known reservoirs under existing economic and operating conditions.

The recovery factor, that is, the relationship between proved reserves and total oil in place, varies according to local conditions and can vary in time with economic and technological changes.

For the United States and Canada the data include oil, which it is estimated can be recovered from proved natural gas reserves.

The data exclude the oil content of shales and tar sands.

Sources: American Petroleum Institute for the United States, Canadian Petroleum Association for Canada, and estimates published by the *Oil & Gas Journal* for all other areas. Table originally published in British Petroleum, *Statistical Review of the World Oil Industry–1974* (London, 1975), p. 4.

FIGURE 1.1

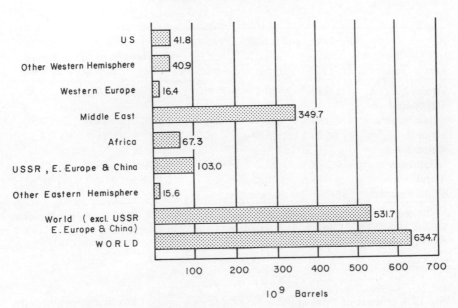

World "Published Proved" Oil Reserves at End of 1973
(thousand million barrels)

U S	41.8
Other Western Hemisphere	40.9
Western Europe	16.4
Middle East	349.7
Africa	67.3
USSR , E. Europe & China	103.0
Other Eastern Hemisphere	15.6
World (excl. USSR E. Europe & China)	531.7
W O R L D	634.7

10^9 Barrels

Increasing import volumes have been accompanied by a shift to greater dependence on oil from the Eastern Hemisphere, particularly from the Middle East and Africa. In 1973, the United States drew approximately 36 percent of its oil imports from the Eastern Hemisphere, and the NPC has estimated that by 1985 this share could rise to 75 percent.[7]

If anything, these trends have accelerated in the post-1973 embargo period. Statistics for 1974 compiled by the Bureau of Mines indicate that crude oil imports from the Persian Gulf and Africa rose from 46 percent of U.S. crude oil imports in early 1973 to 60 percent (these statistics exclude crude shipments to Caribbean refineries and petroleum product imports). By late 1974, Nigeria had emerged as the leading foreign crude oil source for the United States, followed by Canada and Saudi Arabia.[8] Table 1.2 provides a comparison of regional sources of U.S. crude oil imports during June-October 1973 and June-October 1974. An FEA study for the first quarter of 1975 revealed that Saudi Arabia had become the leading foreign crude oil supplier to the United States on a direct-shipment basis, accounting

TABLE 1.2

Regional Sources of Direct U.S. Oil imports
(thousands of barrels per day)

Direct Source	June-October 1974	Percentage of imports	Percentage of demand	June-October 1973	Percentage of imports	Percentage of demand
Arab countries	1,356.3	20.3	8.2	1,310.6	19.0	7.8
Other Eastern Hemisphere	2,194.1	32.9	13.3	1,655.7	14.0	9.8
Canada	906.3	13.6	5.5	1,285.8	18.7	7.6
Other Western Hemisphere	2,218.3	33.2	13.5	2,640.4	38.3	15.6
Total imports	6,674.8	100.0	40.5	6,892.5	100.0	40.8
Total demand	16,483.0	–	–	16,873.0	–	–

Source: *Petroleum Intelligence Weekly*, December 30, 1974, p. 5. Reprinted in Ragaei El Mallakh, "American-Arab Relations: Conflict or Cooperation?" *Energy Policy* 3 (September 1975): 173.

for 13.4 percent of total imports.[9] The decision of the Canadian government to reduce its oil exports to the United States by one-third in January 1976 and to terminate its exports to the United States entirely by 1981 will almost certainly increase U.S. dependence on Eastern Hemisphere sources of crude oil even further.[10] The evolving pattern of U.S. crude oil imports in the period 1930-74 is depicted in Figure 1.2.

These trends have developed despite the existence of sufficient domestic crude oil resources to support substantial increases in production. However, the production cost structure and the impact of government regulation (particularly leasing and environmental restrictions) have inhibited domestic exploration and production while encouraging greater reliance on petroleum imports.* Efforts to

---

*During 1975, domestic production of crude oil declined by 5 percent, while imports rose by 17 percent to 7.4 million barrels per day (*Science* 187 [January 10, 1975] : 42). A recently instituted federal program for leasing areas on the outer continental shelf for oil

FIGURE 1.2

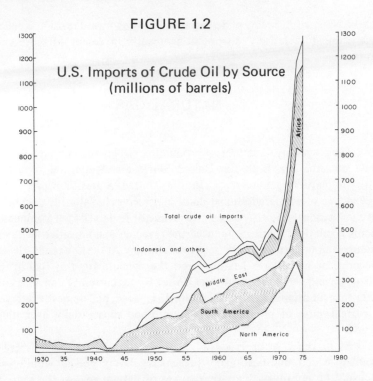

U.S. Imports of Crude Oil by Source
(millions of barrels)

Source: Twentieth Century Petroleum Statistics–1975 (Dallas: DeGolyer and Mac-Naughton, 1975).

develop Alaskan and offshore crude oil reserves in the future will further increase the cost of domestic production. The Bureau of Mines estimates that by 1985, 30 percent of crude oil production in the lower 48 states will be located in offshore areas, in contrast to 18 percent today.[11]

One difficulty that has hampered the formulation of energy policy involves the continuing uncertainty over the size of the domestic crude oil resource base. If this base is relatively limited, additional incentives to stimulate more aggressive domestic exploration may not yield significant increments to existing reserves. In this regard, the U.S. Geological Survey released revised estimates of U.S. "undiscovered recoverable resources" of crude oil in May 1975, which represented a decrease of its 1974 estimates of from 200 to 400 billion barrels to 50 to 127 billion barrels. The later estimate is more consistent with those of the oil industry

---

exploration and production is expected to increase the amount of acreage leased by the federal government in the next decade to a level five times greater than all federal government leasing in the past 20 years, and this should remove a major obstacle to the expansion of domestic exploration efforts (*Science* 188 [April 11, 1975] : 135).

and the National Academy of Sciences, and the downward revision is believed to be largely due to relatively disappointing results in recent offshore exploration efforts.[12]

NATURAL GAS

The geography of natural gas production displays certain similarities with the crude oil situation. Both the United States and Western Europe have major domestic natural gas reserves. In the United States, however, exploration expenditure to locate additional domestic reserves has steadily declined over the last two decades, primarily as a consequence of Federal Power Commission (FPC) pricing regulations that have reduced the revenues and incentive necessary for gas producers to undertake additional exploration.[13] At the same time, the artificially low price of natural gas has increased the demand for this fuel in relation to petroleum and coal. As a result, the United States currently consumes natural gas faster than additional reserves are being discovered, and domestic reserve capacity at current rates of production has diminished substantially over the last two decades.

As in the case of crude oil, there is considerable controversy over the extent to which modifications of present regulatory policies would result in the discovery of additional domestic reserves of natural gas. At the same time that the U.S. Geological Survey revised its estimates of "undiscovered recoverable resources" of domestic crude oil downward, it issued similar revisions in its estimates of "undiscovered recoverable resources" for natural gas. Whereas in 1974 it had estimated that 990 to 2,000 trillion cubic feet of recoverable natural gas resources remained to be discovered, the new estimates lowered these figures to 322 to 655 trillion cubic feet.[14] In Western Europe, production of natural gas is expected to increase rapidly over the next five years and then begin to stabilize, unless major additional discoveries of reserves are reported in the North Sea or elsewhere.[15]

Demand for natural gas, however, will remain high in view of its desirable qualities as a fuel. As a consequence of the supply/demand factors in the major consuming regions and technological advances in the liquefaction and maritime transportation of natural gas, it is probable that international trade in liquefied natural gas (LNG) will expand during the late 1970s. Overall investment and operating cost projects for liquefaction, transportation, and delivery of LNG have risen sharply over the past year or so, and the economics of LNG imports into some important markets are no longer as favorable as had previously been estimated.

The NPC, for example, estimated that natural gas imports to the United States might reach 5.9 to 6.6 trillion cubic feet per year by 1985, accounting for 15 to 29 percent of domestic consumption.[16] Current informed estimates run about half this amount.[17] Among the major exporters of natural gas will be Algeria, Libya, Nigeria, Indonesia, and the Soviet Union, as well as the Middle Eastern oil-producing countries.

IMPLICATIONS OF RECENT PRICE CHANGES

The projections of greater reliance on crude oil imports over the next decade are particularly disturbing in the context of recent transformations in the world petroleum price structure. The increasing dependence of the major consuming areas on crude oil imports from OPEC countries and the absence of satisfactory short-run substitutes created favorable conditions for substantial increases in the price of crude oil from these countries. In addition, several short-term supply constraints that emerged in the Middle East during 1970 provided the final impetus for the producing governments to demand the substantial increases in the "posted" price* of crude oil that were granted in the Teheran and Tripoli agreements of early 1971. A series of subsequent negotiations and the major supply disruptions created by the Arab petroleum production cutbacks and selective boycott in late 1973 further raised the price of crude oil exports from OPEC countries. The posted price for Arabian light crude free on board (f.o.b.) at Ras Tanura escalated from $1.80 per barrel in December 1969 to $11.65 per barrel in January 1974. In a series of more moderate price rises in 1974 and early 1975, the posted price for Arabian light crude escalated even further to $12.37 per barrel in October 1975. Other major exporters of crude oil have correspondingly raised their posted prices, with adjustments for quality and freight differentials.[18] Market prices currently range from the posted level to somewhat lower than this posted level, representing increases over historical levels roughly comparable to those for posted prices.

When these unprecedented increases in crude oil prices were originally announced, economists and political leaders expressed great concern over the serious problems such developments might raise for the balance-of-payments situation in the major consuming countries. Similarly, many felt that the sudden, rapid growth of government revenues in the Middle Eastern countries might

---

*"Posted" prices are prices for crude oil that are formally quoted by producing companies and these prices serve as the basis for computing the tax obligations of private oil companies engaged in the production and export of crude oil. As such, posted prices are a major issue in negotiations between international oil companies and oil exporting governments. However, market prices—the prices at which crude oil is actually sold—often differ considerably from the posted prices.

substantially reduce incentives for several of these countries, in particular Saudi Arabia, to expand production at the rate necessary to satisfy the growth in demand.[19]

Recent trends, however, indicate that these problems may not be as severe as many had originally anticipated. A combination of high crude oil prices and economic recession in the industrialized consuming nations resulted in a 2.5 percent drop in crude oil exports from the major oil-exporting countries in 1973-74, whereas crude exports had been expected to increase by 7.5 percent over the same period. As a consequence, the estimated revenues of the major oil-exporting countries were $88.8 billion, in comparison with forecasts of revenues totaling $98.4 billion.[20]

Even more important, import expenditures by the major oil-exporting countries have increased at a very rapid rate, thereby further reducing the balance-of-payments problems confronted by the industrialized oil-consuming countries. Morgan Guaranty Trust has issued a study that is highly critical of earlier estimates of massive cash surpluses accumulating in the OPEC nations. It points out that lower exports and higher imports have combined to nearly halve the rate at which OPEC countries are accumulating cash surpluses—from $17 billion in the fourth quarter of 1974 to $9 billion in the first quarter of 1975.[21]

While economic recovery in the oil-consuming nations may once again stimulate the growth of oil exports from the OPEC countries, it is doubtful that this growth will reach the rates that had been predicted. In any event, for the moment, considerably less attention is being paid to the need to provide the OPEC nations with the incentives necessary to expand their productive capacity. Instead, the OPEC nations are demonstrating growing concern over the evidence of a surplus-producing capacity that may gradually erode the posted price structure for crude oil.

While the impact of the crude oil price increases on the international economic system has not been as catastrophic as some had warned, it is nevertheless true that the sudden shift of monetary resources to the OPEC countries has generated certain strains in the system as it seeks to adjust itself to the new situation. The less developed economies of the Middle Eastern producing countries possess only limited short-term absorptive capabilities for productive domestic investment. Development plan budgets are being steadily expanded, but critical bottlenecks for additional investment have already begun to emerge in such areas as skilled manpower and construction capabilities. Unable to expand domestic investment beyond a certain rate, many producing countries must divert their massive petroleum revenues into the international capital markets. Up until now, however, most producing governments have demonstrated a marked reluctance to undertake long-term investment outside their own countries. As a result, they have adopted financial policies oriented primarily to maintaining a position of short-term liquidity. In view of the recent instability of the international currency markets and continuing inflation, these financial policies entail considerable risks which increasingly concern the Middle Eastern governments.

While such difficulties in discovering profitable investment opportunities for the cash surpluses accumulating in OPEC countries may contribute to the reluctance of some of these countries to expand their productive capacity in response to future increases in demand, the producing countries do not all have the same ability to absorb additional revenues. Several, including Iran, Iraq, Algeria, and Indonesia, have major incentives to continue to expand production so that they can finance ambitious development programs for their populous countries. Moreover, the difficulties experienced by other countries in locating productive outlets for their revenues are, to some degree, short-term in nature, resulting from a sudden and unprecedented expansion of government revenues. Nevertheless, the consuming nations will confront an important challenge over the next decade as they restructure the international economic system to adjust to the new flows of monetary resources and to provide incentives for a steady expansion of Middle East crude oil production to meet the future growth in demand for crude oil.

Economic considerations are not the only factors in determining the availability of increasing crude oil supplies from the Middle East, however. Political instability in the Middle East, especially the persistent tensions generated by the Arab-Israeli conflict, limit the reliability of crude oil imports from this region. It would be premature to dismiss the possibility of future breaks of hostilities until a permanent settlement has been achieved—particularly until a satisfactory resolution of the Palestinian refugee problem has been negotiated. The magnitude of the Arab-Israeli conflict has furthermore overshadowed two additional sources of political instability: inter-Arab rivalries and the possibility of domestic upheavals. The interests of national security place a high priority on reliable energy supplies, and increasing dependence on crude oil imports from this unstable region is a situation that should be avoided if at all possible.

Current trends therefore indicate continuing expansion of demand for petroleum and natural gas in the consuming countries over the next decade, accompanied by increasing dependence on high-cost and potentially unreliable imports. Economic and national security considerations make this an undesirable energy supply pattern, and it is therefore necessary to examine possible alternative sources as a basis for evaluating the policy options available to the consuming governments.

CONTINUED UNCERTAINTY OVER
FUTURE PRICE TRENDS

Before proceeding, it is necessary to emphasize the enormous degree of uncertainty involved in any comparative economic evaluation of alternative energy sources. Such an analysis requires the forecasting of total energy demand and the evaluation of relative resource economics involving, for various forms of energy, consumer prices, investment requirements, and operating costs. At the present time, none of these factors can be predicted with confidence. There is no way of knowing with certainty, for example, what future levels of crude oil prices will be, nor can the impact of oil prices on consumer demand or competitive energy development be accurately foretold. Worldwide inflation has pushed up investment and operating costs. Lead times required for the design and construction of facilities are growing to five years and more. Opposition on environmental grounds to many projects for development of energy resources is strong. There is a pervasive uncertainty about the future course of the economies of virtually every individual country and the world economy as a whole. Finally, and perhaps most important of all as regards mobilizing the huge amounts of capital required for energy investment, there is a lack of clear-cut government policy and direction in dealing with energy problems.

As an illustration of the prevailing uncertainty in evaluating the energy outlook in the United States, in December 1972 the NPC published a comprehensive study entitled *U.S. Energy Outlook*, which, under normal circumstances, would have been expected to serve as a reliable guide to the economics of U.S. alternative energy resources for some years to come.[22] Less than two years later, in September 1974, the NPC issued a report entitled *Emergency Preparedness for Interruption of Petroleum Imports into the United States*, in which the "high" projection of U.S. energy consumption to 1985 and beyond was very close to the "low" growth forecast given in the 1972 report.[23] It is also generally recognized among authorities in the field that the 1972 NPC forecasts of investment and lead times required for significant development of non-oil alternative energy resources in the United States are no longer valid.[24]

In November 1973, President Richard M. Nixon announced "Project Independence," aimed at attaining U.S. self-sufficiency in energy by 1980. This target was soon criticized as being unrealistic, although a report submitted to the president in December 1973 by the chairman of the Atomic Energy Commission (AEC) concluded that national energy self-sufficiency could be attained by 1985, provided that a five-year, $10 billion energy research and development program were adopted.[25] By way of contrast, in November 1974, the FEA sent to President Gerald Ford their *Project Independence Blueprint*, which neither set forth a national energy policy nor recommended specific programs or target dates but rather outlined an array of options and the results that exercising them could achieve by 1985 and after.[26] The blueprint does focus on the importance of various elements in the task of developing and implementing energy policy and on the uncertainties involved in predicting them. It recognizes both the importance of crude oil prices and their unpredictability but evaluates differences in the U.S. energy demand and supply outlook to 1985 and related economics at world prices of $7 and $11 per barrel. The FEA blueprint is an important document and should be useful in the development of U.S. energy policy.

More recently, President Ford sought to revive the objective of achieving "energy independence" for the United States by 1985, and in October 1975, he submitted to Congress a ten-year, $100 billion financing plan for the commercial development of domestic alternative energy sources. The proposed legislation would make loans, loan guarantees, and price supports available to private corporations that undertake long-term capital investments in alternative energy projects. The entire program would be administered by a newly created Energy Independence Authority (EIA). This plan immediately provoked considerable controversy, and congressional approval, at least in its present form, appears increasingly unlikely.[27]

NOTES

1. Bruce C. Netschert and Sam H. Schurr, *Energy in the American Economy, 1850-1975* (Baltimore: Johns Hopkins University Press, 1960), p. 36.

2. British Petroleum, *Statistical Review of the World Oil Industry: 1974* (London, 1975), p. 16.

3. British Petroleum, op. cit., p. 4. The estimate of the Saudi share of world crude oil reserves is provided in *Economist Intelligence Unit*, "Oil in the Middle East," *Quarterly Economic Review*, annual supplement (London, 1975).

4. "Nine Million b/d from New Areas," *Petroleum Economist* 42 (February 1975): 44.

5. The 1975 estimate is provided by Chase Manhattan Bank (cited in *Petroleum Intelligence Weekly*, August 4, 1975, p. 5).

6. The FEA statistics were reported in the New York *Times*, October 29, 1975, pp. 1, 69.

7. National Petroleum Council, Committee on U.S. Energy Outlook, *U.S. Energy Outlook* (Washington, D.C., 1972), p. 59.

8. *Petroleum Intelligence Weekly*, May 5, 1975.

9. *Petroleum Intelligence Weekly*, June 2, 1975, p. 3.

10. New York *Times*, November 21, 1975, pp. 63, 65.

11. "U.S. Eyes the Continental Shelf," *Petroleum Economist* 16 (August 1974): 299-301; and *Oil and Gas Journal*, November 12, 1973, p. 132.

12. *Petroleum Economist*, June 1975, p. 228.

13. Paul W. MacAvoy, "The Regulation Induced Shortage of Natural Gas," in *Regulation of the Natural Gas Industry*, ed. Keith C. Brown (Baltimore: Resources for the Future, 1972).

14. *Petroleum Economist*, June 1975, p. 228.

15. *Petroleum Press Service*, December 1972, pp. 445-46.

16. *U.S. Energy Outlook*, op. cit., pp. 29-32.

17. Interview with J. Whittlesey, Petroleum Information Foundation, New York, June 1974.

18. For differing interpretations of the events surrounding these price rises in OPEC crude oil exports, see Morris A. Adelman, *The World Petroleum Market* (Baltimore: Johns Hopkins University Press, 1972), pp. 250-65; Christopher T. Rand, *Making Democracy Safe for Oil* (Boston: Little, Brown, 1975), pp. 232-353; and George H.M. Schuler, "The International Oil 'Debate' since 1971," *Petroleum Intelligence Weekly*, supplement, April 22, 1974, pp. 1-36. Other analyses are available in Taki Rifai, *The Pricing of Crude Oil* (New York: Praeger, 1974), and Edith Penrose, "The Development of Crisis," *Daedalus* 104 (fall 1975): 39-57.

19. Some representative articles on this subject include M.A. Adelman, "Is the Oil Shortage Real? Oil Companies as OPEC Tax Collectors," *Foreign Policy*, no. 9 (winter 1972-73), pp. 69-107; James E. Akins, "The Oil Crisis; This Time the Wolf Is Here," *Foreign Affairs* 51 (April 1973): 462-90; Khodadad Farmanfarmaian et al., "How Can the World Afford OPEC Oil?" *Foreign Affairs* 53 (January 1975): 201-22; Walter J. Levy, "World Oil Cooperation or International Chaos," *Foreign Affairs* (July 1974): 690-713; Robert Mabro and Elizabeth Monroe, "Arab Wealth from Oil: Problems of Its Investment," *International Affairs* 50 (January 1974): 15-27; and Gerald A. Pollack, "The Economic Consequences of the Energy Crisis," *Foreign Affairs* 52 (April 1974): 452-71.

20. *Petroleum Economist*, March 1975, p. 84.

21. *Petroleum Intelligence Weekly*, June 2, 1975, p. 7.

22. *U.S. Energy Outlook*, op. cit.

23. National Petroleum Council, *Emergency Preparedness for Interruption of Petroleum Imports into the United States* (Washington, D.C., 1973).

24. For more recent assessments, see National Academy of Engineering, Task Force on Energy, *U.S. Energy Prospects: An Engineering Viewpoint* (Washington, 1974); and Massachusetts Institute of Technology Energy Laboratory, Policy Study Group, "Energy Self-Sufficiency: An Economic Evaluation," *Technology Review* 76 (May 1974).

25. U.S. Atomic Energy Commission, *The Nation's Energy Future*, report submitted by Dixy Lee Ray (Washington, D.C.: Government Printing Office, 1973).

26. Federal Energy Administration, *Project Independence Report* (Washington, D.C., 1974).

27. *Wall Street Journal*, October 13, 1975, p. 4.

2

STATUS OF RESEARCH
AND DEVELOPMENT:
NONCONVENTIONAL
CRUDE OIL SOURCES

The next four chapters will summarize the status of current development programs on alternative energy sources. An evaluation of their technical and economic feasibility at their present stage of development will be provided and the principal problem areas that remain to be solved, identified. A significant document in this connection is the report entitled *The Nation's Energy Future* submitted by Dixy Lee Ray, chairman of the AEC, in response to President Nixon's directive to recommend an integrated energy research and development program for the United States. Table 2.1 summarizes these recommendations, to which further reference will be made in the ensuing discussion of energy resource alternatives. Estimates regarding the size and location of existing known reserves of alternative fuel supplies are included, together with a discussion of the potential environmental impact of specific alternative energy sources. As a basis of comparison, Table 2.2 offers an overview of the U.S. federal energy research and development budget for fiscal years 1973, 1974, and 1975.

Discussions regarding alternative energy sources frequently display a preoccupation with long-term, "exotic" alternatives, such as solar energy and nuclear fusion, which tends to obscure the tremendous underdeveloped potential of existing fossil fuel sources. In particular, coal (which will be discussed in the next chapter), tar sands, and oil shale are much more realistic alternatives for energy resource development over the next ten to 15 years.

Tar sands and shale can be processed to yield crude oil (sometimes known as "synthetic crude" or "syncrude"), while coal can be burned directly or converted into syncrude or gas. Estimates of the amount of crude oil ultimately recoverable from these nonconventional sources are complicated by variable recovery factors, which depend on the existing state of the technology and the different geological characteristics of each deposit. However, even at a low recovery rate of 10 percent, crude oil supplies available from these sources

TABLE 2.1

Summary Schedule of Federal Energy Research and Development Programs, Fiscal Years 1975/79, by Task
(millions of dollars)

Self-Sufficiency Task	1973	1974 (planned)	1975/79 Energy Research and Development Programs (recommended)						1975/79 Agency Projections
			1975	1976	1977	1978	1979	1975/79	Agency Projections
Conserve energy and energy resources									
Reduced consumption									
tion	12.1	22.3	29.9	43.7	51.5	44.4	40.5	210.0	15.0
Increased efficiency	40.7	40.0	136.3	223.4	267.0	287.8	315.5	1,230.0	80.0
Subtotal	52.8	62.3	166.2	267.1	318.5	332.2	356.0	1,440.0	95.0
Increase domestic production of oil and gas									
Production	12.8	11.2	31.7	89.1	79.5	59.5	50.2	310.0	50.0
Resource assessment	7.2	8.3	20.0	23.0	29.5	37.5	40.0	150.0	40.0
Subtotal	20.0	19.5	51.7	112.1	109.0	97.0	90.2	460.0	90.0
Substitute coal for oil and gas on a massive scale									
Mining			45.0	57.0	64.0	77.0	82.0	325.0	
Direct combustion			30.0	35.0	40.0	44.0	51.0	200.0	
High-Btu gasification			35.0	75.0	92.0	81.0	57.0	340.0	
Coal liquefaction			75.0	75.0	75.0	75.0	75.0	375.0	
Low-Btu gasification			30.0	37.0	42.0	48.0	43.0	200.0	
Synthetic fuels—industry pioneering			100.0	100.0	55.0	50.0	50.0	355.0	
Environmenatal control technology			70.0	50.0	42.0	45.0	53.0	260.0	
Supporting research and development			20.0	22.0	24.0	27.0	27.0	120.0	
Subtotal	88.8	167.2	405.0	451.0	434.0	447.0	438.0	2,175.0	842.0

Validate the nuclear option								
Safety and other	42.7	51.7	90.6	125.6	143.0	170.5	189.5	719.2	609.9
Uranium enrichment	50.3	56.8	64.2	54.8	57.4	58.4	59.4	294.2	284.5
High-temperature gas reactor	7.2	14.2	40.0	44.7	24.2	26.9	28.0	163.8	128.6
Light water self-sustaining reactor	29.5	29.0	21.4	17.7	9.8	9.8	9.8	68.5	68.5
Liquid metal fast breeder reactor	253.8	356.8	477.0	538.6	510.8	524.2	506.0	2,446.6	2,470.6
Gas-cooled fast breeder	1.0	1.0	17.0	23.0	29.0	33.0	38.0	140.0	27.0
Advanced technology	11.3	7.8	21.5	24.5	30.5	34.0	37.2	147.7	83.2
Subtotal	394.8	517.3	731.7	828.9	804.7	856.8	867.9	4,090.0	3,672.3
Exploit renewable energy sources to the maximum extent feasible								
Fusion—confinement	39.7	55.8	135.0	230.0	261.0	338.0	376.0	1,340.0	1,132.0
Fusion—laser	35.1	42.9	10.0	20.0	25.0	25.0	30.0	110.0	27.0
Solar	4.2	13.2	32.5	39.9	41.4	42.2	44.0	200.0	80.0
Geothermal	3.8	11.1	40.0	41.0	40.8	35.7	27.5	185.0	20.0
Subtotal	82.8	123.0	217.5	330.9	368.2	440.9	477.5	1,835.0	1,232.0
Total	640.2	889.3	1,572.1	1,990.0	2,034.4	2,173.9	2,229.6	10,000.0	5,931.3

Summary Schedule of Federal Energy Research and Development Programs, Fiscal Years 1975/79 (millions of dollars)

	1975/79 Energy Research and Development Programs					
	1975	1976	1977	1978	1979	1975/79
Operating expenses	1,062.1	1,311.0	1,451.4	1,519.3	1,618.8	6,962.6
Equipment	160.7	233.4	211.3	242.4	250.3	1,098.1
Construction	349.3	445.6	371.7	412.2	360.5	1,939.3
Total	1,572.1	1,990.0	2,034.4	2,173.9	2,229.6	10,000.0

Source: The Nation's Energy Future (Report to Richard M. Nixon, president of the United States, submitted by Dixy Lee Ray, chairman of the U.S. Atomic Energy Commission), p. 29.

TABLE 2.2

U.S. Federal Energy Research and Development Budget, Fiscal Years 1973, 1974, and 1975 (millions of dollars)

	1973 Amount	1973 Per-centile	1974 Amount	1974 Per-centile	1975 Amount	1975 Per-centile
Liquid metal fast breeder reactors	253.7		357.3		473.4	
Other breeders[a]	5.6		4.0		11.0	
High-temperature reactors	7.3		13.8		41.0	
Light water reactors	29.5		29.0		21.4	
Uranium enrichment	50.3		57.5		66.0	
Other[b]	60.1		68.9		111.9	
Nuclear fission	406.5	(60.5)	530.5	(41.8)	724.7	(31.5)
Oil, gas, and shale	18.7		19.1		41.8	
Coal − mining	1.7		7.5		55.0	
− health and safety	28.2		27.0		27.7	
− gasification	37.1		54.3		116.0	
− liquefaction	11.0		45.5		108.5	
− direct combustion	1.5		15.9		36.2	
− other[c]	5.6		14.2		72.1	
Fossil fuels	103.8	(15.5)	183.5	(14.4)	457.3	(19.8)
Fusion	74.8		101.1		168.6	
Geothermal	4.4		10.9		44.7	
Solar	4.0		13.8		50.9	
New energy sources	83.2	(12.4)	125.8	(9.9)	264.2	(11.4)
Residential and commercial	−		15.0		27.9	
Conversion, transmission, storage	11.0		23.8		55.0	
Transport	21.2		27.2		45.7	
Energy conservation	32.3	(4.8)	66.0	(5.2)	128.6	(5.6)
Sulphur oxides	19.0		43.9		94.0	
Other fuel pollutants	8.8		13.1		57.0	
Other[d]	10.6		8.5		27.5	
Environmental control	38.4	(5.7)	65.5	(5.2)	178.5	(7.8)
Environmental and health effects	−		169.7	(13.4)	303.4)	(13.2)
Basic research and manpower development	−		100.8	(7.9)	183.1	(8.0)
Miscellaneous	8.1	(1.2)	28.8	(2.3)	62.8	(2.7)
Grand Total	672.2	(100.0)	1270.6	(100.0)	2302.6	(100.0)

[a]Includes gas-cooled, molten salt, and light water breeders.

[b]Includes reactor safety, waste management, and resource assessment. The biggest increase is in reactor safety.

[c]Includes resource assessment, common technology, and synthetic fuels pioneer program. The latter accounts for the bulk of the increase.

[d]Includes thermal pollution and automotive emissions.

Source: Federal Energy Administration, *Project Independence*, November 1974, pp. 436-37. Reprinted in John Surrey and William Walker, "Energy Research and Development: A U.K. Perspective," *Energy Policy* 3 (June 1975): 115.

would exceed by several times the world's "published proved" reserves of conventional crude (635 billion barrels).[1] Major concentrations of these sources are located in the Western Hemisphere. The United States itself possesses massive domestic reserves of coal and oil shale.

None of these sources yields crude oil through conventional production techniques, and only the development of tar sands has progressed to the commercial stage. The lengthy lead times and highly capital-intensive nature of the recovery processes involved make extensive research and development programs essential if commercial development of these sources is to be accelerated. The high cost and potential unreliability of crude oil imports intensify the need for maximizing the contribution of these sources to U.S. energy supplies.

Unfortunately, there are major obstacles involved in formulating a realistic cost-benefit comparison of these energy alternatives during the early stages of their development. Available studies employ widely differing methods for estimating costs and are based on differing stages of development, thus inhibiting a valid comparison. The technical processes also vary considerably, and each process is expected to have a different environmental impact.

It is therefore difficult to estimate the probable sequence of the development of syncrude processes. Since the technology required for production of crude oil from nonconventional sources is considerably simpler for tar sands than for oil shale and coal, earlier development of this resource has generally been considered likely. Tar sands offer the best prospects for early development among all the syncrude sources, and limited production on a commercial scale has been going on since late 1967. The availability of major domestic reserves of oil shale in the United States, as well as certain desirable qualities of the syncrude product from oil shale, favor accelerating the commercial development of this resource. Coal liquefaction offers a promising long-term synthetic fuel alternative, and accelerated pilot plant development of several coal liquefaction processes can therefore be anticipated over the next few years.

The FEA blueprint suggested that synthetic fuels would not play a major role in the U.S. energy picture until after 1985. With the exception of tar sands in Canada and oil shale in Brazil, the outlook for significant syncrude production elsewhere in the world is even more remote.

TAR SANDS

Tar sands remain the only commercially developed source of nonconventional crude oil and represent the best candidate for accelerated development. Major reserves of tar sands are located in Canada and Venezuela, while considerably smaller reserves also exist in the United States.[2] The Athabasca tar sands in northeastern Alberta have been the focus of most research and development programs, and recoverable oil reserves from these deposits are estimated at 26 billion barrels. It is also estimated, however, that once the technology is developed to provide access to some of the deeper deposits of tar sands, as much as 250 billion barrels of crude oil may be recoverable from the tar sands deposits.[3]

The tar sands contain a very heavy crude oil of relatively high sulfur content. Where the overburden covering the tar sands is sufficiently thin, conventional strip-mining techniques may be employed. The crude tar, or bitumen, extracted from the mined tar sands must undergo preliminary processing to yield a lighter, low-viscosity synthetic crude before it can be pipelined to the refinery. Ten percent of the Athabasca tar sands deposits are believed to be recoverable in this manner, yielding a syncrude recovery efficiency of 70 to 80 percent.[4]

However, strip mining has an adverse environmental impact and poses major problems regarding the continuous handling of vast quantities of materials. A 100,000-barrels-per-day processing plant could require 200,000 cubic yards per day of tar sands, and in order to supply this amount, two to three times this volume of material would have to be stripped and eventually replaced.[5]

The thick overburden covering the rest of the Athabasca tar sands prevents the use of strip-mining techniques, and research is currently being pursued on several alternative methods of in situ production of the heavy crude oil. Some type of thermal recovery will probably be required. In situ production would also eliminate the enormous material handling and waste problems that accompany strip-mining techniques. While such extraction methods are technically possible, they do not yet constitute an economically viable alternative to strip mining.[6]

Thus far, Great Canadian Oil Sands Ltd. (GCOS), an affiliate of Sun Oil, has been the only company to operate a commercial processing plant using the Athabasca tar sands. The 45,000-barrels-per-day plant in Fort McMurray began operation in late 1967, following unanticipated increases in the initial capital investment requirements. It has operated at a loss since its opening, but the annual losses have progressively diminished as its average production rate and sales revenues have increased. In 1974, higher crude oil prices enabled GCOS to achieve its first year of profitable operations, although reports indicate that it experienced new operating losses in 1975. Moreover, continued problems with equipment breakdowns and a lack of capital have delayed plans to expand the capacity of the plant to an authorized level of 65,000-barrels-per-day.[7]

Syncrude Canada, Ltd., owned by a group of oil companies, is expected to bring Canada's second commercial tar sands processing plant on stream in 1978. This plant will have a capacity of 125,000-barrels-per-day and will represent in excess of $2 billion in capital investment, in contrast with the $400 million investment originally anticipated.[8] The soaring construction costs prompted Atlantic Richfield's decision to withdraw from its construction, and the remaining partners reorganized the consortium to include 30 percent participation by government bodies (15 percent by the Canadian government, 10 percent by Alberta, and 5 percent by Ontario) as well as an additional infusion of capital from the corporate partners.[9] The escalating construction costs for the syncrude project suggest that the capital cost of each barrel-per-day producing capacity in the plant will be $16,000, in contrast with the $6,500 capital cost of each barrel per day of capacity of GCOS and the $3,800 of the North Sea oil fields.[10] Although three other permits for commercial plants have been requested, other companies appear to be adopting a cautious attitude pending completion of the Syncrude project before committing major investment capital for additional projects.

In addition to providing financial assistance to the Syncrude project, Alberta announced an Energy Breakthrough Project in January 1974 which authorized the creation of an Alberta Oil Sands Technology and Research Authority with $100 million in funding available over a five-year period. The provincial government has opposed implementation of crash programs for the development of its tar sands resources and instead has favored a "phased and orderly development" of the resources which would seek to achieve a 3 million-barrel-per-day output of syncrude from tar sands in approximately 20 plants by the year 2000.[11]

OIL SHALE

Although the commercial exploitation of oil shale reserves presents more difficult technical problems than that of tar sands, oil shale has several points in its favor as a source of syncrude for the United States. Potential crude oil supplies from shale are greater, and, equally important, the availability of massive domestic reserves offers security against potential disruptions of supply. Furthermore, the crude oil from shale has a higher hydrogen-carbon ratio, which reduces the amount of additional hydrogen required in order to upgrade it for use as refinery feedstock.

The largest oil shale reserves in the world are located in the United States and the Soviet Union, although substantial accumulations are also located in Brazil and in mainland China. Estimates regarding potential syncrude available in these reserves are more uncertain than in the case of tar sands, since the oil content of shale is highly variable, ranging from 10 to 70 gallons per ton of shale. The NPC estimates that U.S. oil shale deposits, concentrated primarily in the Green River formation in Colorado, Utah, and Wyoming, contain 1.8 trillion barrels of shale oil. Of this amount, 129 billion barrels are located in higher-grade deposits of oil shale, containing more than 30 gallons per ton of shale, and in seams over 30 feet thick, which are considered most readily recoverable.[12]

Unlike the crude oil found in tar sands, the crude oil in shale is present not as a liquid but in the form of kerogen, a solid hydrocarbon. The crude oil can therefore only be extracted by applying intense heat to the shale and thermally deomposing the kerogen. This process yields a crude oil with a higher nitrogen content and high viscosity, which must be further processed by distillation, coking of residue, and/or hydrogenation.

Most technically feasible processes currently under development for syncrude production from oil shale involve mining the shale and retorting it on the surface to decompose the kerogen.[13]Although strip mining may be feasible for some of the more shallow shale deposits, most of the oil shale deposits are deep and require underground mining techniques. The only mining method for oil shale that has actually been demonstrated is room-and-pillar mining. Mining and surface extraction of crude oil from shale poses an unprecedented material handling and disposal problem with a serious environmental impact. There is also the disconcerting complication that spent shale actually occupies over 25 percent more volume following extraction of its crude oil than it did in its original form. A study done by the National Academy of Engineering has pointed out that at this rate, oil shale plants producing one million-barrels-per-day of syncrude would require associated mining operations to obtain 500 million tons of rock per year, which is almost equal in tonnage to the output of the entire U.S. coal mining industry in 1973.[14]

An additional problem that may emerge as a rigid constraint on the rapid expansion of shale oil processing capacity involves the large quantities of water required for shale processing. According to the NPD report, 3.4 barrels of water will be needed for each barrel of syncrude produced.[15] Since the Green River oil formation is located in an area with limited natural supplies of water that may already be overcommitted for other uses, either new retorting processes that minimize water intake must be devised or expensive ancillary systems will be required to tap water supplies from other regions.[16]

Some research is being devoted to the feasibility of in situ retorting of the kerogen in oil shale. This alternative could reduce the high cost and adverse environmental impact of surface retorting processes and might prove adaptable to a wider range of oil shale deposits than conventional mining techniques. However, in situ retorting requires preliminary fracturing of the oil shale formation to create sufficient permeability for the injection of retorting fluids, and reliable fracturing methods have not yet been developed.*

---

*Occidental Petroleum Company received considerable publicity in 1973 when it announced its successful operation of a pilot plant employing an in situ process for oil shale

The largest oil shale prototype plant in operation in the non-Communist world is located at the Irati oil shale deposits in Brazil. This government plant was placed in operation in 1972 and currently processes 2,200 tons of shale per day and produces 1,000-barrels-per-day of shale oil. Plans to construct a large commercial shale oil plant have been announced by the Brazilian government.[17]

Three distinct surface retorting processes have been tested on a sufficient scale to evaluate the retorting operation. Commercial development of domestic U.S. shale reserves depends heavily on federal government energy policy in general and, in respect to shale, on leasing policy in particular, since roughly 80 percent of known high-quality oil shale deposits in the United States are located on federal land.[18] The government initiated an oil shale leasing program in January 1974, and the successful bid for leasing the first tract of oil shale land in Colorado was $120 million, which seems to indicate a considerable degree of commercial interest in this resource.[19]

The FEA blueprint mentions that at $11 per barrel crude price (in constant 1974 dollars), shale oil recovery might reach one million-barrels-per-day by 1985.[20] However, the prevailing uncertainties concerning eventual costs of production for shale oil, and persistent concern over the adverse environmental consequences associated with shale oil development, have served to dampen much of the enthusiasm exhibited by companies in the bidding for leases in 1974. As a result, some authorities consider the FEA projection for 1985 production as optimistic. The National Academy of Engineering, for instance, estimates that only 500,000-barrels-per-day of commercial production from shale oil will be achieved by 1985, and even this more modest level of production will require between $3 and $5 billion in capital investment.[21]

The continuing delays in the commercial development of oil shale and other synthetic fuels prompted a congressional measure that would have provided $6 billion in federal loan guarantees for the construction and operation of commercial synthetic fuel plants. This measure specifically envisioned assistance for the construction of two 50,000-barrels-per-day commercial oil shale plants as well as facilities for coal gasification. Energy Research and Development Administration (ERDA) officials believed that such a measure would ensure 350,000-barrels-per-day of synthetic fuels by the early 1980s and ultimately 10 million-barrels-per-day of synthetic fuels by the year 2000. However, in December 1975, the House of Representatives unexpectedly rejected

---

extraction at a cost of $1 per barrel of syncrude. These early reports were subsequently revealed to be premature (London *Times*, November 24, 1973, p. 1). For an evaluation of the research necessary to develop reliable fracturing methods, see National Science Foundation, *Energy Research Needs*, report prepared by Resources for the Future, in cooperation with Massachusetts Institute of Technology Environmental Laboratory (Washington, D.C., 1971), pp. IV-8,9.

this Senate- approved legislative proposal by a wide margin in a move that was interpreted as a major defeat for proponents of accelerated development of alternative energy sources.[22] Less than two weeks after this legislative defeat, Atlantic Richfield and Oil Shale Corporation announced their decision to withdraw from an oil shale venture that had been organized to develop a 5,100-acre federal lease in Colorado. Both companies cited rising costs, the unavailability of capital and lack of government support as reasons for their withdrawal. The construction costs for the 50,000-barrels-per-day oil shale facility are anticipated to exceed $850 million, in contrast with cost estimates of $250 to $300 million cited in 1973. The remaining participants in the venture, Shell Oil and Ashland Oil, intend to continue with the project, but they indicated that the withdrawal of the other companies would delay their progress.[23]

NOTES

1. M.W. Clegg, "New Sources of Oil: Oil Sands, Shales and Synthetics" (Paper presented to the Institute of Petroleum Summer Meeting, Harrogate, England, June 5-8, 1973), p. 1.

2. Ibid., p. 2.

3. "Alberta Looks to Oil Sands," *Petroleum Economist* 41 (August 1974): 288-91.

4. Clegg, op. cit., p. 2.

5. Ibid., p. 4.

6. Ibid., p. 6. For a brief summary of more recent efforts by companies to develop in situ recovery methods, see "Alberta Looks to Oil Sands," op. cit.

7. New York *Times*, October 12, 1975, section 3, p. 2.

8. "In Energy Impasse, Conservation Keeps Popping Up," *Science* 187 (January 10, 1975): 42-45.

9. *Petroleum Economist*, March 1975, p. 108.

10. New York *Times*, op. cit.

11. "Alberta Looks to Oil Sands," op. cit.

12. National Petroleum Council, Committee on U.S. Energy Outlook, *U.S. Energy Outlook* (Washington, D.C., 1972), p. 4.

13. For a technical description of the three leading surface retorting processes, see Hoyt C. Hottel and Jack B. Howard, *New Energy Technology* (Cambridge: Massachusetts Institute of Technology Press, 1971), pp. 196-99.

14. National Academy of Engineering, Task Force on Energy, *U.S. Energy Prospects: An Engineering Viewpoint* (Washington, D.C., 1974), p. 71.

15. *U.S. Energy Outlook*, op. cit., p. 54.

16. *U.S. Energy Prospects: An Engineering Viewpoint*, op. cit., p. 72.

17. *Petroleum Press Service*, July 1973, p. 250.

18. *U.S. Energy Outlook*, op. cit., p. 51.

19. New York *Times*, January 9, 1974, p. 15.

20. Federal Energy Administration, *Project Independence Report* (Washington, D.C., 1974), p. 132.

21. *U.S. Energy Prospects: An Engineering Viewpoint*, op. cit., p. 73.

22. *Wall Street Journal*, December 12, 1975, p. 7; and November 6, 1975.

23. *Wall Street Journal*, December 22, 1975, p. 5; and New York *Times*, November 3, 1974, section 3, p. 2.

3

STATUS OF RESEARCH AND DEVELOPMENT: COAL AND COAL CONVERSION PROCESSES

Coal offers the major short-term alternative energy source to crude oil and natural gas, particularly for power generation and industrial use, and it also represents the most abundantly available fossil fuel, over the long term, in the world. But despite vast untapped reserves in the United States and other parts of the world, coal has a rapidly declining share of the total energy consumption in each of the major consuming regions. In 1920, coal supplied 75 percent of the energy requirements of the United States; as recently as 1950, it accounted for only approximately 35 percent. By 1972, however, coal's share of total energy consumption was reduced to approximately 17 percent.[1] In the other two major consuming regions of the non-Communist world, this trend has been even more dramatic, occurring as it did at a relatively later date and at a more rapid pace.

The relative decline of coal's position in the supply of energy can be largely attributed to three factors: (1) increasing competition from petroleum and natural gas as less expensive and more convenient energy sources, (2) environmental legislation restricting the use of high-sulfur coal, and (3) increased production costs. In the United States, coal has been, and still is, less expensive than domestic crude oil, at their respective sources and on an equivalent energy content basis. However, higher transportation and handling costs and other disadvantages of coal more than counterbalance this differential at the point of consumption.

The long-term availability of coal reserves provides a major incentive to increase the role of this fossil fuel in the supply of energy. The NPC report *U.S. Energy Outlook* cites an estimate of domestic coal resources made by the U.S. Geological Survey of 3.2 trillion short tons (this figure includes both identified and probable reserves). Comparable estimates suggest that total world reserves

FIGURE 3.1

Coal Resources of the World
(10^{12} metric tons)

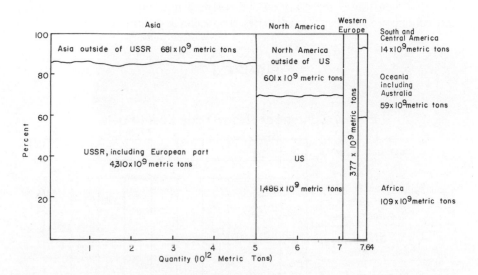

Note: The figures represent the total initial resources of minable coal, which is defined as 50 percent of the coal actually present. The horizontal scale gives the total supply. Each vertical block shows the apportionment of the supply in a continent. From the first block, for example, one can ascertain that Asia has some 5×10^{12} metric tons of minable coal, of which about 86 percent is in the Soviet Union.

Source: M. King Hubbert, "The Energy Resources of the Earth," *Scientific American* 224 (September 1971): 64.

range between 9 and 12 trillion tons. One estimate of world coal resources based on information compiled by Paul Averitt of the U.S. Geological Survey is depicted in Figure 3.1.

The NPC believes that 150 billion tons of U.S. coal reserves are currently recoverable using existing mining technology, and it suggests that even at maximum projected production rates over the next 15 years, less than 10 percent of existing recoverable reserves will be consumed by 1985. Moreover, since recoverable reserves represent only 5 percent of total domestic reserves, there is a major opportunity for expanding the size of recoverable reserves by introducing more efficient mining technology.[2] Figure 3.2 illustrates graphically the overwhelming importance of coal reserves in the world's initial supply of recoverable fossil fuels.

Despite reassuring estimates regarding aggregate coal reserves, numerous problems emerge in a more detailed analysis of the locale of existing reserves and of legislative restraints on expanded coal production. Recent environmental legislation constitutes the most serious potential restraint on coal production and consumption in the United States. The secondary sulfur dioxide emission

FIGURE 3.2

Energy Content of Recoverable Fossil Fuels

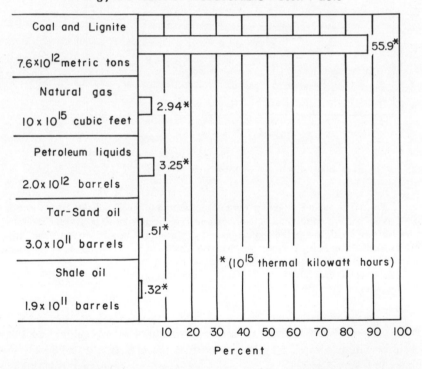

Note: Energy content of the world's initial supply of recoverable fossil fuels is given in units of 10^{15} thermal kilowatt-hours. Coal and lignite, for example contain 55.9 x 10^{15} thermal kilowatt-hours of energy and represent 88.8 percent of the recoverable energy.

Source: M. King Hubbert, "The Energy Resources of the Earth," *Scientific American* 224 (September 1971): 66.

control standards stipulated in the federal Clean Air Act of 1970 for electric generating plants could render 40 percent of the estimated coal reserves in the eastern part of the United States unusable because of their high sulfur content. Currently, approximately 95 percent of domestic coal production is located east of the Mississippi, and implementation of these emission control standards could entail a massive shift of production to western coal regions and substantially increased transportation costs to the major eastern markets.[3]

In addition, coal producers argue that the Coal Mine Health and Safety Act of 1969 imposed excessive restrictions on mining operations which contributed to declining productivity levels and to the high cost of labor. While coal mining productivity has decreased by 30 percent since 1970, wildcat labor strikes and the use of increasingly obsolescent mining technology have also been cited as factors. Most of the coal production in the eastern United States employs deep-mining techniques, and the declining productivity levels have considerably reduced the profitability of these operations. Since 1969, there have been 1,500 underground mines closed down in the United States.[4]

Increasing labor costs and other factors have accelerated the shift of domestic production from underground mines in the eastern United States to surface mining in the western United States. In 1971, total domestic coal production from surface mines surpassed that from deep mines, and the share of surface-mined coal is likely to increase rapidly over the next decade.[5] Perhaps one of the greatest paradoxes of recent environmental legislation has been the role of sulfur dioxide emission controls in accelerating the trend toward surface mining of coal, which has in turn been heavily criticized for its adverse impact on the landscape. However, 83 percent of domestic reserves of relatively low-sulfur coal are located in the western United States in large deposits, many of which can only be efficiently extracted using surface-mining techniques.[6] Prohibition of surface mining accompanied by strict emission control standards would effectively eliminate the short-term potential of the vast domestic reserves of coal in minimizing energy shortages and would probably considerably aggravate the existing energy crisis. On the other hand, greater reliance on surface mining would increase the availability of low-sulfur coal.

Industry projections suggest that considerable potential exists for increasing the current production levels of approximately 640 million tons per year. In the short term, it would be possible to produce an additional 50 million tons per year of coal over previous targets. This additional coal production would be sufficient to permit the conversion of electric power generating stations from scarce oil and gas supplies to coal. Some coal industry representatives further believe that current coal output could be doubled by 1980 and tripled by 1985 to reach an annual production level of about 1.8 billion tons. All of these estimates, however, assume increasing reliance upon surface mining, relaxation of existing legislative restraints, and labor stability.[7] On the other hand, the National Academy of Engineering report, *U.S. Energy Prospects*, offers a considerably less optimistic projection, forecasting that the coal industry will be able only to double current production by 1985. This report stresses potential mining equipment bottlenecks which might delay the expansion of production. For example, there are currently only two manufacturers in the United States of large power shovels, and both are quoting deliveries in 1979.[8] The FEA *Project Independence Report* concludes that domestic coal production will reach 1.1 billion tons per year in 1985 under a "business as usual" scenario, while accelerated development might raise this level to 2.1 billion tons.[9]

The current desirability of expanding surface-mining production to meet short-term energy requirements should not obscure the urgency of developing more efficient deep-mining techniques. First, surface mining involves an undeniable adverse impact on the land surface, and although limited land reclamation may be possible in many areas at costs ranging from $200 to $800 per acre, some areas, such as farmland and steep terrain, cannot be reclaimed using existing methods. Full reclamation would involve costs of $1,500 to $4,000 per acre.[10] The crucial consideration for each mining operation, however, will be the cost of reclamation per ton of coal mined, and this will vary according to the mine. In the long run, less than one-third of the recoverable coal reserves in the United States can be extracted with surface-mining techniques, and major additions to existing recoverable reserves will depend largely on innovations in underground mining technology.

A substantial research and development program could expand the application of more efficient continuous mining systems, improve the efficiency of removal systems from the mine to the surface to match accelerated extraction rates, and reconcile the objective of efficient, low-cost extraction with concern for the safety of the miners and for potential adverse environmental impact. Greater automation of underground mining systems would minimize the exposure of miners to unpredictable safety hazards. In particular, the longwall system of mining may offer advantages over existing room-and-pillar techniques. Thus far, however, longwall mining has only been successful in a limited range of mines, and additional research and development programs are necessary to increase the applicability of this technique.[11]

One potential bottleneck in the future expansion of domestic coal production involves a growing hopper car shortage for coal transportation by railroad. Several construction companies have responded to this problem by seeking federal action granting them the power of eminent domain to obtain rights of way for the construction of long-distance coal slurry pipelines. The technology necessary for such pipelines is relatively well known—it involves grinding the coal to a fine powder which can be suspended in water for transportation. At the other end of the pipeline, centrifuges extract the coal particles from the water, leaving a pulverized coal fuel for use in power plant boilers.

Five such coal slurry pipelines are currently in the planning stages, with the most advanced project involving a 1,030-mile pipeline connecting Wyoming coal mines with utilities in Arkansas, Louisiana, and Mississippi. Proponents of coal slurry pipelines argue that they constitute a far more efficient method of coal transportation, thereby extending the geographical area in which the output of a coal mine can be profitably marketed. The railroads, however, have generally opposed these proposals, arguing that they would divert much needed business and further weaken the already precarious financial conditions of the railroad companies.[12] One major constraint that may emerge in the construction of coal slurry pipelines involves the availability of large amounts of water needed as a suspension medium.

TOWARD A RESOLUTION OF THE SULFUR PROBLEM

Coal Combustion Processes

The expansion of coal production from underground mines will also require research and development programs for sulfur extraction from coal to permit more extensive use of high-sulfur coal without raising sulfur dioxide emissions above acceptable levels. Experiments with two new coal combustion processes suggest that the combustion of high-sulfur coal in a pressurized, fluidized bed boiler system containing a sulfur acceptor (limestone or molten iron) could significantly reduce sulfur emissions. These processes have reached the pilot plant stage and may become commercially available by the late 1970s, although they will require changes in boiler designs.

Stack Gas Scrubbing

Several years ago, optimistic projections suggested that stack gas scrubbing systems would provide the least expensive method of sulfur dioxide emission control. These systems remove sulfur dioxide from the flue gas of power generating stations and can be attached to existing facilities. Although these systems have already been installed in several power generating stations, their performance has been disappointing, and electric utilities are searching for other alternatives.[13] The manufacturers of the scrubbing systems and the Environmental Protection Agency (EPA) argue that scrubbing systems remain the most inexpensive methods of emission control and that more reliable technology will be commercially available by 1976. Other authorities disagree with these projections and believe that the problems involved in removing relatively small quantities of sulfur dioxide from large amounts of flue gas constitute a major obstacle to the development of reliable stack gas scrubbing systems.

PRECOMBUSTION SULFUR REMOVAL

The prospect of further delays in the perfection of these systems has increased interest in several alternative methods for the precombustion removal of sulfur from coal. Precombustion removal of sulfur is believed to be more technologically feasible and probably less expensive in the long run than stack gas scrubbing systems, since the sulfur content of coal is much more concentrated at this stage. In particular, three processes at differing stages of development are receiving high priority in coal research and development programs: (1) conversion of coal into low-Btu (British thermal unit) gas, (2) solvent refining of coal to produce a low-ash, low-sulfur solid, and (3) coal liquefaction.[14] However, the widely varying properties of coal and its condensed chemical structure pose major problems for processes that attempt to alter its chemical composition. Both coal gasification and liquefaction also require the introduction of large quantities of hydrogen during the conversion process. As a result, coal conversion processes will require the development of new technologies that operate efficiently and reliably in large-scale units.

Low-Btu Coal Gasification

Coal gasification to produce a low-Btu, low-sulfur gas suitable as a fuel for electric power generating stations is the only coal conversion process now commercially available. As early as 1936, Lurgi Gesellschaft developed a process for coal gasification in Germany which is currently used in approximately 60 small European plants to produce either town gas or chemical feedstock from coal. Several alternative processes are under development and offer the potential for more efficient and less expensive coal gasification. These processes would yield a gas containing sulfur in the form of hydrogen sulfide, which can be inexpensively removed during a subsequent purification stage by using methods that are already commercially available.

However, the major attraction of the low-Btu gasification process is that it provides an ideal fuel for gas turbines in the advanced combined cycle power generators which are nearing commercial application. In the combined cycle, newly developed stationary gas turbines are linked with steam turbines to yield a very high thermal efficiency. According to current estimates, the simultaneous development of low-Btu gasification processes and advanced combined cycle generating systems will provide an economically competitive alternative to conventional fossil fuel plants equipped with sophisticated stack gas scrubbing systems.[15]

However, there are also several disadvantages associated with low-Btu gasification of coal. The conversion process might entail a loss of 25 percent in the original heating value of coal. It is not economically feasible to transport low-Btu gas over long distances; therefore, the gasification plant must be located reasonably near the electric power generating station. Furthermore, there is no method for storing large volumes of hot low-Btu gas, and this renders the power generating plant highly vulnerable to disruptions in fuel supply as a result of possible malfunctions in the gasification plant.

The Lurgi process employs a low-temperature fixed bed gasifier which has limited thermal efficiency and imposes major restrictions on maximum coal processing capacity and unit size. As a consequence, the Office of Coal Research has awarded several contracts for the development of alternative coal gasification processes that would overcome these drawbacks.[16] Ray's report recommends that $200 million be allocated to a research and development program on low-Btu gasification processes during the fiscal years 1975/79. Under this program, contracts would be awarded to build and operate three to five pilot plants to test various gasification processes as well as to build and operate two integrated combined cycle demonstration plants.[17] At this pace of development, commercial low-Btu gasification plants will probably not be on stream before 1980. The FEA *Project Independence Report* contains the far more conservative estimate that commercial production of low-Btu gas will not begin in the 1980s.[18]

Available estimates suggest that conversion from coal to clean, low-Btu gas as a fuel in a conventional power plant with 38 percent thermal efficiency would sharply increase the cost of power generation. However, if the gasification process is considered in conjunction with an advanced combined cycle generating plant operating at a thermal efficiency of 45 percent, the cost differential declines substantially and would probably be more than eliminated if the comparison were made with a conventional coal burning plant with stack gas scrubbing for emission control. These estimates were made on the basis of currently available technology, and projections indicate that second-generation gasification processes and combined cycle plants in the 1980s will generate power for less than conventional plants even before the added costs of stack scrubbing systems are considered.[19] While these cost estimates may change as development of the processes continues, they nevertheless suggest the possibility that low-Btu gasification of coal may soon provide an economically competitive fuel for electric utilities currently relying on conventional fossil fuels. The M.W. Kellogg Company recently announced that its low-Btu coal gasification system, using bituminous coal at $20 per ton, can produce fuel gas at a cost competitive with $10-per-barrel oil.

High-Btu Coal Gasification

Existing technology for the low-Btu gasification of coal has also served as a basis for efforts to develop high-Btu content pipeline-quality gas from coal. The successful commercial application of these more sophisticated systems may ultimately provide the largest new market for coal and provide a flexible alternative to dwindling domestic natural gas reserves. In order to provide a feasible substitute for natural gas, however, synthetic gas from coal will require a high methane content to increase its Btu value. High-Btu gas can then be used as a substitute in a wide variety of appliances that currently rely on natural gas, and it will be economical to transport the synthetic gas over long distances. However, coal gasifiers that can operate at much higher pressures during the conversion process must be developed to maximize the methane content of the gas, and then the gas will have to undergo catalytic methanation (or some alternative enrichment process) to increase its methane content even further.

The urgency of developing synthetic gas processes is illustrated by the fact that gas pipeline companies have already announced plans to construct commercial high-Btu gasification plants using the currently available Lurgi process followed by an additional methanation stage. There are at present five projects in this field for which all planning and design work has been completed. The five plants together will produce 420,000 million cubic feet of synthetic natural gas annually while consuming over 40 million tons of coal. Production costs for pipeline-quality synthetic gas from these plants appear to be competitive with those of imported LNG, although its price is much higher than the current regulated price for "new" domestic natural gas.[20]

Several more efficient processes for the production of high-Btu gas are being developed, and at least four are at the pilot plant stage (Hygas, CO_2-Acceptor, Synthane, and Bigas).[21] Little consensus exists as to their relative merits, although the results from pilot plant operation will provide a good indication of the problems involved in scaling up each process. At least some of the pilot plant operations will probably be successful, leading to the construction of commercial plants employing these new processes. It is also probable, however, that escalating investment costs, the normal expectation of technical problems, long lead times in equipment procurement, and other factors will mean that they will not make any substantial contribution to U.S. gas supplies much before 1985. The FEA *Project Independence Report* estimates that under an "accelerated development" program, 1 trillion cubic feet per year of synthetic high-Btu gas could be produced by 1985, but under a "business as usual" scenario, the annual production by 1985 would be only one-half of this level.[22]

In the meantime, an active research and development program will continue over all phases of the coal conversion process, while additional basic research will focus on the physical behavior of coal. More efficient processes for coal conversion to high-Btu gas might also be adapted for coal conversion to low-Btu gas.

The reliability of existing cost estimates for the production of pipeline-quality synthetic gas is questionable in view of the differing methods of cost calculation employed and the highly competitive situation in the development of alternative processes. Promoters of each process are reluctant to publish cost estimates that exceed those of alternative processes, and there is the additional fear that cost estimates that exceed the anticipated price of natural gas by too much might reduce federal support for research and development programs. As a result of the narrow cost differentials among the various processes and the lack of adequate pilot plant data, precise economic criteria to evaluate each process do not yet exist. Approximate estimates, based on 1974 dollars, suggest that pipeline-quality synthetic gas could be priced in the range of $2.00 to $2.50 per million Btu, although some estimates are now as high as $3.65 per million Btu.* The lower estimates would, as noted, be competitive with imported LNG and would of course reinforce the attractiveness of coal gasification from a national security standpoint.

---

*Harry Perry, in his report to the Senate Committee on Interior and Insular Affairs, estimated that production costs of synthetic gas from a plant using the existing Lurgi process coupled with a subsequent methanation stage would range between $1.25 and $1.40 (U.S. Congress, Senate, Committee on Interior and Insular Affairs, *Energy Research and Development: Problems and Prospects,* report prepared by Harry Perry [Washington, D.C.: Government Printing Office, 1973]). An estimate prepared on May 2, 1973, by Frederic Holloway, vice president for science and technology of Exxon Corporation, indicated that production costs in a Lurgi process plant built in 1976 would roughly approximate $1.50 per million Btu, whereas a plant built in 1981 using one of the technologies currently under development would have production costs of $1.55 (Frederic A. Holloway, "Synthetic Fuels: Why, Which Ones and When?" [Paper presented to *Oil Daily* "Synthetic Energy: The Immediate Outlook" forum, May 2, 1973]). The higher, and more recent, estimates cited in the text were obtained from discussions with researchers in the field and reflect greater experience with the developing technologies. An even more recent and pessimistic estimate of the cost of synthetic high-Btu gas made from coal through the Lurgi process indicates that the cost could be as high as $3.65 per million Btu (Ogden Hammond and Martin B. Zimmerman, "The Economics of Coal-Based Synthetic Gas," *Technology Review* 78 [July-August 1975]: 43-51).

Coal as a Source of Liquid Fuels

Research and development programs for coal liquefaction have lagged considerably behind those for coal gasification because of the availability of adequate supplies of conventional crude oil at reasonable costs. However, crude price increases, together with mounting concern over available crude oil reserves and security of supply, have brought about additional research and development commitments in coal liquefaction.

Coal liquefaction essentially involves a chemical reaction of coal with hydrogen at high temperatures and pressures to yield a variety of products: light hydrocarbon gases, a wide range of liquid hydrocarbons, and a mixture of solid materials. Most liquefaction processes yield two to three barrels of syncrude for every ton of dry coal feed. The interaction of hydrogen with the sulfur, oxygen, and nitrogen in the coal during the liquefaction process results in the partial purification of the gas and liquid products.

As in the case of coal gasification, it was Germans who pioneered in the development of coal liquefaction processes, having employed two different methods commercially during World War II—hydrogenation and catalytic synthesis. The Fischer-Tropsch process for the catalytic synthesis of hydrocarbons from coal was developed in 1925 and is currently being used in a South African coal liquefaction plant to produce 62 million gallons of gasoline per year. Syncrude production costs using this process have substantially exceeded $10 per barrel.[23] Three alternative processes are currently at the pilot plant stage of development: (1) solvent refining of coal with minimum hydrogenation to produce a very heavy ash-free and sulfur-free fuel oil, (2) pressure hydrogenation, and (3) staged pyrolysis.[24] Pyrolysis has thus far produced a lower liquid yield than hydrogenation, but it may prove economically competitive as part of a multiproduct system at the mine-head. Such a system would fully utilize a variety of coal products resulting from coal liquefaction—pipeline-quality and low-Btu gas, crude oil, gasoline, chemical by-products, and low-sulfur coke.*

Solvent Refining of Coal

Solvent refining is a technically appealing approach to achieving increased utilization of high-sulfur coal. It is in fact a semiliquefaction process designed to

---

*FMC Corporation currently operates the only coal liquefaction pilot plant using a multiproduct system. Finely pulverized coal is used to produce a medium-Btu synthetic gas, synthetic crude, and residual char (Lawrence Lessing, "Capturing Clean Gas and Oil from Coal," *Fortune*, November 1973, p. 130).

provide a sulfur-free coal product at economically attractive prices. In this process, solvents are used to dissolve high-sulfur coal, and then a purification stage removes the sulfur from the dissolved coal. The liquid product may either be finally resolidified into a dense refined coal which is nearly free of ash or remain a highly viscous liquid which must be heated in order to be pumped through pipelines. While researchers believe that it may be possible to reduce the sulfur content of the coal considerably during the refining process, initial tests indicate that adequate sulfur removal has not yet been achieved. The high-Btu content of either end-product makes it economical to transport over long distances and may eventually provide a viable substitute for low-sulfur conventional coal or low-sulfur residual oil. This process is considerably simpler than full-scale liquefaction of coal because it requires the introduction of relatively small quantitities of hydrogen at low pressures and minimizes the by-products. Assuming that existing sulfur removal problems can be satisfactorily overcome, precombustion desulfurization by solvent refining of coal appears to offer an attractive alternative to sulfur emission control with stack gas scrubbing systems on the basis of tentative cost estimates.* Unlike low-Btu coal gasification, solvent refining of coal also permits the separation of coal conversion facilities from the electric power generating plant, thus increasing flexibility in choosing the location of these facilities.

Federal research and development expenditures for coal liquefaction processes during fiscal year 1973 amounted to $5.1 million, and Ray recommended raising annual expenditures in this field to $75 million.† The FEA *Project Independence Report* suggests that under its "accelerated case" scenario, 500,000-barrels-per-day production of synthetic liquids from coal could be achieved by 1985, although the more conservative "business as usual" scenario indicates that no commercial production of synthetic liquids from coal will be achieved by 1985.[25] The Task Force on Energy of the National Academy of Engineering estimated that an ambitious research and development program would permit the production of 300,000 barrels per day of synthetic crude from coal by 1985.[26] In addition to supporting research on the processes outlined

---

*Hoyt C. Hottel and Jack B. Howard include an estimate in their study on new energy technology that solvent refining of coal would entail additional costs of 3.3 to 18.8 cents per million Btu (depending on the percentage of coking involved in the process) versus 22 cents per million Btu additional fuel cost for a stack gas scrubbing system (Hoyt C. Hottel and Jack B Howard, *New Energy Technology* [Cambridge: Massachusetts Institute of Technology Press, 1971], p. 165).

†U.S. Atomic Energy Commission, *The Nation's Energy Future*, report submitted by Dixy Lee Ray (Washington, D.C.: Government Printing Office, 1973), p. 19. This research and development budget would be used to finance the construction of three pilot plants to test competing coal liquefaction processes and to finance the design of a major demonstration plant.

above, there is an urgent need for an expanded basic research program focusing on hydrogenation techniques and the development of catalysts capable of working at high temperatures and pressures. Uncertainties similar to those noted earlier for syncrude production from shale also apply to any attempt at the economic analysis of coal liquefaction. Current informed judgement indicates that a crude price of at least $12 to $14 per barrel (in 1974 dollars) will be required to support commercial operation.*

NOTES

1. Federal Energy Administration, *Project Independence Report* (Washington, D.C., 1974), pp. 98-99.

2. National Petroleum Council, Committee on U.S. Energy Outlook, *U.S. Energy Outlook* (Washington, D.C., 1972), pp. 139-45. The NPC figures are based on the widely cited U.S. Geological Survey, *Coal Resources of the United States*, Bulletin no. 1275, study prepared by Paul Averitt (Washington, D.C.: Government Printing Office, 1967). *Petroleum Press Survey* provided one estimate of world coal reserves at 9 trillion tons (*Petroleum Press Survey*, July 1973, p. 249). The comparison of reserve estimates from two or more sources is often made difficult by the differing measurement criteria employed by each source.

3. *U.S. Energy Outlook*, op. cit., p. 158.

4. *Newsweek*, November 12, 1973, p. 51.

5. Edmund A. Nephew, "The Challenge and Promise of Coal," *Technology Review* 76 (December 1975): 21.

6. Hoyt C. Hottel and Jack B. Howard, *New Energy Technology* (Cambridge: Massachusetts Institute of Technology Press, 1971), p. 73.

7. These conclusions were reached at a series of Energy Workshops held at Cornell University under the sponsorship of the AEC in September and October 1973. A summary of the concluding report is available in the New York *Times*, January 6, 1974, p. 52.

8. National Academy of Engineering, Task Force on Energy, *U.S. Energy Prospects: An Engineering Viewpoint* (Washington, D.C., 1974), pp. 34-35.

9. *Project Independence Report,* op. cit., pp. 106-08.

10. Nephew, op. cit., p. 24.

11. An analysis of research and development requirements for the development of more efficient mining technologies is available in Nephew, op. cit., and in U.S. Congress, Senate, Committee on Interior and Insular Affairs, *Energy Research and Development:*

---

*This price range was derived from discussions with researchers in the field and, once again, reflects a substantial increase over earlier, more optimistic estimates offered when less experience with the operating characteristics of the processes was available. For example, the NPC's 1972 study concluded that a 30,000-barrel-per-day commercial demonstration plant using western coal would be able to produce syncrude for a "price" of $7.75 to $8.28 per barrel (in 1970 dollars) with a 15 percent discounted cash flow rate of return on capital investment (National Petroleum Council, Committee on U.S. Energy Outlook, *U.S. Energy Outlook* [Washington, D.C., 1972], p. 46).

Problems and Prospects, report prepared by Harry Perry (Washington, D.C.: Government Printing Office, 1973), especially pp. 125-26.

12. For an account of the controversy surrounding coal slurry pipelines, see "The Fight Over Moving Coal by Pipeline," *Business Week*, July 27, 1974, p. 36.

13. A rather favorable evaluation of various scrubbing system technologies can be found in J.T. Dunham, C. Rampacek, and T.A. Henrie, "High-Sulfur Coal for Generating Electricity," *Science* 184 (April 19, 1974): 346-51. Some of the difficulties encountered in the commercial application of such systems are discussed in *Business Week*, April 21, 1973, p. 55.

14. An extensive (although somewhat dated) discussion of the various coal conversion technologies currently under development is available in Hottel and Howard, op. cit., pp. 103-86. A less technical survey of these technologies is provided by Wilson Clark, *Energy for Survival* (New York: Doubleday, Anchor Books, 1974), pp. 254-62.

15. H. C. Hottel and J. B. Howard, op. cit., pp. 275-82.

16. Lawrence Lessing, "Capturing Clean Gas and Oil from Coal," *Fortune*, November 1973, p. 210.

17. U.S. Atomic Energy Commission, *The Nation's Energy Future*, report submitted by Dixy Lee Ray (Washington, D.C.: Government Printing Office, 1973), pp. 19, 103-04.

18. *Project Independence Report*, op. cit., p. 138.

19. Hottel and Howard, op. cit., p. 282.

20. *Petroleum Economist*, March 1975, p. 111; and Lessing, op. cit., p. 214.

21. For a detailed comparison of these technologies, see Hottel and Howard, op. cit., pp. 103-36.

22. *Project Independence Report*, op. cit., p. 137.

23. Perry, op. cit., p. 93.

24. For a detailed technical comparison of the major competing coal liquefaction processes currently in the research and development stage, see Hottel and Howard, op. cit., pp. 170-85.

25. *Project Independence Report*, op. cit., pp. 137-38.

26. *U.S. Energy Prospects: An Engineering Viewpoint*, op. cit., p. 47.

4

STATUS OF RESEARCH
AND DEVELOPMENT:
NUCLEAR ENERGY

GENERAL BACKGROUND

The history of the commercial development of nuclear energy has paradoxically been characterized by continuing enthusiasm regarding its long-term potential accompanied by persistent disappointment over its actual attainments. Optimistic projects of the contribution of nuclear energy to overall energy supply often obscure the fact that so far the only practical commercial application of nuclear energy has been in the field of electric power generation. Therefore, the foreseeable role of commercial nuclear energy will be largely limited to this one sector of energy supply, and its long-term contribution will depend on the relative importance of electric power in the advanced industrial economies. Moreover, even in this limited context, it is sobering to consider that after roughly 15 years of commercial development in the United States, nuclear energy currently accounts for only 5 percent of the total installed electric generating capacity and slightly more than 1 percent of the nation's energy supplies.[1]

By the end of 1973, the United States had 25,000 megawatts of installed nuclear generating capacity with operating licenses and an additional 53,000 milliwatts had received construction permits but had not yet entered into operation.[2] The AEC, which has repeatedly been compelled to revise downward its overly optimistic projections for accelerated growth of nuclear generating capacity in the United States, had projected a few years ago that nuclear plants would supply 150,000 milliwatts of electrical energy (equivalent to 22 percent of overall electric power generation) by 1980. Recent difficulties in nuclear plant projects have prompted the commission to lower this estimate to 102,000 milliwatts, and some experts question the realism of even this more modest target.[3]

Outside the United States, the Soviet Union, Great Britain, France, and Canada pioneered in the commercial development of nuclear energy, and during the late 1960s, other countries in Western Europe as well as Japan launched programs of their own. Nine countries currently account for 90 percent of the world's nuclear power generating capacity, and four countries—the United States, Great Britain, West Germany, and Japan—alone account for 75 percent of the world's capacity.[4] This pattern is likely to persist at least throughout the rest of this decade. Table 4.1 indicates the distribution of world nuclear power reactors by the middle of 1973.

The average size of nuclear power generating units under construction has increased steadily as a result of considerable economies of scale, and during the period 1969-77, average size is projected to more than double—from 361 to 771 milliwatts. This trend is most advanced in the United States, where one-half of the nuclear generating capacity over the next five years will be in the 950-to-1,200-milliwatt range.[5] Although the AEC recently placed a ceiling of 1,300 milliwatts on the size of new units for light water reactors (LWRs) and 1,500 milliwatts for high-temperature gas-cooled reactors (HTGRs) in order to encourage standardization of design, nuclear generating units of 1,700 milliwatts are now considered technically feasible.

The multinational development of commercial nuclear energy has resulted in the emergence of three basic categories of nuclear reactors which vary in terms of fuel, moderator, and coolant. All three categories derive most of their energy from the slow neutron fission of a scarce uranium isotope, U_{235}. The fission, or "splitting," of the nucleus of a U_{235} atom releases additional neutrons which generate a self-sustaining reaction. In addition, it produces a number of fission products and a certain amount of energy, which is released as heat. However, the U_{235} isotope constitutes only one part in 140 of natural uranium, which consists primarily of U_{238}. Some nuclear reactor models are capable of using natural uranium as a fuel, while other models require the preliminary enrichment of natural uranium in order to increase the content of the isotope U_{235} to 2 to 3 percent. Unless the neutrons in the chain reaction are retarded, they will be absorbed by the U_{238} in the fuel and the reaction will not be sustained; this function is performed by the moderator. A coolant is also necessary in order to absorb the heat generated by the nuclear reaction within the reactor core and to transfer it either directly or indirectly to the turbine-generator.

Despite the presence of a moderator, some neutrons are inevitably absorbed by the predominant U_{238} isotope to form a substantial amount of plutonium (Pu_{239}). Some of the plutonium by-product fissions in the reactor, but most of it is removed during the fuel reprocessing stage and stored to be used as a fuel in breeder reactors. The plutonium may also be recycled and used as a fuel in present-day reactors, although the AEC (and now its successor, the Nuclear Regulatory Commission) has repeatedly delayed approval of plutonium recycling in existing LWRs.

TABLE 4.1

Distribution of World Power Reactors by Type and Size
(100 Megawatts or More)

Country/Area	Units	Operating Light Water Reactors	Average Size (Megawatts)	Units	Under Construction Light Water Reactors	Average Size (Megawatts)
United Kingdom	22	0	192.5	8	0	636.2
France	7	1	364.4	1	1	850.0
West Germany	6	5	344.5	6	6	1186.3
Italy	3	2	202.3	1	1	783.0
Benelux	1	1	450.0	3	3	810.0
Subtotal	39	9	154.1	19	11	856.3
Switzerland	3	3	335.3	1	1	850.0
Spain	3	3	357.6	6	6	902.0
Sweden	2	2	600.0	3	3	686.6
Other Western Europe	0	0	–	1	1	720.0
Subtotal	8	8	409.8	11	11	796.5
United States	22	21	607.2	54	53	901.2
Japan	7	6	426.9	8	8	731.9
Canada	6	0	415.0	0	0	–
Latin America	0	0	–	1	1	318.0
Asia and other	5	2	261.0	5	3	–
Total	87	46	383.1	98	87	841.2

	On Order			Proposed			Total		
	Units	Light Water Reactors	Average Size (Megawatts_e)	Units	Light Water Reactors	Average Size (Megawatts_e)	Units	Light Water Reactors	Average Size (Megawatts_e)
United Kingdom	2	0	660.0	8	0	1051.2	40	0	476.4
France	3	3	900.0	0	0	–	11	5	554.6
West Germany	5	5	984.8	15	15	908.4	32	31	866.7
Italy	0	0	–	1	1	750.0	5	4	428.0
Benelux	0	0	–	3	3	550.0	7	7	647.1
Subtotal	10	8	894.4	27	19	905.0	95	47	627.0
Switzerland	1	1	850.0	1	1	850.0	6	6	592.7
Spain	0	0	–	3	3	1110.0	12	12	817.9
Sweden	4	4	820.0	5	5	740.0	14	14	731.4
Other Western Europe	1	1	720.0	5	4	537.5	7	6	548.3
Subtotal	6	6	808.3	14	13	754.8	39	38	703.8
United States	68	62	1030.4	18	16	1088.6	162	152	936.3
Japan	6	6	939.5	25	25	961.6	46	45	837.4
Canada	4	0	750.0	0	0	–	10	0	549.0
Latin America	2	2	713.0	6	6	466.7	9	9	504.9
Asia and other	4	4	591.0	9	7	458.2	23	16	450.6
Total	100	88	962.7	99	86	863.3	384	307	775.1

Note: Table does not include estimates for Communist countries.

Source: U.S. Atomic Energy Commission, *Nuclear Power 1973-2000*, 1972; additional data provided by the commission's Division of International Programs, May 1973. Reprinted in Joseph A. Yager and Eleanor B. Steinberg, *Energy and U.S. Foreign Policy* (Cambridge: Ballinger, 1974), p. 336.

TYPES OF NUCLEAR REACTORS

Nonbreeding Fission Reactors

In the United States, the LWR has dominated the commercial nuclear reactor market, and this model has been widely adopted in other areas, particularly in Western Europe and Japan. The LWR uses enriched uranium as a fuel and employs conventional light water both as a moderator and as a coolant. One variety of the LWR—the pressurized water reactor (PWR)—represents 60 percent of the LWRs installed in the United States.[6] In the PWR, the light water is pressurized to 2,250 pounds per square inch so that its boiling point is raised to above 600 degrees Fahrenheit. Once the pressurized water absorbs the heat from the nuclear reaction, it is circulated to a steam generator, where the heat is transferred to water at a lower pressure (with a corresponding lower boiling point), thus generating steam to power a steam turbine. The other major variant of the LWR—the boiling water reactor (BWR)—uses water at considerably lower pressures (1,000 pounds per square inch). As a result, the water boils in the reactor itself, and the resulting steam is utilized directly in a steam turbine, thus eliminating the need for an intermediate steam generator.

As a consequence of the relatively low steam temperatures generated in an LWR nuclear power plant (506 degrees Fahrenheit versus 1,000 degrees Fahrenheit in a conventional fossil fuel generating plant), these reactors can only attain thermal efficiencies of 32.5 percent, in comparison with a thermal efficiency in the range of 40 to 44 percent possible in a conventional power plant.[7] Lower thermal efficiencies in turn imply not only higher costs but greater thermal pollution, and it is estimated that an LWR generating plant releases 50 percent more warm water than an equivalent fossil fuel generating plant.[8] One consequence of this is that nuclear generating plants must either be located near large natural bodies of water capable of absorbing the excess heat with minimum adverse effect or else utilize cooling towers. The additional costs entailed in the disposal of waste heat provide a major incentive for the development of nuclear energy systems with higher recoverable heat characteristics.

Gas-cooled reactors constitute the second major category of nuclear reactor models. Although this category has received relatively little research and development support in the United States, it has served as the basic model for Great Britain's commercial nuclear energy program. The Magnox reactors, developed by the British during the 1950s and early 1960s, represented the first stage of gas-cooled reactor development. The more compact and more efficient advanced gas-cooled reactor (AGR) was introduced in the mid-1960s as an improved version of the Magnox design, and since 1965 it has been the only model ordered by the British Central Electricity Generating Board (CEGB). Construction delays have thus far prevented the commercial operation of any AGR generating plants, and growing disillusionment with this particular model has prompted the British Atomic Energy Authority to abandon the AGR model and to adopt an alternative reactor design.

In the meantime, the European Nuclear Energy Agency of the OECD and Gulf Oil Corporation have separately pursued research and development programs on a third variant of the gas-cooled reactor—the HTGR—which they believe will offer significant advantages over either of the LWR models.[9] The HTGR uses a mixture of enriched uranium and thorium as a fuel, and instead of light water, it uses graphite as a moderator for the nuclear reaction. The HTGR differs from previous gas-cooled reactor designs by using helium as the coolant, and this has permitted the attainment of higher coolant outlet temperatures (800 to 1,000 degrees Fahrenheit) than had been possible in any other commercial reactor design. As a result, the HTGR, in a design for a twin reactor producing 1,260 milliwatts, is believed to be capable of thermal efficiencies of 42 percent, which is roughly equivalent to the thermal efficiency of conventional power generating stations.[10] Moreover, proponents of the HTGR point out that a helium coolant can be heated to high temperatures and then used directly in a gas turbine as the first stage in an advanced combined cycle generating plant. Such an arrangement would raise the thermal efficiency to 45 percent, which is higher than has been obtained in any conventional fossil fuel generating plant.[11] Additional technological advances in gas turbines may raise the thermal efficiency of the HTGR even higher than is currently possible.

Although the capital costs of a commercial HTGR model would be higher than for an equivalent LWR, more efficient use of the fuel in the HTGR would significantly reduce the differential in long run operating costs. The higher thermal efficiency of the HTGR and the enhanced flexibility entailed by the use of thorium as a fuel have been cited as significant advantages of the HTGR over alternative designs. A report by the European Nuclear Energy Agency summarizing its work on the Dragon high-temperature reactor project maintained that the HTGR is now economically competitive with other reactor models.[12]

Gulf Oil Corporation has sponsored an ambitious private research and development program on the HTGR which includes the operation of a 40-milliwatt prototype HTGR built in 1967. The first commercial HTGR (330 milliwatts) in the United States has begun operation in Colorado, and Gulf has announced that seven additional commercial plants ranging from 330 to 1,160 milliwatts have already been ordered.[13] Royal Dutch-Shell recently organized a joint venture with Gulf to sponsor an additional three-year, $200 million research and development program on the HTGR. Although the AEC has primarily concentrated its own research and development program on LWRs, its recent proposal for a federal energy research and development budget for fiscal years 1975/79 includes additional support for HTGR development.*

---

*The AEC report entitled *The Nation's Energy Future*, submitted to President Nixon on December 1, 1973, envisioned an increase in the research and development budget for

The third major category of nuclear reactor models consists of heavy water reactors, primarily represented by the Canadian Deuterium Uranian (CANDU) model sponsored by Atomic Energy of Canada, Ltd. (AECL).[14] This model uses heavy water as a moderator and pressurized heavy water as the coolant which then boils light water in a heat exchanger. The major attraction of the CANDU model, however, is that it is the only advanced nonbreeder reactor design that uses natural, rather than enriched, uranium as a fuel and increases the energy yield per ton of uranium fuel. The lower long-run fuel costs are somewhat offset by the 10 percent higher initial capital costs over comparable LWRs, however. Long-run operating cost estimates vary. The AEC withdrew from a joint project with AECL in 1971 because it believed that LWRs were more economical than the CANDU model. AECL, on the other hand, continues to argue that the long-run cost differentials between the two categories of reactors are more favorable to the CANDU.*

Commercial CANDU power generating stations are already in operation in Canada, and more are scheduled. One attractive aspect of the CANDU model is the quick start-up and early operating success of these commercial generating stations. Thus far, few CANDU reactors have been built outside of Canada, although CANDU manufacturers recently undertook a vigorous campaign to persuade the British CEGB to adopt the CANDU design for its next generation of commercial nuclear reactors. While the British authorities ultimately rejected the CANDU model, the steam generating heavy water reactor (SGHWR) model they eventually selected is a hybrid design incorporating features of both the CANDU and the BWR models.

The increasing commitment to nuclear reactors in the major energy-consuming regions has naturally produced concern over the adequacy of

---

HTGRs from \$7.2 million in fiscal year 1973 to \$40 million in fiscal year 1975, with expenditures of \$128.6 million projected over the period of 1975/79. However, the ERDA budget request for fiscal year 1976 submitted to Congress in February 1975 reported an estimated fiscal year 1975 expenditure of \$21.9 million for the gas-cooled thermal reactor program—almost 50 percent lower than the earlier AEC estimate. The budget request for fiscal year 1976 has been similarly scaled down from the \$44.7 million mentioned in the AEC report to \$31.4 million. The ERDA budget request for fiscal year 1976 is summarized in *Nuclear News*, March 1975, pp. 28-34.

Business Week, in its August 5, 1972, issue, carried an article, " 'Heavy' Reactors Seek a Market," analyzing the CANDU reactor model and the controversy over its long-run operating costs. While the capital costs of the CANDU reactor are higher because of the more complicated internal plumbing required, its supporters point out that annual fuel costs for the CANDU are roughly one-half the fuel costs for a comparable LWR. While the heavy water required for the CANDU reactor is relatively expensive (approximately \$39 per pound), it represents a once-only purchase, since the heavy water is recirculated in the reactor and only insignificant additional purchases are required to replace losses from leaks and evaporation (amounting to roughly 1 percent of the reactor's heavy water inventory each year).

uranium reserves to satisfy accelerating demand. This issue is particularly important in the continuing controversy over the development of fast breeder reactors (FBRs). The FBR is capable of "breeding" additional fuel during the nuclear reaction process by placing a blanket of U_{238} around the reactor core to absorb some of the escaping neutrons. This absorption process "breeds" plutonium (Pu_{239}), which can then be chemically treated and used as a fuel. Since the rationale for the development of the FBR depends heavily on the evaluation of available uranium reserves, estimates of these reserves are a critical variable in the debate over this new technology. The problem of reserve estimates is complicated by the fact that uranium exploration programs have not been extensively undertaken, and it is considered likely that major additional reserves exist that have not yet been discovered. Moreover, estimates have usually calculated reserves in terms of recovery costs using existing extraction technology.

Aside from the obvious point that extraction technology may undergo substantial improvement as the demand for uranium fuels increases, this also raises the difficult question of the precise impact of uranium fuel prices on overall electricity generating costs using nuclear reactors. Since fuel costs constitute a much smaller proportion of operating costs in nuclear reactors than in conventional fossil fuel generating plants, prices of uranium have a reduced impact on the cost of electricity. High-grade uranium deposits are generally considered to be those recoverable at under $10 per pound of uranium oxide. A 1971 Massachusetts Institute of Technology (MIT) study concluded, however, that a substantial rise in uranium prices from $8 per pound to $18 per pound would yield only a 7 percent increase in the price of electricity from an LWR plant, and more recent estimates suggest that the final increase might be even less.[15]

The United States currently accounts for approximately one-third (33.4 percent) of the world's known reserves of uranium, while additional major reserves exist in Canada (18.9 percent) and South Africa (20.5 percent).[16] Recent exploration suggests that various African countries as well as Australia contain sizable uranium reserves. The Soviet Union and mainland China are also known to possess large reserves. The OECD has published one set of estimates of world uranium reserves, which is reproduced in Table 4.2. According to AEC estimates, 275,000 tons of proved domestic reserves of uranium concentrate (U_3O_8) were recoverable at a forward cost* of $8 per pound or less as of January 1, 1974. At a higher forward cost of $15 per pound or less, proved domestic reserves of U_3O_8 increase to 525,000 tons. When "estimated additional" resources are added to proved domestic reserves, the AEC estimates

---

*"Forward cost" is an incremental cost which does not include sunk costs or return on investment, so actual prices will be substantially greater than forward costs.

TABLE 4.2

Uranium Resources by Major Countries, 1973
(thousands of short tons)

	Price Range up to $10 per pound U_3O_8*		Price Range $10 to $15 per pound U_3O_8	
	Reasonably Assured Resources	Estimated Additional Resources	Reasonably Assured Resources	Estimated Additional Resources
Angola	–	–	–	17.0
Argentina	12.0	18.0	10.0	30.0
Australia	92.0	102.0	38.3	38.0
Brazil	–	3.3	0.9	–
Canada	241.0	247.0	158.0.	284.0
Central African Republic	10.5	10.5	–	–
Denmark (Greenland)	7.0	13.0	–	–
Finland	–	–	1.7	–
France	47.5	31.5	26.0	32.5
Gabon	16.0	6.5	–	6.5
India	–	–	3.0	1.0
Italy	1.6	–	–	–
Japan	3.6	–	5.4	–
Mexico	1.3	–	1.2	–
Niger	52.0	26.0	13.0	13.0
Portugal	9.3	7.7	1.3	13.0
South Africa	263.0	10.4	80.6	33.8
Spain	11.0	–	10.0	–
Sweden	–	–	351.0	52.0
Turkey	2.8	–	0.6	–
United States	337.0	700.0	183.0	300.0
Yugoslavia	7.8	13.0	–	–
Zaire	2.3	2.2	–	–
Total	1,127.7	1,191.1	884.0	820.8

*Dollar value of March 1973: $1 = 0.829; European Monetary Agreement units of account = 0.829 Special Drawing Rights. This dollar value corresponds to $42.22 per fine ounce of gold.

Source: Organization for Economic Cooperation and Development, *Uranium Resources Production and Demand,* joint report by the OECD Nuclear Energy Agency and the International Atomic Energy Agency (Paris, August 1973), p. 14. Reprinted in Joseph A. Yager and Eleanor B. Steinberg, *Energy and U.S. Foreign Policy* (Cambridge: Ballinger, 1974), p. 457.

of the domestic U_3O_8 resource base rise to 675,000 tons and 1,525,000 tons at forward costs of $8 per pound and $15 per pound or less, respectively.[17]

These resource estimates should be evaluated in the context of current projections of demand for uranium concentrate in the decades ahead. One recent estimate suggests that cumulative U.S. uranium requirements through the year 2000 will reach approximately 2 million tons of U_3O_8. Equally important, however, is the fact that the cumulative lifetime requirements of the nuclear plants in operation at that time will be in the range of 5 million tons.[18] These estimates assume that plutonium recycling operations will be begun by 1982, and they would have to be revised upward if breeders do not achieve commercial application by the early 1990s. Under present projections for the expansion of nuclear power generating capacity, present uranium production capacity will have to quadruple over the next ten years, requiring capital investment of $5 billion in exploration and development programs, uranium mines, and associated mills.[19]

In view of the lengthy lead times associated with the development of new mining facilities (currently eight years), it seems highly probable that at least a short-term tightness in the supply of uranium will be experienced at the beginning of the next decade. The long-term supply situation, while still plagued by considerable uncertainty, seems to offer more reason for at least guarded optimism. Since less than 10 percent of the area in the United States considered geologically favorable for uranium deposits has been explored, there is still a great probability that major additional reserves will be discovered as exploration efforts intensify.[20] In 1974, the base price of uranium increased substantially to the $15-per-pound range, in comparison with the 1964 base price of $8 per pound. The AEC (now the ERDA) only recently initiated the first systematic attempt to gather the data necessary to evaluate the ultimate size of domestic uranium reserves, and it will be several years before definitive results from this study—the National Uranium Resource Evaluation (NURE)—will become available.[21] The substantial increases in the price of uranium occurred only in the period following 1974, and while they provide a strong incentive for the expansion of producing and milling capacity by the uranium supply industry, these price increases are too recent to have had much impact on current levels of supply.

On a global level, an OECD study revealed that known worldwide reserves of high-grade uranium ore increased by one-third during 1970-73. This study also anticipated that global resources of high-grade uranium would actually prove to be 15 times larger than most current estimates suggest.[22] While growing imports of uranium ore (currently prohibited) represent one possible response to future limitations under domestic study, this option is undesirable if one of the objectives of national energy policy is to minimize dependence on foreign energy supplies.

The controversy over the adequacy of domestic reserves of uranium ore has tended to divert attention from other potential constraints on the accelerated development of a commercial nuclear energy associated with the nuclear fuel cycle. The nuclear fuel cycle encompasses a complex series of operations required to supply nuclear reactors with adequate fuel supplies and to process the fuel once it has been used in the reactors.

In addition to the exploration and mining of uranium ore and the initial milling and refining of the ore to produce the uranium concentrates, these concentrates must go through an enrichment process in which they are converted to uranium hexafluoride (UF_6) and then enriched to increase the proportion of the isotope U_{235}. Following enrichment, there is a process for the fabrication of nuclear reactor fuel involving the conversion of the enriched uranium hexafluoride into uranium dixoide and then pellitizing the uranium dioxide, encapsulating it in rods, and assembling the final fuel elements. Once the spent fuel leaves the reactor, it must be reprocessed to recover "unburned" uranium and plutonium from the radioactive wastes, and then the radioactive wastes must be indefinitely stored under maximum safety conditions to guard against leakage. Each stage of this process usually involves some transportation of highly radioactive materials as well as storage of uranium inventories. As can be seen, the nuclear fuel cycle requires an extensive industrial infrastructure designed to service the growing fuel needs of commercial nuclear reactors, and bottlenecks in any stage of the cycle would seriously hamper the accelerated expansion of nuclear power generation in the United States.

The two major areas of concern in the nuclear fuel cycle involve potential limitations in uranium enrichment capacity and in fuel reprocessing capacity. At present, the U.S. government owns and operates three uranium enrichment plants with a combined capacity of 17 million separative work units (SWU) per year, and these plants supply all the needs of all domestic reactors, as well as a number of reactors operated by foreign utilities.[23] While there is currently a surplus capacity in domestic enrichment facilities, there is some concern regarding the capability to meet the additional demand for enriched uranium which would arise under any program to accelerate the expansion of nuclear reactor capacity in the next decade. Present plans call for an expansion of capacity in the three existing plants to 28 million SWU by 1983, but many experts believe that additional plants should be built to ensure reliable enriched uranium supplies.[24] A seven-to-nine-year lead time is generally required for the design and construction of an enrichment plant, and recent uncertainties in this area have tended to discourage investment in this area.

The U.S. government has indicated its desire to end the government monopoly currently dominating the field and to encourage private investment in the future expansion of enrichment capacity, but until recently, no detailed policy had been formulated to provide the incentive necessary for private investors to commit the billions of dollars required for a single enrichment plant.

In June 1975, however, President Ford announced such a policy, which met with a receptive response from Uranium Enrichment Associates, a private joint venture considering the construction of an enrichment plant with a 9 million-SWU capacity estimated to cost $3.5 billion (in 1976 dollars).[25]

Another uncertainty that has tended to restrain expansion of enrichment plant capacity involves the decision as to whether to continue to rely on the proven method of gaseous diffusion enrichment or to adopt the unproven method of centrifugal enrichment, which permits greater flexibility in plant size and a significant reduction in the electricity consumption associated with the enrichment process.[26] Proponents of the centrifugal enrichment process argue that it will render gaseous diffusion obsolete within a decade. Thus far, however, U.S. enrichment plants have been designed for the gaseous diffusion process, and there are no definite plans for a commercial application of the centrifuge process. More recently, there have been encouraging reports regarding progress in the development of new laser enrichment techniques, both in the United States and in Israel.[27] These techniques could improve the enrichment process while permitting a substantial cost reduction.

The other problem area in the nuclear fuel cycle concerns a potential national shortage of uranium fuel reprocessing capacity. Unexpected technical difficulties have left the United States without a single commercial nuclear fuel reprocessing plant in working order.[28] The most recent setback involved General Electric's announcement that its Midwest Fuel Recovery Plant did not work and would have to be fundamentally redesigned.[29] General Electric had pioneered in the development of a new "Aqua Fluor" process which had generated considerable optimism in its early stages of development, but the recent problems encountered in scaling up this process suggest that it is not yet ready for commercial application.

The growing disillusionment over commercial fuel reprocessing has prompted increasing support for the concept of a "throwaway fuel cycle," in which spent fuel rods would simply be stored indefinitely without reprocessing. However, the government has postponed its plans to construct a national repository, and existing storage basins for spent fuels and radioactive wastes are rapidly reaching their capacity. By 1979, a national backlog of 2,300 tons of used but unprocessed reactor fuel is anticipated.[30] In addition to the logistical problems associated with radioactive waste management, there is also a major safety problem, as indicated by numerous reports of radioactive waste leakage from tanks and storage drums located on AEC facilities.[31] While it is true that recent cancellations of orders for nuclear reactors by electric utilities have prompted more conservative estimates regarding the growth of nuclear power generation, it is also necessary to recognize that virtually any program of national energy independence will probably involve an accelerated expansion of nuclear power generation and will therefore require the resolution of these problems in the nuclear fuel cycle.

Cost comparisons among alternative energy sources are notoriously difficult to make, and attempts to compare the economic costs of electric power generation from conventional fossil fuel plants and from various models of nuclear reactors have encountered even greater obstacles. One difficulty stems from the different cost structures of various nuclear models and conventional power plants. In general, capital costs account for an overwhelming share of nuclear generating costs, while fuel costs in fossil fuel plants assume a much more important share of total costs. In view of these differences, the only viable method of comparison involves estimates of long-run system costs for each alternative, and these in turn depend on assumptions concerning such uncertain variables as probable plant operation patterns and future trends in fuel prices. Since the location of the plants often has a major impact on long-run costs, detailed comparisons are only feasible for specific locations, and attempts to generalize from these comparisons are highly unreliable.

In a 1973 article in *Energy Policy*, A.J. Surrey attempted to make a rough general comparison of long-run system costs for a 1,000-milliwatt LWR plant and an equivalent fossil fuel generating plant.[32] Assuming that a 1,000-milliwatt LWR plant ordered in mid-1973 would require capital costs of $450 million, while a comparable fossil fuel plant would involve $350 million in capital costs, Surrey concluded that a nuclear reactor plant would be economically competitive with a conventional plant once fossil fuel prices exceeded 42 cents per million Btu. This estimate assumed a 15 percent capital charge rate and a 75 percent load factor.

Since average coal and fuel oil prices in the United States during 1972 were 40 cents per million Btu and 60 to 70 cents per million Btu, respectively, Surrey believed then that nuclear reactor plants were already generally competitive, particularly in the Northeast, which lacked any local fossil fuel reserves. Since Western European coal prices are substantially higher than U.S. coal prices, a major additional price incentive exists in Europe for the accelerated development of nuclear energy. Although the transformation of the crude oil price structure during 1973 and prospects for continuing high prices of fossil fuels were expected to further strengthen the economic competitiveness of nuclear energy in every major energy-consuming region, this effect was at least somewhat counterbalanced by the quadrupling of the price of uranium that occurred over the same period.

Proponents of commercial nuclear energy have expressed growing concern over recent trends that suggest that the demand for nuclear generating plants by electric utilities has weakened considerably. The Atomic Industrial Forum recently reported that utilities have deferred 77 of the 181 nuclear units currently under construction or once firmly planned.[33] While utilities have deferred plans for many conventional power generating units as well, because of the unanticipated slowness in the growth of demand for electricity as well as lower earnings, a variety of factors have contributed to a fundamental reevaluation of the comparative economics of nuclear energy.

The rapid escalation of construction costs for nuclear reactors has proved particularly disturbing. One recent study indicated that construction costs for nuclear plants increased at an average of $31 per kilowatt per year between 1969 and 1975, while construction costs for coal plants increased at a rate of only $13 per kilowatt per year.[34] As a result, although nuclear plants may still be competitive in the fuel-scarce Northeast, there is now considerable doubt as to whether nuclear reactors are in fact any longer economically competitive with conventional power plants in other parts of the country.

Moreover, comparisons between nuclear-generated electricity and fossil fuel-generated electricity that are restricted to economic cost estimates ignore broader factors which will have a substantial role in determining the pace of commercial nuclear energy development. Nuclear reactor plants represent major long-term commitments of capital (almost half a billion dollars for a 1,000-milliwatt plant ordered in 1973), and electric utilities have demonstrated considerable reluctance to undertake such commitments as a result of persistent uncertainties regarding long-term energy policies and demand. Commercial nuclear reactor development is still at a relatively early stage, and the rapidly evolving technology inhibits attempts to standardize reactor designs. As a result, only limited commercial operating experience which would permit an accurate assessment of future performance has accumulated for any particular design (except for Magnox reactors, which are now considered obsolescent). The lengthy lead times currently experienced between initiation and commercial operation of a nuclear plant project (approximately ten years) also increase the possibility that reactor designs ordered today will have undergone substantial improvement by the time the reactor enters operation.

Mounting concern over the safety of the LWRs and resulting restrictions on their construction and operation have further increased the reluctance of the utilities to invest heavily in nuclear technology. Future FBRs pose even greater safety problems, since they operate much closer to the margins of an uncontrolled fission reaction than thermal reactors, and the consequences of an accident would probably be more serious. Any energy strategy that seeks to promote the accelerated development of commercial nuclear energy must include policies designed to minimize these obstacles. In the meantime, electric utilities will avoid committing a large share of future base load capacity to nuclear energy and will instead place the emphasis of their investment programs on the diversification of fuel sources.

Lead times for the construction of nuclear power generating plants have gradually lengthened from five to ten years, and both construction delays and licensing procedures have been singled out as major contributing factors.[35] The National Environmental Protection Act of 1970 requires all nuclear plants to obtain an operating license as well as an initial construction permit in order to promote full public disclosure of the projected environmental impact of each plant. The construction permit must be obtained before construction can begin, and the period from initial application to final issuance of a construction permit ranges from 20 to 30 months, while operating license applications usually require an additional 24 to 30 months.[36] These procedures are further complicated by design modifications which are usually requested by utilities when they order nuclear plants. A nuclear plant manufacturer will prepare approximately 3,000 different documents for a typical reactor sale, and of these approximately 25 percent will be modified by either the purchaser or the AEC.[37] Construction delays attributable to strikes, the replacement of poor-quality materials, and delays in component deliveries have also constituted a major obstacle in fulfilling orders. The economic impact of these various delays is significant: reactor start-up delays cost the utilities $100,000 to $200,000 per day in interest charges and in the cost of obtaining supplementary interim power.

In 1973 several steps were taken to reduce the lead time in nuclear plant construction, and President Nixon stated that these lead times should ultimately be reduced to six years. In an effort to promote standardization of reactor designs and simplify licensing procedures, the AEC announced in March 1973 that it would restrict the size of proposed LWR and HTGR units to 1,300 milliwatts and 1,500 milliwatts, respectively, and that it would consider applications from nuclear plant manufacturers for a blanket operating license for a specific standardized reactor design. These measures should provide a major incentive for the development of standardized models and increase the reluctance of utilities to order design modifications. General Electric has already developed a standardized package design for its 1,220-milliwatt BWR/6 model and has asked the AEC to grant this design a blanket operating license.[38] While such steps offer a significant potential for reducing lead times, it is important to ensure that standardization of reactor designs does not restrict continuing technological innovation in this field.

Probably the most serious obstacle to the accelerated development of commercial nuclear energy involves the growing concern over the safety of the LWRs, which will constitute 85 percent of the nuclear generating units constructed during 1969-85. Ironically, one major advantage of nuclear reactors over conventional fossil fuel generating plants is that they minimize the harmful atmospheric emissions usually associated with fossil fuel plants. While a 1,000-milliwatt fossil fuel generating plant annually emits 10 million tons of carbon dioxide, several hundred thousand tons of sulfur dioxide, nitrogen oxide, and ash particles, comparable nuclear plants emit virtually no atmospheric pollutants.[39] Multiple barriers within the nuclear reactor and associated nuclear facilities reduce atmospheric emissions of radioactive substances during normal operations to minimal levels which are hardly distinguishable from natural background radiation.

The focus of concern, however, has been on the accidental release of radioactive emissions during various stages of the nuclear fuel cycle. The AEC minimizes the potential for accidents and points to an unblemished safety record of over 100 reactor-years of commercial operation for LWRs without any accident resulting in deaths or injuries to the public having occurred. However, confidence in this safety record has been increasingly reduced by reports of component failures and corrosion problems in operating nuclear reactors.[40]

In particular, critics of the LWRs have cited the dangers involved in potential loss of coolant accidents (LOCAs), in which a malfunction occurs in the cooling water system. Such a malfunction would require the automatic shutdown of the nuclear reactor and the activation of the emergency core cooling system to flood or spray the hot core with cold water. Failure of either of these steps would result in the runaway heating of the reactor core and melt the multiple barriers surrounding the core within several minutes, releasing large quantities of fission products into the atmosphere. It has been estimated that such a release would be fatal within 100 miles downward of the reactor and would cause injuries over an area extending tens of thousands of square miles.[41] In view of the seriousness of such an accident, it is essential to determine the probability of a LOCA's occurring and the reliability of the emergency core cooling system.

A recently published report by the AEC estimates that the failure rate for the reactor coolant system may be as high as 0.1 percent per reactor-year, and major pipe failures may be even more frequent.[42] In fact, several pipe failures which required shutdown of operating LWRs have already been reported, although there has so far been no cooling system failure in such a situation. On the basis of elaborate computer simulations, the AEC estimates cooling system reliability to be from 99 to 99.9 percent, with total effectiveness during operation.[43] However, a wide variety of experts have challenged the validity of these computer simulations, arguing that they depend on inadequate knowledge of the physical effects associated with the prolonged exposure of various metals to radioactive emission. Unanticipated corrosion and damage to fuel elements in nuclear reactor experiments involving relatively low temperatures raise additional doubts concerning the reliability of the AEC computer simulations.

Critics of the AEC's safety policies point out that a task force of reactor safety specialists commissioned by the AEC in 1966 to evaluate manufacturer's designs of emergency cooling systems cited a variety of technical shortcoming in these systems and recommended more research on the capabilities of such systems before the AEC should proceed to license future reactors. However, the report was never officially issued by the AEC and has been virtually unobtainable from the commission.[44] A series of tests conducted in late 1970 and early 1971 on miniature nine-inch-high models of reactor pressure vessels at the National Reactor Testing Station in Idaho provide additional cause for concern.

In what may be the only actual test of the emergency core cooling system, these models were drained of coolant water, and six successive attempts to flood the reactor cores with emergency water met with failure, since only 10 percent of the emergency cooling water reached the core.[45] The AEC has attempted to discredit the test results by arguing that miniature reactor core models cannot adequately reproduce conditions encountered in commercial nuclear reactors. However, in the absence of full-scale field testing, critics of the AEC insist that computer simulations offer no greater reliability in evaluating safety mechanisms than scale-model testing and that in the presence of conflicting data regarding the operation of these mechanisms, major additional research in the area of reactor safety technology is urgently required.

The controversy over the reliability of safety devices in the LWRs served as the focus for almost 18 months of public hearings held by the AEC at Bethesda, Maryland, in 1972 and 1973. Rather than resolving the issue, testimony accumulated during the hearings only raised further doubts regarding the AEC's conclusion that LWRs were adequately safe. The most disturbing aspect of the controversy is that many of the AEC's own reactor safety experts, including the director of the Nuclear Safety Division at the AEC Oak Ridge National Laboratory, have challenged the AEC's official position on this issue.*

The AEC made one further attempt to satisfy the growing concern over nuclear reactor safety with the publication in August 1974 of an 11-volume report summarizing the results of a two-year study directed by N.C. Rasmussen, a professor of nuclear engineering at MIT. This study, which soon became known as the "Rasmussen Report," concluded that although there were potential hazards associated with the commercial development of nuclear energy, the risks were "smaller than many other man-made and natural risks."[46] The study concentrated on the LOCA issue and employed a methodology known as "fault-free analysis," an approach initially developed for the aerospace industry to predict the effects of failures of small components in large, complex systems.

As with the public hearings held earlier at Bethesda, the Rasmussen Report seemed to raise more questions than it answered regarding nuclear reactor safety. The Sierra Club and the Union of Concerned Scientists jointly issued a critique of the report, arguing that the methodology employed was inappropriate for an evaluation of nuclear reactor safety, the study had relied on an improper and incomplete statistical data base, and the results of the study did not support the conclusions of the report.[47] As a result, the controversy over the risks associated

---

*William Cottrell, who in addition to serving as director of the Nuclear Safety Division at the AEC Oak Ridge National Laboratory is the editor of *Nuclear Safety*, wrote: ". . . we are not certain that the Interim Criteria for ECCS [emergency core cooling system] adopted by the AEC will . . . 'provide reasonable assurances that such systems will be effective in the unlikely event of a loss-of-coolant accident' " (quoted in "Reactor Core Cooling Hearings," *Energy Digest*, March 28, 1972, pp. 59-64). Other representative quotes by AEC personnel critical of the AEC's official assurances regarding the effectiveness of emergency systems in LOCAs can be found in Wilson Clark, *Energy for Survival* (New York: Doubleday, Anchor Books, 1974), pp. 287-88.

with the LOCA has not been satisfactorily resolved and remains a major obstacle to any program for the accelerated development of commercial nuclear energy.

While the LOCA has received the most publicity, concern has also been expressed regarding possible failures of the steel pressure vessels that hold the cooling water around the reactor core as well as accidental emissions of radioactive materials during the transportation of nuclear fuels and the long-term storage of radioactive wastes. The transportation and storage problems will become increasingly prominent as the quantity of radioactive materials grows.[48] Current reactor models are characterized by a low fuel burn-up per cycle which requires a high ratio of recycling and refabrication of fuels, further increasing the handling problems in the nuclear fuel cycle. The conversion of many light water plants to recycled plutonium as a fuel will further increase the hazards associated with handling nuclear fuels, since plutonium is one of the most toxic radioactive substances known.

These safety problems cannot be ignored.* The occurrence of one major accident would not only cause widespread injury or death, but it could also effectively halt the commercial development of nuclear energy.† Public concern over these safety issues has already significantly delayed reactor construction lead times in the United States and has had a major impact on LWR development programs abroad. If the accelerated development of commercial nuclear energy is desired, it will be necessary to undertake major additional research and development programs to improve the safety characteristics of existing LWR designs.

Detailed comparisons of the safety features of alternative reactor designs are also required, and studies should be made of the economic and safety implications of various proposals for the underground construction of nuclear reactors or for the isolation of nuclear generating plants with associated processing and storage facilities in relatively remote areas to minimize the adverse impact of an accidental release of radioactive substances. A study by the Nuclear Regulatory Commission concluded that while there were advantages to

---

*Perhaps even more disturbing than the evidence that the AEC, in its eagerness to promote accelerated development of commercial nuclear energy, has not been sufficiently sensitive to continuing concern by some of its own experts regarding nuclear reactor safety is the growing evidence that the AEC has on occasion actively attempted to suppress critical reports by its personnel. Accounts of these incidents are summarized in "AEC Files Show Effort to Conceal Safety Perils," New York *Times*, November 10, 1974, pp. 1, 64.

†The urgency of the situation was highlighted by an incident on March 22, 1975, at the Tennessee Valley Authority's Brown's Ferry, Alabama, nuclear reactor plant. In what has been described as "the worst accident in light water reactor history," an accidental fire was brought under control only after several emergency systems (including the emergency core cooling system) had failed to function. For an account of this incident, see *Business Week*, November 17, 1975, p. 105.

the construction of nuclear energy centers encompassing up to 20 commercial nuclear power plants on one site, such centers would not offer any significant improvement in safety in comparison with dispersed power plants. While the study estimated that nuclear energy centers would permit a 15 percent reduction in construction costs over building plants individually, it also indicated that such centers would require large quantities of water for cooling and could alter local weather patterns as a consequence of the dissipation of large amounts of waste heat into the atmosphere.[49]

The proposed federal energy research and development budget for fiscal years 1975/79 submitted to President Nixon by the chairman of the AEC included a substantial expansion of research funds allocated to improve reactor safety and to accelerate development of the HTGR model.[50] These programs constitute a necessary response to the potential obstacles for accelerated commercial development posed by nuclear reactor safety problems.

Fast Breeder Reactors

The federal government's research and development strategy for alternative energy has undergone a major shift in emphasis regarding the development of a second generation of nuclear reactors—FBRs—which are capable of generating additional fuel during the nuclear reaction process. In June 1971, President Nixon announced that the commercial development of the FBR would serve as the primary goal in the government's program to develop new energy sources, and this policy commitment was clearly reflected in federal budgetary allocations.* Four years later, in June 1975, the newly organized ERDA submitted a program to Congress for energy research and development that reflected a far more restrained attitude regarding the prospects for FBR technology. While affirming the ERDA's commitment to an aggressive research and development program in FBR technology, ERDA administrator Robert Seamans expressed growing concern over "significant problems" associated with FBR technology, particularly in the areas of reactor safety and waste management, and deliberately remained noncommittal regarding the eventual commercial applicability of this technology.[51]

The FBR permits a more efficient conversion of the thermal energy in the nuclear fuels and for this reason requires a smaller core than current fission

---

*In fiscal year 1973, $253.8 million was allocated to the liquid metal fast breeder reactor (LMFBR) program, representing the largest single allocation among all federal energy research and development programs and almost 40 percent of the $640.2 million allocated for all such programs. U.S. Atomic Energy Commission, *The Nation's Energy Future*, report submitted by Dixy Lee Ray (Washington, D.C.: Government Printing Office, 1973).

reactors. No moderator is employed, and a coolant that does not slow neutrons—either pressurized helium or liquid sodium—is used. The FBR uses a mixture of plutonium and U_{238} rather than the scarcer isotope U_{235} as a fuel. The fission of each plutonium nucleus by a fast neutron releases thermal energy and 2.5 additional neutrons, one of which continues the chain reaction while the others are absorbed by U_{238}, converting it into Pu_{230}, which may then be chemically separated and stored for later use as a fuel. This breeding cycle might be capable of generating an amount of plutonium fuel equivalent to the quantity originally employed every eight to nine years (known as its doubling time), although some believe that this estimate is too optimistic.[52] In addition to permitting the use of abundant natural U_{238} resources, the more efficient breeder reactor requires only 1.3 tons of uranium per million kilowatt-years of electricity generation, in comparison with the 171 tons required by LWRs.[53] As a result, the costs of electricity generation using breeder reactors would become virtually independent of fuel costs, enabling the exploitation of relatively expensive uranium reserves. The implication of these factors is that at the existing level of electricity generation in the United States, breeder reactors could fulfill all the electricity requirements for the next 64,000 years by merely using currently known domestic uranium reserves.* The FBR would therefore dramatically reduce future dependence on limited reserves of natural uranium, and this has been a central element in the rationale for its development.

However, a serious question exists as to whether the FBR can become economically competitive with either conventional fossil fuel generating plants or the existing generations of nonbreeding reactors in the foreseeable future.[54] Projections regarding FBR designs suggest that the capital costs of a commercial FBR generating plant would exceed current capital costs for nonbreeding reactor generating plants by perhaps $200 per kilowatt of generating capacity.[55] These projections would probably have to be revised upward even further as a result of escalating construction costs. This differential in capital costs stems largely from the need for more sophisticated component designs to withstand the high temperatures generated in the FBR core. On the basis of these estimates, nonbreeding reactors would have economically competitive operating costs even if the cost of uranium fuel were to almost double to $15 per pound.† Thus, the

---

*Manson Benedict, "Electric Power from Nuclear Fission," *Technology Review*, October-November 1973. This estimate assumes that a breeder reactor could still operate economically if uranium prices were to rise to $100 per pound.

†U.S. Congress, Senate, Committee on Interior and Insular Affairs, *Energy Research and Development: Problems and Prospects*, report prepared by Harry Perry (Washington, D.C.: Government Printing Office, 1973), pp. 146-47. Another analysis concludes that breeder reactors would be competitive if breeders could be built at a capital cost of $50 or less per kilowatt than a comparable LWR and if uranium prices were to rise above $50 per

case for FBR development critically depends upon the accuracy of current estimates regarding the limited availability of uranium reserves recoverable at $15 per pound. As has already been indicated, these estimates are based on very limited exploration data, and many authorities believe that additional uranium reserves will be discovered sufficient to permit economic operation of commercial nonbreeding reactors until at least the end of this century.

Despite these reservations regarding the economic competitiveness of the FBR, the United States and other countries—primarily the Soviet Union, Great Britain, and France—have launched major FBR development programs. Most of these programs have focused on the development of the LMFBR, which uses liquid sodium at low pressures as a coolant and has been considered preferable to the other major FBR, the gas-cooled fast breeder reactor (GCFR).[56] The sodium coolant has major advantages as a result of its very high thermal conductivity. Its high boiling point permits it to attain temperatures of 1,150 degrees Fahrenheit in the reactor, thereby increasing thermal efficiency to 40 percent.

However, the handling of liquefied sodium, which reacts violently with either air or water, introduces major new engineering problems in reactor design. These problems are further complicated by the fact that the liquid sodium coolant becomes intensely radioactive in the reactor core so that it becomes necessary to interpose a secondary nonradioactive sodium coolant loop to transfer the heat from the reactor to the steam generator. Another disadvantage of the liquid sodium coolant is its opaqueness, and in current reactor designs, refueling and other operations within the reactor core must therefore be performed "blind."

The second most prominent breeder design—the GCFR—utilizes approximately the same mixture of plutonium and uranium as a fuel, but instead of liquid sodium, pressurized helium gas is used as the coolant. Although the heat transfer capability of helium is inferior to that of liquid sodium, its transparency, inertness, and freedom from bubble formation offer significant advantages over liquid sodium as a coolant. The GCFR may also benefit by current research on the HTGR, since both designs present similar technological problems. However, one serious implication of the lower heat transfer capability of helium is that the loss of pressure or other malfunctions in the coolant system may produce uncontrollable overheating in the reactor core. Such an accident could have even more serious consequences than the LOCAs in nonbreeding reactors as a result of the larger inventory of highly radioactive plutonium.

---

pound, but that if the capital cost differential were to rise above $125 per kilowatt of capacity and if uranium costs remained within the range of $8 to $15 per pound, a breeder reactor could not economically compete with the present generation of fission reactors (Irvin C. Bupp and Jean Claude Derian, "The Breeder Reactor in the U.S.: A New Economic Analysis," *Technology Review,* July-August 1974, p. 34).

Both of these fast breeder designs present serious problems which have not as yet been satisfactorily resolved. Perhaps even more important, the intense heat and neutron radiation levels generated within the reactor core require highly resistant component metals. Increasing evidence of unpredicted corrosion and damage to the metals employed in nonbreeding reactors at relatively low temperature and radiation levels illustrates our current lack of adequate knowledge regarding the impact of prolonged exposure to radioactive processes on metals. Until our knowledge in this field can be substantially increased through further research programs, the difficulties in designing reliable components for the FBR will prove to be a major obstacle to its commercial development.[57] In addition to problems associated with reactor design, the large inventories of plutonium which will be required at all stages of the nuclear fuel cycle in a commercial breeder reactor system substantially increase the dangers associated with accidental releases of radioactive materials. Not only is plutonium one of the most radioactive and toxic substances known, but it is an essential component of nuclear weaponry. The widespread presence of plutonium in a commercial FBR supply network and the possibility of international trade in plutonium fuels present major security risks.

Like the present generation of LWRs, FBRs have been the target of growing concern over safety features to minimize the potential of uncontrolled chain reactions. A variety of characteristics of the LMFBRs make them potentially more hazardous than present commercial reactors: "higher power density; higher operating temperatures; higher fuel enrichment; greater sensitivity to control; and chemical problems with the sodium coolant, including fire and radioactive hazards associated with sodium."[58] Concern over breeder reactor safety is not without foundation—two of the three experimental breeder reactors that have been operated in the United States have experienced fuel meltdowns.[59]

Four countries—Great Britain, West Germany, France, and the Soviet Union—have more advanced FBR research and development programs than the United States. All of these programs concentrate on development of the LMFBR model and involve the construction of large prototype facilities over the next five years.[60] The U.S. research and development program similarly gives priority to development of the LMFBR model and includes construction of both a Fast Flux Test Facility in Hanford, Washington, to test breeder components and a 350-milliwatt demonstration breeder reactor at Oak Ridge, Tennessee.[61]

However, the research and development strategy currently being pursued by the AEC has been subjected to growing criticism. An advisory panel headed by Hans Bethe has recommended major design changes and a change in emphasis for both of the FBR facilities that the AEC will operate.[62] In particular, concern has been expressed over mounting cost overruns and construction delays at the Hanford test facility. At the same time, the estimated completion date for the Oak Ridge demonstration project has been extended from 1980 to 1982, and its projected cost has more than doubled.[63] Despite the problems that have been encountered in LMFBR research and development, funding has increased steadily, and during fiscal year 1974, the operating budget for LMFBR research and development reached $193 million. In fiscal year 1975, it is estimated that this allocation will increase to $250 million, while the proposed ERDA program for fiscal year 1976 envisions an additional 4.5 percent increase to $261.3 million.[64] The continuing heavy bias in favor of the LMFBR model is illustrated by the fact that the GCFR is expected to receive an operating budget of only $6 million for fiscal year 1975, or roughly 2 percent of the proposed LMFBR allocation.[65]

Even at the current level of support, a demonstration LMFBR will not be in operation before 1982, and it is therefore unlikely that commercial breeder reactors will be available in the United States before 1990. At this rate of development, FBRs would not represent a significant share of base load electric generating capacity until at least the end of this century. The more advanced state of breeder reactor development abroad makes it likely that commercial use of the LMFBR will occur somewhat earlier outside the United States.

Nuclear Fusion Reactors

Nuclear fusion reactors constitute a third stage in reactor development and have aroused considerable enthusiasm in view of their potential for supplying virtually unlimited quantities of energy with minimal adverse environmental impact. As suggested by its name, a nuclear fusion reactor produces a net release of energy from the fusion of the nuclei of fuel atoms which have been heated to extremely high temperatures in order to overcome the repellant forces that normally separate the positively charged nuclei. To produce energy in sufficient quantity, it is necessary to confine the fuel in the form of a dense plasma at extremely high temperatures (100 million degrees Centigrade) for a minimum period of time (approximately one second). The major obstacles to the development of a satisfactory fusion reaction design have been the relative lack of knowledge regarding high-temperature plasma physics and the inability to design confinement systems capable of meeting the minimum criteria for controlled fusion reactions. Since no known metals are capable of withstanding the extreme temperatures required for fusion reactions, research has focused on the experimental development of several magnetic field configurations which would contain the fuel plasma in a relative stable equilibrium at the necessary density and temperature. More recently, attention has also focused on the potential of laser-induced fusion as an alternative method of satisfying the necessary criteria.

Although theoretically a number of fuels may be employed to generate a nuclear fusion reaction, the most feasible fuel for initial nuclear fusion reactors will most likely be a 50-50 mixture of two heavy hydrogen isotopes, deuterium and tritium.[66] Deuterium is an isotope that can be obtained from ordinary water, while tritium can be derived from lithium ores. Since the extraction of deuterium from sea water provides a virtually limitless supply of this isotope, the only constraint in fuel supply would be the availability of lithium. As in the case of uranium, relatively limited exploration makes it difficult to provide detailed estimates of lithium reserves. Major reserves are known to exist in the United States, Canada, and Africa (particularly Rhodesia), and current estimates suggest that world land reserves of lithium ores exceed by five times the land reserves of uranium available at current prices.[67] M. King Hubbert has estimated that the fusion energy obtainable through the deuterium-tritium reaction with known and inferred reserves of lithium would approximately equal the energy content of the world's fossil fuel reserves.[68] Figure 4.1 summarizes Hubbert's estimates regarding world reserves of lithium.

While most evaluations of the potential of nuclear fusion reactors have focused on the abundance of nuclear fuel supplies that would be available for such reactors, relatively little attention has been given to potential problems in the availability of essential materials for the manufacture of components of the reactor structure. Two characteristics of fusion reactor designs account for these problems: the relatively large reactor size, attributable primarily to the need for increased shielding, requires large quantities of materials, and the high temperatures generated within the reactor core require components fashioned from relatively scarce elements.

Not only will the large materials demands require more intensive development of the limited reserves known to exist for many of these elements, but many of these elements are simply unavailable in the necessary quantities from domestic reserves, and large-scale nuclear fusion reactor development will therefore involve increasing dependence on foreign sources for a few essential elements. The elements that might present the greatest problems from this point of view are niobium and vanadium (refractory metals suitable for withstanding high temperatures); tin and titanium (materials for the superconducting magnet); manganese, chromium, and nickel (essential ingredients in the manufacture of nonmagnetic stainless steel); and beryllium (used as a neutron multiplier or cooling component).[69]

A major potential advantage of a nuclear fusion reactor using the deuterium-tritium fuel over conventional nuclear fission reactors (as well as breeder reactors) is its minimal impact on the environment and, in particular, its greater safety. The amounts of radioactive substances associated with the operation of a fusion reactor are very small in comparison with fission reactors. One major problem, however, is that the high-speed bombardment of neutrons against the walls of the reactor structure during the nuclear fusion process will render a large part of the structure radioactive, and at the end of the 20-year life cycle of a nuclear fusion reactor, it will be necessary to dispose of large quantities of radioactive materials from the reactor structure itself. Fortunately,

FIGURE 4.1

World Reserves of Lithium

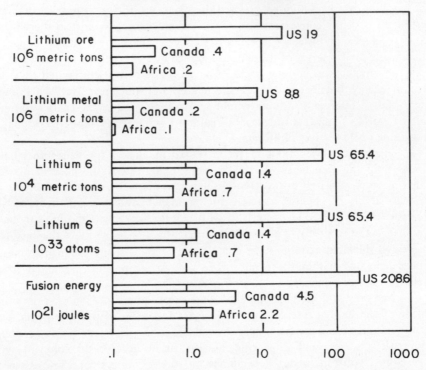

Note: World reserves of lithium, which would be the limiting factor in the deuterium-tritium fusion reaction, are stated in terms of lithium 6 because it is the least abundant isotope. Even with this limitation, the energy obtainable from fusion through the deuterium-tritium reaction would almost equal the energy content of the world's fossil fuel supply.

Source: M. King Hubbert, "The Energy Resources of the Earth," *Scientific American* 224 (September 1971): 70.

most of these radioactive materials consist of nonvolatile metallic elements having relatively short half-lives. While inevitably there is the possibility of accidents occurring during the operation of the nuclear fusion process, even the most serious of such accidents (for example, a liquid lithium fire) would have little potential for causing damage to the population in the area surrounding the nuclear fusion reactor.[70]

Neither the primary fuels (deuterium or lithium) nor the main reaction products (mainly helium) of a fusion reactor are radioactive, thus eliminating the hazards associated with the fuel cycle in conventional fission reactors. Although the secondary fuel, tritium (generated within the reactor from lithium), is radioactive, it can be processed and reinjected into the reactor relatively quickly, and the very small amounts involved significantly reduce the potential damage associated with accidental leakages.

A nuclear fusion reaction is theoretically capable of a 48 percent thermal efficiency, which would reduce the thermal pollution from a fusion reactor by a factor of two in comparison with current fission reactors.[71] However, such a thermal efficiency does not represent a significant improvement over thermal efficiencies in conventional steam generating plants, and therefore nuclear fusion plants would generate comparable levels of thermal air and water pollution. While fusion power reactors eliminate chemical atmospheric emissions such as sulfur dioxide and carbon monoxide, the normal operation of fusion reactors will entail minimal emissions of radioactive tritium. It is nevertheless estimated that the radioactive emissions associated with the operation of nuclear fusion reactors would be less than the emissions from existing fission reactors or even coal-fired plants, and, as a consequence, replacement of these plants by fusion reactors could significantly reduce the biological hazard potential (BHP) of radioactive emissions in power generation processes.*

Although the deuterium-tritium fusion reaction is currently regarded as the most easily attainable because of the lower minimum temperatures required to sustain it, scientists believe that it may ultimately be possible to confine the fuel plasma at the higher temperatures that would be required if deuterium alone were used as a fuel. If this were to become possible, society would in effect have acquired an inexhaustible energy source.

Research on the commercial application of controlled nuclear fusion to power generation began in the early 1950s following the development of the hydrogen bomb. Initial optimism regarding the commercial potential of controlled thermonuclear energy soon dissipated as scientists began to realize the need for substantial additional basic research in high-temperature plasma physics. Broad international cooperation in this field finally resulted in a series of major scientific advances beginning in the mid-1960s and revived earlier optimism regarding the feasibility of producing controlled thermonuclear reactions.

Research on magnet containment systems for fuel plasma has focused on three distinct configurations.[72] Small experimental systems have been built for each of these configurations, and attempts have been made to attain one or more of the minimal conditions believed necessary for a controlled thermonuclear

---

*Biological hazard potential (BHP) is measured for various radioactive isotopes by determining the volume of air necessary to dilute the isotopes to their maximum permissible concentration levels (Gerald L. Kulcinski, "Fusion Power: An Assessment of Its Potential Impact in the U.S.A.," *Energy Policy*, June 1974, pp. 121-22.

reaction. Each configuration has its own strengths, but great interest has been aroused particularly by a series of experiments with the Soviet-developed toroidal Tokamak system. Experiments with the containment systems have now produced the capability of achieving plasma densities and temperatures that approach thermonuclear reactor interest, and confinement times have been increased to one-tenth of a second.[73]

The potential of each configuration can only be verified by building larger systems capable of generating plasma conditions that simulate those of a prototype reactor so that the results can be extrapolated with reasonable confidence. Two such systems using the Tokamak design concept are currently under construction in the Soviet Union and the United States, while a third system (also using the Tokamak concept) is planned by Euratom.[74] Researchers now believe that the scientific feasibility of controlled thermonuclear energy will be definitively established within the next decade.[75]

Once this is accomplished, the research and development program for commercial nuclear fusion reactors will confront major technological and engineering problems associated with the design of large-scale commercial reactors. The most important of these problems stems from the necessity of shielding the magnetic field coils from the intense temperatures and gamma radiation generated during the fusion reaction. With the technology currently available, severe limits would be placed on the permissible heat flux at the protective blanket-plasma interface, and these limitations would raise the capital cost per unit of power considerably, making it difficult to compete with fission reactors or conventional power generators.[76] Moreover, the serious lack of knowledge regarding the damage to component materials—particularly swelling—produced by prolonged exposure to radiation constitutes a major obstacle to the design of reliable commercial fusion reactors. An economically competitive fusion reactor will also require the reduction by a factor of ten of the present cost of superconducting magnets.[77] The AEC has already begun large-scale funding of preliminary research on the technological difficulties associated with nuclear fusion reactors, and unless this work is pursued vigorously, the commercial development of fusion reactors will be significantly delayed, even following confirmation of the scientific feasibility of controlled thermonuclear reactions.

In response to the technological problems anticipated in the design of commercial fusion reactors, proposals have been advanced suggesting that a complementary fusion-fission system that would permit earlier commercial application for nuclear fusion might be designed.[78] Since the respective advantages and limitations of nuclear fission reactors and nuclear fusion reacts are complementary, such a combined system could maximize the contributions of both while eliminating their shortcomings. Since fusion reactors with existing technology can generate power only at a high cost but can breed new fuel at an extremely rapid rate, they could be modified to breed fuel for a fission reactor.

The fission reactor, on the other hand, can generate power at a much lower cost than any currently conceivable fusion reactor, but it can breed fuel only with a significant sacrifice in safety. In the combined system, the nuclear fuel would be bred by a fusion reactor for use in an adjacent fission reactor, which would reduce the high safety risks anticipated in the commercial generation of FBRs.

Although most research and development work on controlled thermonuclear energy has concentrated on experiments with magnetically contained high-temperature plasma, an alternative approach involving laser-induced fusion is also receiving budgetary support in the United States. Rather than attempting to confine relatively dilute plasmas for increasing periods of time, laser-induced fusion would attempt to heat a deuterium-tritium fuel pellet at normal density with the intense heat generated by a focused laser pulse, thus reducing the minimum required containment time for a thermonuclear reaction to less than a microsecond. The ensuing energy release from the fuel pellet would be in the form of an explosive pulse, and there would be a limit to the maximum amount of energy released in each pulse.[79]

Laser beams capable of delivering sufficient energy in extremely rapid pulses are not as yet technologically feasible, and research has therefore concentrated on the development of laser technology, as well as on computer simulations of the physical effects that might be produced in such a fusion system. Unlike research in other forms of nuclear energy, much of the recent advance in laser-induced fusion research has occurred in the private sector, most notably in the research laboratories of KMS Fusion, Inc.[80] Official government research in fusion energy has thus far tended to concentrate heavily on magnetically contained fusion reactor systems, and most of the research on laser-induced fusion has been related to weapons development programs.* As a result, until recently much of the work in this field has been heavily classified.

However, a major breakthrough in the field of laser-induced fusion occurred in October 1974, when researchers from KMS Fusion reported to a meeting of the American Physical Society that their experiments had demonstrated for the first time that a fuel pellet would implode when evenly illuminated with laser light.[81] Largely as a result of its success in these landmark experiments, KMS Fusion received a $350,000 contract from the ERDA to conduct a series of laser test shots, and additional funding appeared to be assured once this initial series is completed.[82]

---

*In fiscal year 1974, the operating budget for magnetically confined fusion systems reached $52.97 million, whereas the laser-induced fusion operating budget was $36.85 million. This imbalance increases even further in the proposed ERDA fiscal year 1976 budget, which allocates $120 million and $54 million, respectively, to the operating budgets of these two programs ("The FY 1976 Nuclear Budget," *Nuclear News*, March 1975, p. 31).

The renewed interest in the potential of laser-induced fusion resulted in the appointment by the ERDA of a four-man panel headed by Lawrence Hafstad to conduct a major review of the government's laser fusion program. The report of this panel, released in March 1975, recommended broader funding for the program, particularly under the sponsorship of universities and private corporations, but also warned against excessive optimism regarding the potential use of laser-induced fusion for the commercial production of electricity.[83] The report was more optimistic regarding the potential usefulness of laser-induced fusion in weapons development through the simulation of nuclear weapons explosions, and also regarding the possible use of laser-induced fusion processes in hybrid fusion-fission plants for the eventual commercial production of electricity.

Major obstacles remain, including the need to achieve a minimum fuel pellet energy gain of 75-fold and a minimum fuel pellet compression of 5000-fold, before laser-induced fusion can realistically be considered for commercial applications in energy production. To achieve the necessary minimum pellet compression would require a 1 million-joule laser, whereas the largest existing laser has only a 1,000-joule capability, and even the ambitious $25 million laser construction project at the ERDA's Lawrence Livermore Laboratory is designed to produce a laser with only a 10,000-joule capability.[84] The extremely high capital costs involved in constructing the laser to ignite the pellet, even after it becomes technologically possible, would severely limit its economic feasibility. Current experiments with laser prototypes at the Lawrence Livermore Laboratory also raise another potential problem: The lasers have had relatively short lives, requiring dismantling and overhauling every 30 shots. The fuel pellets themselves might represent a significant cost component of any laser-induced fusion system, since a vast number will be required and each one will consist of a multiple shell structure which will require an extremely delicate polishing operation within narrow tolerances.[85]

The 10,000-joule laser under construction at the Lawrence Livermore Laboratory is scheduled for completion early in 1977, and scientists hope to use this laser to demonstrate, first, a significant thermonuclear burn, and then a "break-even" situation (in which the minimal conditions are achieved for a net gain in energy through a laser-induced thermonuclear reaction).[86] Since laser fusion research remains at a relatively early stage, projections regarding its future pace of development are still highly speculative.

The potential advantages of commercial fusion reactors have prompted governments in all the major consuming regions to allocate increased financial support for fusion research and development programs. U.S. government funding of fusion research and development programs has increased from $89.82 million in fiscal year 1974 to an estimated $124.43 million in fiscal year 1975, and the recent proposed budget by the ERDA for fiscal year 1976 includes both $174 million for operating expenses and a $24.2 million allocation for construction funds in fusion research projects.[87] While it represents significant increases over research allocations in preceding years, the fiscal year 1976 proposed budget still does not match the recommendations made for fusion research funding in Ray's proposed federal budget for energy research and development in the period for fiscal years 1975/79. In her proposal, Ray had recommended gradually increasing annual support for fusion programs over the five-year period to $406 million in fiscal year 1979 and included a total allocation of $1,450 million for fusion research and development over the entire period.[88] The British government decided in 1973 to step up its spending on fusion research after progressive cutbacks in funding over the preceding five years. Western European participants in Euratom are currently considering a proposal for a five-year plan for fusion research that would include the construction of a Joint European Tokamak. Japan is also reported to be substantially increasing its funding for fusion research during the next decade.[89]

At the current rate of development, the scientific feasibility of both magnetic containment and laser-induced fusion systems could be confirmed within the next decade. Only when this is accomplished will it be possible to think realistically about demonstration reactors that will bear some valid ancestral resemblance to eventual commercial practice. Even with scientific feasibility established, the ensuing development and engineering problems will undoubtedly be enormous. A commercial fusion power plant can probably be anticipated within 30 years after a controlled fusion reaction is obtained in the laboratory. One of the problems involved in attempting to accelerate this development schedule is that it is still considered too early to select a particular type of basic fusion device, and therefore, work must be pursued simultaneously on several alternatives. Nevertheless, some of the technological problems that fusion development will entail can be foreseen in broad terms, and it is essential to expand research in these problem areas now.

NOTES

1. Federal Energy Administration, *Project Independence Report* (Washington, D.C., 1974), p. 118.

2. National Academy of Engineering, Task Force on Energy, *U.S. Energy Prospects: An Engineering Viewpoint* (Washington, D.C., 1974), p. 57.

3. "In Energy Impasse, Conservation Keeps Popping Up," *Science* 187 (January 10, 1975): 43-44.

4. A.J. Surrey, "The Future Growth of Nuclear Power: Part I. Demand and Supply," *Energy Policy* 1 (September 1973): 113.

5. Ibid., p. 114.

6. Manson Benedict, "Electric Power from Nuclear Fission," *Technology Review*, October-November 1971, p. 32.

7. Ibid., p. 34.

8. Ibid.

9. A detailed technical analysis of the HTGR is available in "Large HTGR Enters Market," *Electrical World*, February 15, 1974, pp. 45-48.

10. *Petroleum Press Service*, August 1972, p. 307.

11. Ibid., pp. 307-8.

12. The conclusions of the report by the European Nuclear Energy Agency on the Dragon high-temperature reactor project are summarized in ibid.

13. *Petroleum Press Service*, July 1973, p. 260.

14. For a more detailed description of the CANDU reactor model, see F.C. Boyd, "Nuclear Power in Canada: A Different Approach," *Energy Policy*, June 1974, pp. 126-35.

15. Hoyt C. Hottel and Jack B. Howard, *New Energy Technology* (Cambridge: Massachusetts Institute of Technology Press, 1971), pp. 229-30.

16. Albert Parker, "World Energy Resources: A Survey," *Energy Policy* 3 (March 1975): 63.

17. These AEC estimates are displayed in tables in "The Quest for U.S. Energy Sufficiency: National Mission for the 1970s," *Coal Age* 79 (April 1974): 80.

18. John F. Hogerton, "U.S. Uranium Supply and Demand, Near Term and Long Range," *Nuclear News*, May 1975, p. 49.

19. *U.S. Energy Prospects: An Engineering Viewpoint*, op. cit., p. 62.

20. National Petroleum Council, Committee on U.S. Energy Outlook, *U.S. Energy Outlook* (Washington, D.C., 1972), p. 187.

21. Hogerton, op. cit., p. 50.

22. Irvin C. Bupp and Jean Claude Derian, "The Breeder Reactor in the U.S.: A New Economic Analysis," *Technology Review*, July-August 1974, pp. 27-28.

23. *U.S. Energy Prospects: An Engineering Viewpoint*, op. cit., p. 63.

24. Ibid.

25. *Nuclear Industry*, June 1975, p. 3.

26. For a general discussion of work on the centrifuge process and a comparison with the present gaseous diffusion process, see William D. Metz, "Uranium Enrichment: U.S. 'One Ups' European Centrifuge Effort," *Science* 183 (March 29,1974): 1,270-72.

27. "Uranium Enrichment: Rumors of Israeli Progress with Lasers," *Science* 183 (March 22, 1974): 1,172-74.

28. *Science* 188 (May 23, 1975): 818.

29. *Science* 185 (August 30, 1974): 770-71.

30. Ibid.

31. Wilson Clark, *Energy for Survival* (New York: Doubleday, Anchor Books, 1974), pp. 309-10.

32. A.J. Surrey, "The Future Growth of Nuclear Power: Part 2. Choices and Obstacles," *Energy Policy* 1 (December 1973): 215-21.

33. "In Energy Impasse, Conservation Keeps Popping Up," op. cit., pp. 42-45.

34. This study and others are review in the New York *Times*, November 6, 1975, pp. 1, 58. See also "Why Atomic Power Dims Today," *Business Week*, November 17, 1975, pp. 98-106; and New York *Times,* October 5, 1975, section 3, pp. 1, 7.

35. *Business Week*, April 21, 1973, p. 56.

36. William W. Lowe, "Creating Power Plants," *Technology Review*, January 1972, pp. 25-30. Lowe provides an account of the procedures required to obtain permission to construct and operate nuclear plants.

37. *Business Week*, May 26, 1973, p. 89.

38. Ibid.

39. Benedict, op. cit., p. 35.

40. Amory B. Lovins, a physicist associated with the Friends of the Earth, published a strong critique of the safety features of the LWR which discussed the unexpected component failures and corrosion problems that have been encountered in commercial reactors (London *Sunday Times*, November 25, 1973, p. 62). Lovins also reported that unexpected damage (sufficient to keep water from entering the reactor core) had been discovered in Oak Ridge experiments at fuel temperatures of more than 500 degrees Fahrenheit below the maximum safety levels established by the AEC. For another critical evaluation of reactor safety problems, see Clark, op. cit., pp. 276-92.

41. Lovins, op. cit., p. 62.

42. U.S. Atomic Energy Commission, *The Safety of Nuclear Power Reactors (Light Water-Cooled) and Related Facilities*, report no. WASH-1250 (Washington, D.C., 1973). For an evaluation of a preliminary draft of this report, see Robert Gillette, "Nuclear Safety: AEC Report Makes the Best of It," *Science* 179 (January 26, 1973): 360-63.

43. Lovins, op. cit., p. 62.

44. U.S. Atomic Energy Commission, *Advisory Task Force on Power Reactor Emergency Cooling, Emergency Core Cooling*, report submitted by William K. Ergen (Washington, D.C.: Government Printing Office, 1967). This report is discussed in Clark, op. cit., pp. 283-85.

45. Clark, op. cit., pp. 285-86.

46. Officially, this report is U.S. Atomic Energy Commission, *Reactor Safety: An Assessment of Accident Risks in U.S. Commercial Power Plants*, draft report no. WASH-1400 (Washington, D.C., 1974). A brief summary of its conclusions is available in Robert Gillette, "Nuclear Safety: Calculating the Odds of Disaster," *Science* 185 (September 6, 1974): 838-39.

47. *Nuclear News* 18 (January 1975): 31.

48. A variety of these issues are raised in Theodore B. Taylor and Mason Willrich, *Nuclear Theft: Risks and Safeguards* (Cambridge, Mass.: Ballinger, 1974).

49. This report is summarized in an article in the *Wall Street Journal*, December 16, 1975, p. 10.

50. U.S. Atomic Energy Commission, *The Nation's Energy Future*, report submitted by Dixy Lee Ray (Washington, D.C.: Government Printing Office, 1973), p. 29.

51. *Nuclear Industry* 22 (June 1975): 5.

52. U.S. Congress, Senate, Committee on Interior and Insular Affairs, *Energy Research and Development: Problems and Prospects*, report prepared by Harry Perry (Washington, D.C.: Government Printing Office, 1973), pp. 147-48.

53. Benedict, op. cit., p. 37.

54. An early critical evaluation of the economic feasibility of the FBR can be found in Thomas B. Cochran, *The Liquid Metal Fast Breeder Reactor* (Baltimore: Resources for the Future, 1974). For an alternative, more optimistic evaluation of the economics of FBRs, see K.M. Horst and R.S. Palmer, "Cost Targets for Commercial LMFBR's" (Paper delivered to American Power Conference, Chicago, April 1974). Also see T.R. Stauffer, R.S. Palmer, and H.L. Wyckoff, "An Assessment of the Economic Incentive for the Fast Breeder Reactor" (Paper delivered to Seminar on Energy Policy, Harvard University, December 4, 1974).

55. This estimate is based on interviews with authorities in the field and reflects the growing concern over the escalating capital costs experienced at FBR test facilities.

56. For a brief technical comparison of the two leading FBR designs, see Benedict, op. cit., pp. 37-40.

57. A brief summary of some of the major design difficulties associated with each of the leading FBR models is included in Hottel and Howard, op. cit., pp. 254-59.

58. Clark, op. cit., p. 301.

59. Ibid., p. 295. A detailed account of one of the most serious fuel meltdown incidents, at the Enrico Fermi reactor near Detroit, is provided in John G. Fuller, *We Almost Lost Detroit* (New York: Reader's Digest Press, 1975).

60. Manson Benedict, "Electric Power from Nuclear Fission," op. cit., p. 40.

61. Ibid. Far more limited budgetary support has been given to three other FBR models. For an interesting analysis of one of these alternative models, the light water breeder reactor, see "Rickover's Reactor Race," *Business Week*, July 13, 1974, pp. 38, 41.

62. The conclusions of this AEC advisory panel are reported in "Breeder Reactor Plan Facing Delays," New York *Times*, December 19, 1973, pp. 1, 48.

63. *Wall Street Journal*, September 18, 1974, p. 11.

64. "The FY 1976 Nuclear Budget," *Nuclear News*, March 1975, p. 29.

65. Ibid.

66. Lawrence Lidsky, "The Quest for Fusion Power," *Technology Review*, January 1972, p. 10.

67. "How Near Is Nuclear Fusion?" *Petroleum Press Service*, August 1973, p. 295.

68. M. King Hubbert, "The Energy Resources of the Earth," *Scientific American* 224 (September 1971): 69-70.

69. A detailed analysis of this problem is presented in Gerald L. Kulcinski, "Fusion Power: An Assessment of Its Potential Impact in the U.S.A.," *Energy Policy*, June 1974, pp. 112-15.

70. Ibid., pp. 118-19.

71. Lidsky, op. cit., p. 12.

72. For a comparison of the three leading configurations for magnetic containment systems and an evaluation of the relative advantages of each, see Lidsky, op. cit., 14-18.

73. For a summary of the status of experimental work in nuclear fusion, see an article by two researchers in the field, R.F. Post and F.L. Ribe, "Fusion Reactors as Future Energy Sources," *Science* 186 (November 1, 1974): 397-407.

74. William D. Metz, "Nuclear Fusion: The Next Big Step Will Be a Tokamak," *Science* 187 (February 7, 1975): 421-23.

75. Post and Ribe, op. cit., p. 402.

76. Lidsky, op. cit., pp. 19-20.

77. D.C. Leslie, "Nuclear Energy 2: From Fission to Fusion" (Paper delivered at Institute of Petroleum Summer Meeting, Harrogate, England, June 5-8, 1973).

78. Lidsky, op. cit., pp. 20-21.

79. A detailed technical description of laser-induced fusion is available in John L. Emmett, John Nuckolls, and Lowell Wood, "Fusion Power by Laser Implosion," *Scientific American* 230 (June 1974): 24-37.

80. Gene Bylinsky, "KMS Industries Bets Its Life on Laser Fusion," *Fortune*, December 1974, pp. 149-56.

81. *Science* 186 (December 27, 1974): 1,193.

82. *Science* 187 (March 7, 1975): 817.

83. The conclusions of this report are summarized in an article in *Science* 188 (April 4, 1975): 32-33.

84. Ibid.

85. *Science* 186 (December 27, 1974): 1,194.

86. Perry, op. cit., p. 86.

87. "The FY 1976 Nuclear Budget," op. cit.

88. Ray, op. cit., p. 115.

89. *Petroleum Press Service*, August 1973, p. 297.

GEOTHERMAL ENERGY

In addition to conventional fossil fuels and nuclear energy sources, there are a number of non-nuclear alternative energy sources that have considerable potential for future development. Of these, geothermal energy is perhaps the most readily accessible.[1] Geothermal energy is the product of heat radiated from the interior of the earth which accumulates in subterranean reservoirs in the form of either steam, hot water, or hot rocks. The high-temperature geothermal reservoirs (with temperatures ranging from 400 to 700° F) which have thus far been discovered are limited to areas of crustal deformation where the heat flow from the earth's interior has been higher than average due to the intrusion of magma into the shallower layers of the earth's crust. These areas of crustal deformation are characterized by frequent earthquakes and volcanic activity. One belt of crustal deformation has been identified along the continental margins encircling the Pacific, while a second belt extends through southern Europe and across the middle of Asia. Similar, although less accessible, belts are known to exist in deep ocean basins as well.

A second type of geothermal reservoir is located in large sedimentary basins that have undergone geological deformation. Rather than high-temperature steam, however, these reservoirs contain large accumulations of hot water (with temperatures usually ranging from 150 to 400°F) at relatively shallow depths. If the temperatures are sufficiently high in these hot water reservoirs, they may be tapped to generate electricity, using one of two possible methods. In one method, steam is flashed from hot water pumped from the reservoir and then used in a low-temperature steam turbine while the residual

73

water is reinjected into the reservoir. Because of the low temperature of the steam, such generating systems are characterized by low conversion efficiencies and require very large turbines. More effective utilization of the heat is possible using a heat exchange method in which a low-boiling liquid such as isobutane is brought into contact with the hot water from the reservoir, and the resulting steam is used to power the turbine.

Lower-temperature hot water reservoirs which are not suitable for the generation of electricity may be developed to provide direct heat for a variety of purposes, including space heating for buildings.[2] Since these liquid-dominated systems are far more prevalent than steam-dominated systems, a United Nations symposium on the development of geothermal resources urged in 1970 that expanded research and development programs be undertaken to maximize their utilization.[3] Hot water reservoirs have been discovered in the Soviet Union, Australia, and several other countries. Large hot water reservoirs containing pressurized water at temperatures as high as 365°F have been discovered along the U.S. Gulf Coast.

Geothermal reservoir heat is also found in hot dry rock systems consisting of an impermeable rock layer over a local heat source. The heat in this type of reservoir might be tapped through the injection of water or low-boiling-point fluids to operate turbine-powered electric generators at the surface. The AEC Los Alamos Scientific Laboratory has proposed tapping the earth's normal heat gradients with a technique involving both boiling and hydrofracturing. The implementation of such a technique would involve drilling to great depths, ranging from three to five kilometers for purposes such as domestic heating, water desalination, and other possible industrial uses and up to nine kilometers to reach heat levels necessary for direct electric power generation. Despite the difficulties such a technique would involve, the AEC considers such projects to be "technically feasible" and to have "economic potential."[4]

The high-temperature steam found in geothermal reservoirs has already been used by a number of countries for electric power generation. By early 1973, world electric generating capacity using geothermal steam was 1,086 milliwatts, and expansion of this capacity can be expected over the next several decades.[5] Italy pioneered in the commercial exploitation of geothermal steam and in 1904 built a small generating plant using geothermal steam from its Lardarello fields. The Lardarello fields have since been exploited to their full capacity, providing steam for approximately 400 milliwatts of generating capacity, and Italy is now exploring other geothermal fields for similar exploitation. New Zealand was the second country to develop its geothermal reservoirs for electric power generation, and numerous other countries along the primary geological belts described earlier have launched geothermal exploration and development programs.

In 1972, the United States had 298 milliwatts of installed electric generating capacity based on geothermal steam from the California Geysers

Field—the largest known dry steam field in the world.[6] A second large dry steam field has been discovered in New Mexico, and a geothermal reservoir of very hot brine (up to 650°F) has been identified in Imperial Valley, California.[7] Thus far, the pace of geothermal development in the United States has been seriously hampered by the government's refusal to lease federal lands where approximately 75 percent of potential geothermal sites are believed to be located.[8] Although the Geothermal Steam Act of 1970 specified leasing procedures that would make federal lands available for geothermal exploration and development, nearly four years elapsed before the first leases were made available for bidding.[9] Despite bureaucratic delays and a lack of fiscal incentives for geothermal drilling, bidding for these leases indicates a substantial increase in interest in the development of the geothermal fields.[10]

Estimates regarding the potential contribution of geothermal energy to U.S., or world, energy supplies vary widely as a result of the relatively limited exploratory data that has been accumulated thus far. A U.S. Geological Survey report estimates that 12,000 megawatts$_e$ of electricity could be generated from geothermal fields in the United States at present prices and with present technology and that this could be increased by a factor of ten provided that more aggressive exploration and research and development programs are undertaken.[11] An even more optimistic estimate by two geologists suggests that U.S. geothermal capacity could eventually reach 30,000 to 100,000 milliwatts.[12] These estimates indicate that geothermal energy could represent between a 2.8 and 24 percent addition to the 424,000-milliwatt installed capacity for electricity generation that existed in the United States at the end of 1973.

On a more immediate level, there is also considerable disagreement over the potential contribution of geothermal energy to U.S. energy supplies by 1985. The NPC study *U.S. Energy Outlook* estimated that geothermal energy could supply between 3,500 and 19,000 milliwatts$_e$ by 1985, depending on a variety of assumptions regarding the pace of future technological development.[13] The more recent FEA *Project Independence Report* presents a more conservative projection of 4,000 to 17,000 milliwatts$_e$ for geothermal energy plants by 1985.[14] Despite the passage of the Geothermal Energy Research Development and Demonstration Act in 1974, it appears that the more conservative estimates regarding the medium-term contribution of geothermal energy are more realistic, a conclusion that is supported by the National Academy of Engineering.[15]

The commercial exploitation of high-quality geothermal steam for electric power generation in both Italy and the United States provides sufficient experience to permit the compilation of comprehensive cost figures for the electric generating plants. The results of these studies suggest that both capital and operating expenses in these plants are considerably lower than in generating plants using either fossil fuels or nuclear energy.[16] Significantly lower construction costs are possible because there is no need for a boiler, and operating costs are reduced because of the elimination of the problems associated with fuel handling and combustion. The only generating plants that are economically competitive are hydroelectric power plants, and, at least in the United States, there is only limited potential for further expansion of hydroelectric generating capacity. The economic factor that is still relatively uncertain for geothermal power generation is the cost of exploration required to discover geothermal reservoirs, but, on the basis of current data, this is not anticipated to emerge in the near future as a major constraint on the commercial development of geothermal reservoirs in the United States.[17] Although geothermal reservoirs that are distant from major consuming centers were until recently considered uneconomical to develop as a result of the high costs associated with long-distance transmission of electricity, the introduction of high voltage transmission lines has increased the economic feasibility of separating power generating plants from major load centers.[18]

Contrary to what one might think, there are significant environmental problems to be solved in developing geothermal heat as an energy source.[19] These problems are greater for the more commonly occurring hot water geothermal systems than for the less common high-temperature steam systems. Large land areas are affected by the drilling of wells and the installation of roads, pipelines, power plants, and auxiliary facilities. There is also the problem of land subsidence, which has been experienced in New Zealand and Mexico, and could be particularly serious in fault-prone areas such as California. Start-up of most geothermal operations is marked by great clouds of steam and a continuous roar, since new wells must generally be vented to the atmosphere for many days to remove sand. Also, the corrosive and abrasive nature of the water and steam handled by geothermal operations increases the risk of blowouts, and these are difficult to bring under control. Cleanup of geothermal steam for power plant operations results in the production of hydrogen sulfide and ammonia with the attendant possibility of significant atmospheric pollution. The atmospheric effluents associated with geothermal plant operation will vary widely because of the distinct geophysics and geochemistry of each hydrothermal reservoir. The waste heat generated by geothermal plants is considerably greater than that of conventional generating plants as a consequence of the very low 7.5 percent thermal efficiency characteristic of geothermal energy production.[20] Finally, geothermal operations generally produce huge quantities of waste water with high salt content and alkalinity which must be reinjected, since it cannot be disposed of by surface drainage. Reinjection operations, which increase the costs associated with geothermal energy production, would have the beneficial effects of minimizing the adverse environmental impact, increasing thermal efficiency, and possibly prolonging the life of the geothermal reservoir.

The commercial development of all varieties of geothermal reservoirs will require an active exploration program supplemented by a research program to develop more accurate exploration techniques. Research and development

programs should also focus on reservoir development and management techniques and on improving the ability of drilling components to withstand high
temperatures and highly corrosive salts. A recent report estimated that as little as
1 percent of the total heat accumulated in geothermal reservoirs can be
extracted with current drilling techniques.[21] Research and development of new
deep-drilling techniques is also urgently needed to reduce the high costs
associated with geothermal drilling operations. Geothermal drilling currently
costs more than twice as much as conventional gas and oil drilling.[22] The federal
geothermal research and development budget for fiscal year 1973 included only
$3.8 million, most of which was devoted to resource identification. Although
the proposed budget for energy research and development over the period of
fiscal years 1975/79 submitted by the chairman of the AEC recommended that
this allocation be increased to approximately $40 million per year, present
expenditure levels have still not matched this ambitious target. The operating
expenses budget for geothermal research and development is estimated to reach
$13.8 million for fiscal year 1975, while the ERDA request for fiscal year 1976
would increase this budget to $28.4 million.[23] Congress recently passed a
measure designed to demonstrate the commercial feasibility of geothermal
energy by the end of the decade. Under this measure, Congress has already
authorized a $50 million loan guaranty program to encourage private corpora-
tions to develop geothermal resources more aggressively.[24]

SOLAR ENERGY

The enormous potential represented by solar energy has always fascinated
researchers interested in developing a virtually inexhaustible supply of energy
that would not generate the pollution associated with more conventional forms
of energy. Although solar energy theoretically yields a very high thermodynamic
potential (the solar energy received by the U.S. land area alone exceeds by 600
times the present rate of energy consumption in the United States), its
extremely dilute influx density and great variability have defied most attempts
to convert this energy economically with existing technology.[25] Nevertheless, a
wide variety of proposals have been advanced, and three in particular have
received much attention: (1) low-temperature, flat-plate fixed collectors for
residential space and hot water heating, (2) thermal conversion systems using
either ground-based conventional collectors or photovoltaic collectors in association with electric power generating plants, and (3) large-scale thermal
conversion systems involving the use of photovoltaic collectors on earth satellites
and the transmission of energy to the earth by means of microwave beams.

Residential Space and Water Heating

Low-temperature, flat-plate fixed collectors offer the most immediate commercial application of solar energy. The technology required for flat-plate fixed solar collectors and heat storage units is already sufficiently advanced to encourage the introduction of commercial solar heating systems for individual residences in many parts of the United States.[26] A solar-powered residential space heating system would include a flat-plate fixed solar collector and a glass- or clear plastic-enclosed heat trap. A fluid or gas is employed to transfer heat from the collector to a heat storage facility which may be either a tank of water, a bin of small rocks, or a fusible salt. Substantial storage volume is generally desirable in a solar-powered system to provide heat during the night as well as during bad weather, and as a result, the heat storage facility represents a major component of the capital cost of the entire system. Air is passed through the heat storage facility and then sent through vents into a conventional forced-air heating system. In an alternative design, solar-heated water may be sent through a pipe system to heat each room of the house.

Most solar-powered space heating systems include an auxiliary heating unit which operates on conventional fuel to compensate for occasional fluctuations in the supply of solar energy resulting from prolonged periods of minimal sunlight.[27] Due to the variability of solar energy and the limited capacity of existing heat storage units, solar heating systems are designed primarily as supplements to, rather than replacements for, conventional heating systems using fossil fuels. Since roughly 20 percent of U.S. energy consumption is devoted to the heating and cooling of buildings, solar energy heating systems offer a potentially significant replacement for conventional fossil fuels in this area.

Cost estimates for solar-powered residential space heating systems tend to support the conclusion that such systems are already commercially feasible, particularly in certain parts of the United States. One detailed study completed in 1973 concluded that solar heating was already competitive with electric heating in six of the eight cities chosen for comparison (Miami and Seattle were the two exceptions), while home furnaces using oil or gas were still less expensive in most of the cities examined.[28] However, this study was concluded prior to the substantial rises that occurred in heating fuel prices during 1973-74, and the competitiveness of solar heating systems has undoubtedly improved in the aftermath of these price rises. Although solar water-heating systems were widely available commercially in Florida and California during the 1920s and 1930s, the subsequent advent of low-cost fuel oil and natural gas led to the gradual disappearance of most of these systems.[29] A recent study indicates that even with improved technology, solar water heaters will not become fully competitive with conventional heating systems for another few years.[30]

Given the availability of technologically feasible solar-powered space and water-heating systems, some of the most difficult challenges remaining in this field involve the task of gaining widespread public acceptance for this new technology. Early efforts in the marketing of solar energy technology produced disappointing results due to the tendency of promoters to make unrealistic claims concerning the capabilities of the new systems and to overestimate production capabilities. Another problem involves the "first-cost syndrome" among potential consumers, who concentrate on the relatively high capital costs associated with the initial installation of the system ($3,500 to $6,000, not including the cost of the conventional heat distribution system)[31] while underemphasizing the fact that this initial capital investment will generate considerable savings in fuel costs over the life of the system.

Arthur D. Little, Inc., a leading research and consulting firm, launched a major new program in May 1973 in an effort to overcome these obstacles. The program, expected to cost between $300,000 and $500,000, is explicitly designed to encourage the growth of "a solar climate-control industry," and it has enlisted the support of a diverse group of electric utilities, oil companies, and chemical companies in a cooperative effort to explore the potential of short-range markets in this field. The program's sponsors optimistically predict that nearly $1 billion in equipment sales for solar climate-control systems will be generated in the next decade.[32] A special panel of solar energy scientists assembled by the National Science Foundation and the National Aeronautics and Space Administration (NASA) reported in 1972 that solar climate-control systems might be installed in 10 percent of all new buildings by 1985, provided that the federal government contribute $24 million for a demonstration program to establish the commercial feasibility of solar technology.[33] It should be noted, however, that even at this rate of development, solar energy will make only a relatively minor contribution to the energy demand for heating and cooling of buildings in the next decade.

Since capital costs constitute such an important element in solar heating systems, more intensive research and development programs on component design for such systems will probably yield significant additional costs savings. One modification being developed for current systems involves the use of solar energy for space cooling (through absorption refrigeration systems) as well as for heating. Combined solar heating/cooling systems have not as yet been demonstrated, and five to ten years will be required before they become commercially available.[34] Another important area of research involves the design of economically competitive solar total-energy systems for large buildings, such as shopping centers, offices, and industrial plants. A recent attempt to develop a rough approximation of the cost of such a system indicates that it is very close to becoming "an economic investment for a typical suburban industrial plant in the middle latitudes of the U.S."[35] With the present level of research, however, such systems will probably not be widely available for ten to 20 years.[36]

Large-Scale Solar-Powered Generating Systems

There have been numerous suggestions regarding the possibility of building large-scale solar-powered generation systems. However, a wide range of technological problems associated with current designs for solar collectors must be solved before such systems become either technically or economically feasible. Most of these systems involve the collection of solar energy through focused concentrators spread over large areas of the earth's surface, the storage of the resulting high-temperature heat in salt or metal tanks, and the use of conventional steam turbines and alternators to generate electricity.

Perhaps one of the most ambitious proposals for a large-scale solar-powered generating system was advanced by two University of Arizona scientists, Aden and Marjorie Meinel, in their book *Power for the People*.[37] They called for the creation of a "national solar power farm" in the southwestern part of the United States and claimed that such an installation, consisting of 1,000 1 million-kilowatt solar power plants, would be capable of supplying the entire national demand for electricity in the twenty-first century. The solar power farm, including support facilities, would cover almost 15,000 square miles of desert land. Each power plant in the complex would require more than six square miles of collection surface, yielding a collection efficiency of approximately 60 percent and an overall generating efficiency of 25 percent. The National Science Foundation's Research Applied to National Needs (RANN) program provided $180,000 in 1971-72 to pursue experimental work to demonstrate the feasibility of the Meinel concept of a solar-thermal power plant.[38]

While such proposals offer a fascinating glimpse of the ultimate technological potential of the development of solar-powered generating systems, present cost estimates offer little hope that such systems will be economically competitive with conventional systems over the next few decades. Current models of focused concentrators are prohibitively expensive, and realistic cost estimates indicate that the installed costs for a large-scale solar-powered generating system could be as high as 15 times the capital costs for conventional generating plants and that overall costs per kilowatt-hour may still be ten times higher than those for a comparable conventional system.[39] Major additional research and development work will obviously be necessary before these large-scale systems reach commercial application.

One variant of the proposal for large-scale solar-powered generating systems would replace the focused conventional collecting surfaces with silicon photovoltaic cells either to generate electricity or to produce hydrogen through the electrolysis of water. If hydrogen were produced, it could then be used either directly by consumers as a nonpolluting gaseous fuel or in a fuel cell to produce electricity.

Although silicon photovoltaic cells have been successfully employed as a source of energy in space vehicles, their low conversion efficiency (10 to 15 percent) and extremely high capital costs ($100 per watt) have effectively limited their use to situations in which no alternative energy sources are available.[40] A variety of active research programs have been undertaken in an effort to improve the conversion efficiency and to reduce the unit costs of photovoltaic cells. Even if the most optimistic cost estimates for photovoltaic cells can be achieved with existing technology, the cost of the photovoltaic cells required in a solar cell power generating plant alone would be approximately equivalent to the total capital costs of a conventional generating plant.[41]

However, recent research conducted by Tyco Laboratories, Inc., in Waltham, Massachusetts, suggests that the currently unfavorable cost estimates may have to be dramatically revised. Tyco has been experimenting with a new silicon ribbon production process which could offer considerable cost savings in comparison with the present, expensive silicon water production process and thereby reduce the costs associated with a major component of solar cells. A.R. Mlavsky, head of Tyco's silicon research program, has estimated that this new process will eventually permit the mass production of finished solar cells at a cost of $180 per kilowatt.[42] Even if this estimate is somewhat optimistic, it is clear that this new process represents a major advance in reducing the costs associated with solar cell technology. Tyco's work in this field has attracted the interest of Mobil Oil Corporation, which has agreed to invest $30 million in a joint venture with Tyco to develop this process.[43]

Another proposal that has received widespread publicity involves mounting photovoltaic cells on enormous panels attached to a satellite in synchronous orbit above the earth.[44] This arrangement would bypass the diffusion of solar energy which accompanies its passage through the earth's atmosphere and would permit solar energy collection on a 24-hour-a-day basis. A 10,000-milliwatt capacity installation would require 13 square miles of photovoltaic panels in space and a 36-square-mile land-based collecting station to receive the microwave beams generated from the satellite.[45] While such a relay system would offer important advantages over alternative land-based collection systems, it would also require major advances in space technology as well as enormous reductions in capital costs. Present satellite launch costs would have to be reduced by a factor of 50 to 1, while solar cell costs would have to be reduced by a factor of 1,000 to 1, in order to make such a system even remotely economically competitive.[46]

Even if the enormous costs associated with the current proposals for large-scale solar-powered generating systems could be substantially reduced, there would still remain some difficult environmental problems which are often underemphasized by proponents of such systems. Although such systems would not generate air or water pollution, they would require large land surfaces for the collection of solar energy, and the fact that the collection surfaces would absorb more solar energy than had been absorbed by the land itself could trigger unpredictable changes in local weather conditions.[47] However, a strict comparison of land-use requirements for both conventional and solar-powered generating plants indicates that the latter might in fact require less land if one were to include the land areas that would be required to mine the coal or uranium to supply conventional power plants. Proposals for microwave transmission of solar energy from orbiting satellites have not adequately dealt with the potentially adverse environmental effects of large-scale microwave radiation.[48]

In an article in *Technology Review*, Walter E. Morrow, Jr., of the Lincoln Laboratory at MIT outlined nine major areas for a solar energy research and development program: the development of low-output-temperature solar collectors for space and water heating applications; the development of inexpensive low-temperature energy storage techniques; the development of low-cost, high-efficiency solar collectors for applications requiring high output temperatures; the development of economical high-temperature thermal energy storage systems; the development of improved photovoltaic solar cells; the development of solar concentrators to use with photovoltaic solar cells; the development of inexpensive electrical energy storage techniques for use with photovoltaic solar cell systems; surveys of solar intensity variations; and systems studies on various applications of solar energy. The most urgent priority in all research areas involves reducing the costs associated with existing solar technology.[49]

Indirect Utilization of Solar Energy

A number of imaginative alternatives may also be available for more indirect utilization of solar energy: new designs for windmills, tapping thermal gradients in the ocean, systematic utilization of photosynthesis in large multipurpose tree farms, and conversion of solid organic wastes into low-sulfur oil and gas. Many of these alternatives have already been demonstrated on a limited scale, and more extensive research and development programs will be necessary to improve the technologies involved and to increase the applicability of these systems at economically competitive costs.

Wind energy is the by-product of the atmospheric absorption of solar energy, and it provided one of the earliest sources of mechanical power through such devices as windmills and sailing ships. Although it is doubtful that wind will ever prove to be a viable substitute for conventional fuels in the large-scale generation of electricity, it already offers considerable potential as a supplementary energy source. Much of the basic technology is already available, and most current research concentrates on the application of aerodynamic techniques developed over the last three decades in an effort to reduce system costs and increase market applications.[50] The two most pressing research and development problems in this field involve the development of reliable materials for use in the construction of blades and the development of blades designed for variable pitch to adjust to variations in wind velocity.

Commercially available wind-powered generators are generally in the one-to-five-kilowatt size range to supply the power needs of farmhouses or remote locations such as harbor beacons, but it is unlikely that such systems will prove to be economically competitive with conventional power sources in the near future.[51] Nevertheless, many proponents of wind-powered systems argue that the environmental advantages of a "clean" power source far outweigh its potentially higher costs.

One of the leading proponents of wind-powered electrical generating systems, William E. Heronemus, a professor of civil engineering at the University of Massachusetts, has even prepared an ambitious proposal for offshore networks of wind generators designed to supply a major portion of U.S. electrical energy requirements.[52] Such projects appear to be far from economic feasibility at this point, but many researchers believe that large-scale wind generators in the 100-kilowatt-to-5-milliwatt range might eventually be integrated into electrical utility grids as supplementary sources of power. The National Science Foundation and NASA are currently funding research programs to develop improved windmill designs to be used in experimental power-generating units in the one-to-five-milli-watt range.[53]

Scientists have long speculated about the possibility of using the temperature gradients in the oceans for the purpose of generating electricity. Research sponsored by the French government immediately following World War II demonstrated that such a power generating system was technically feasible, but the government eventually abandoned its efforts to develop a system that would be economically competitive with conventional power sources.[54] Most proposals for the utilization of the ocean's thermal gradients as a power source involve a vapor turbine and the circulation of a low-boiling-point liquid to transfer heat in a closed system. The fluid, perhaps propane, would boil as it circulates through pipes located in the ocean's warm surface water, and the vaporized fluid would then pass through the turbine. It would be recondensed to its liquid form in a condenser cooled by colder ocean water located far below the ocean's surface.[55] The use of relatively low-temperature heat in the power generating system severely restricts the system's thermal efficiency to an estimated maximum of 6 to 7 percent, and this operates as a major constraint on its commercial application.

Despite this problem, two consulting engineers have prepared detailed plans for the construction of a semisubmerged sea thermal plant which would be located off the coast of Florida.[56] These plans envision a 100-milliwatt plant which might be operated in conjunction with a desalination plant to minimize the cost of such a power generating system. The National Science Foundation has funded studies to develop improved designs for these systems in an effort to increase their economic competitiveness with conventional power systems.[57] At this point, however, the relatively limited research funding available for such projects offers little hope that sea thermal plants will become commercially available before the end of this century.

Solar bioconversion techniques represent another potential avenue for the indirect utilization of solar energy. These techniques can be divided into two broad categories. The first encompasses a variety of proposals for the systematic cultivation of "energy crops" in an effort to minimize the energy yield of photosynthetic processes in plants. Such crops as sugar cane and sugar beets have often been suggested because of their high photosynthetic yield. The sugar and cane cellulose from the harvested plants could be converted into alcohol at a relatively high thermal efficiency (although the thermal efficiency of the original photosynthetic process is generally quite low), and the alcohol could then serve as a source of hydrocarbons.[58] Another proposal, issued by the NPC, suggests the use of uncultivated land areas to grow agricultural grains which would then be used to produce alcohol.[59] Some solar energy experts have proposed the establishment of "energy plantations" which would undertake the harvesting of forests for wood that would then be used as a fuel for conventional power plants.[60]

All of these "solar bioconversion" projects remain at a very early stage of research, and it is still too early to ascertain which, if any, of them will eventually prove to be economically competitive with conventional fuel sources. As with most efforts to harness solar energy, large-scale solar bioconversion processes involving the cultivation of "energy crops" would require extensive land surfaces, and it is doubtful whether any of these processes will every be capable of net energy production.[61]

Another, more promising, category of solar bioconversion involves the conversion of organic wastes into combustible fuels. Three different techniques have been developed on an experimental basis by the Bureau of Mines: hydrogenation, pyrolysis, and natural anaerobic fermentation. These systems have already achieved limited commercial application in several cities throughout the United States. Perhaps the most advanced of these systems is operated by the Union Electric Company in St. Louis and processes 300 tons of garbage each day.[62] As a result of the successful operation of this system, Union Electric has announced plans to build a $70 million power plant which will be designed to generate about 6 percent of its power from the entire solid waste output of the St. Louis metropolitan region (roughly 2.5 to 3 million tons per year), with coal supplying the rest of the fuel needs of the plant. The plant is scheduled to begin operation in 1977.[63] One of the major obstacles remaining for the further commercial development of such waste conversion systems involves the need to minimize the costs associated with the collection of waste and the separation of organic waste from inorganic waste. Since the United States is currently estimated to generate approximately 2 billion tons of organic solid wastes each year, these waste conversion systems offer a promising source of energy, especially for large urban areas.[64]

U.S. support for solar research and development programs was negligible several years ago. In 1973, budgetary support increased to $4.2 million, and in fiscal year 1974, this allocation more than quadrupled to $17 million. Appropriations of $50 million for solar energy research programs in fiscal year 1975 represented a major expansion of research in this field. Moreover, Congress has also authorized a $60 million program over the next five years to demonstrate the feasibility and commercial application of solar climate-control systems for residential and commercial buildings. Another congressional bill provides budgetary support for a wide-ranging solar research and development program to explore various applications of solar energy, including industrial process heating, thermal generation of electricity, photovoltaic conversion, bioconversion, ocean thermal gradient conversion, and wind energy conversion. The initial funding authorized under this bill was $77 million by the end of fiscal year 1976, but the legislation envisions a long-range program ultimately costing $1 billion or more.[65] Proponents of solar energy development regard this as a necessary beginning but believe that ideally a 15-year research and development program costing $3.5 billion would be required to accelerate the commercial application of solar energy.[66]

ELECTRIC BATTERY TRACTION SYSTEMS

While batteries more accurately represent a form of electrochemical energy storage than an entirely distinct alternative energy source, the development of electric battery traction systems may provide a viable alternative to the internal combustion engine as a power source for motor vehicles. A brief summary of the research and development status for such traction systems is therefore included because of its potential impact on the future demand for petroleum products in the transportation sector. The obvious attraction of developing an economically competitive energy source for motor vehicles that would satisfy recent legislative controls on automobile emissions has induced a large number of companies to undertake active research and development programs in this area. At the current rate of development. satisfactory battery traction systems for motor vehicles will probably not be commercially available before the end of this decade, and it will be 1985 before such systems will have a significant impact on the automobile market.[67]

Many people believe that battery traction systems offer a nonpolluting energy source, but this is a misconception that ignores the fact that batteries are simply a form of energy storage. The initial production of energy for storage in batteries would occur in conventional power plants and therefore would entail additional pollution at this stage. It is even possible that with the efficiencies currently attainable in battery traction systems, the overall pollution associated with the production of energy for this system would be greater than that associated with the production of energy using gasoline in internal combustion engines.

The major problem now confronting research and development programs in this field involves the perfection of a design for a high-capacity storage battery of low weight that is able to deliver moderately high performance over an adequate range. The only well-tested electric battery traction system—based on a lead-acid accumulator—has been able to provide a 60-mile range of 30 miles per hour.[68] Various prototypes that have been tested have been able to travel only a relatively short distance before requiring recharging, and this distance was directly proportional to the speed of the vehicle and the gradient of the route. Several research programs are attempting to break through existing speed/range constraints by developing an alternative to the lead-acid accumulator that would be capable of a specific energy storage equivalent to 100 watt-hours per kilogram.[69] Until these constraints can be overcome, electrically powered motor vehicles will be feasible only for relatively limited use in large urban areas, where speed and range are of secondary importance to the nonpolluting features of such cars.

FUEL CELLS

Fuel cells have also been considered as a possible alternative propulsion unit for motor vehicles, but despite significant potential advantages over storage batteries, research to date has not been very encouraging.[70] Fuel cells convert the chemical energy produced by the combination of fuel and an oxidizing agent directly into electrical energy with a very high conversion efficiency and minimal adverse environmental impact. However, the commercial application of fuel cells to either motor vehicles or central station electric power generation has been continually delayed by the disappointing cost and performance characteristics of existing models.[71]

Despite these problems, in 1973, a consortium of electric utilities in cooperation with Pratt & Whitney launched a $42 million private research and development program with the aim of developing a commercial 26-milliwatt fuel cell for use as a supplement to conventional methods of power generation by 1978.[72] Over 50 provisional orders for such a fuel cell have been submitted to the consortium by other electric utilities, and cost estimates of $200 per kilowatt of fuel cell generating capacity are considered competitive with other power sources.[73]

The use of fuel cells as a supplement to conventional power generation would offer significant advantages. Since fuel cells can operate efficiently and reliably in relatively small units, they constitute promising components for a dispersed power supply system consisting of small generating units located near the main areas of power consumption. With minimal atmospheric pollutants and no need for elaborate cooling facilities, these fuel cell generating units could be situated in urban areas, and as a result flexibility in the location of such units would be substantially greater than with conventional generating units. Such a dispersed power supply system would minimize the high levels of energy loss associated with present systems which transmit electricity over considerable distances from the centralized generating units to the points of consumption. Other advantages of fuel cells include low maintenance costs, efficient energy conversion even when operated at less than full capacity, and short start-up times when used as a peaking power unit.[74]

Although fuel cells offer a variety of potential advantages, their contribution to future energy supplies remains critically dependent on success in developing economically competitive methods for fuel cell production. Progress in this field has been hampered by the low levels of government funding for research and development programs. While NASA spent up to $16 million a year in the early 1960s to develop fuel cell technology for application to the space program, the very nature of this program made cost reduction a secondary objective, and in recent years, government funding has virtually disappeared.[75] The ERDA budgetary request to Congress for fiscal year 1976 provided for only $500,000 in operating expenses to be allocated to the fuel cell research and development program—the same level estimated to have been spent in fiscal year 1975.[76]

HYDROGEN FUELS

Hydrogen has often been suggested as a component of fuel cells, and it is believed that hydrogen may eventually provide a versatile alternative to petroleum products and natural gas. The combustion of hydrogen does not produce polluting emissions (the only end-product is water), and it can be used as a fuel for both aircraft and motor vehicles. Hydrogen can also be economically transported over long distances and can be easily stored, even in small quantities. In addition to its potential uses as a fuel, hydrogen is an important industrial feedstock and is an essential ingredient in coal conversion processes to create synthetic gas or crude oil. Despite its relatively high price, world production of hydrogen already exceeds 200 billion cubic meters per year.[77]

It is important to remember that hydrogen is not itself a primary energy source and requires large amounts of energy for its production. The most prevalent methods for hydrogen production involve either partial oxidation and cracking of hydrocarbons or electrolysis of water. The electrolysis of water is in principle a well-known process, but the difficulties involved in the large-scale production of hydrogen by this method at economically competitive costs constitute a major obstacle to the accelerated commercial development of hydrogen fuels. On a calorific value basis, conventionally produced hydrogen in Western Europe is approximately three times as expensive as Dutch natural gas.[78]

Recent experiments with the Mark 1 process developed at the Ispra establishment of the European Economic Community's (EEC) Joint Research Center suggest that an alternative method of hydrogen production may be possible through the decomposition of water at the moderately high temperatures available from HTGR nuclear reactors. Additional research is now being pursued to perfect the process for large-scale commercial application, since it is believed that the Mark 2 process would reduce the cost differential between hydrogen and natural gas by one-half.[79] Moreover, the decomposition of water using nuclear heat diversifies the potential role of nuclear energy, which thus far has been limited exclusively to electric power generation. The Mark 2 process yields oxygen as a by-product which could profitably be utilized in coal gasification processes. The growing industrial market for hydrogen, the technological feasibility of large-scale production units, the increasing scarcity of low-cost natural gas supplies, and the potential market for oxygen by-products provide major incentives for the accelerated commercial development of the Mark 2 process. The initial experience gained from hydrogen production for industrial purposes using the Mark 2 process should permit further cost reductions which will gradually increase the economic competitiveness of hydrogen fuels in the residential and transportation markets.

Ultimately, hydrogen production from water may offer the possibility of virtually inexhaustible supplies of nonpolluting fuels to replace nonrenewable fossil fuels. For the foreseeable future, however, the enormous input of electricity required to produce hydrogen through the electrolysis of water using conventional techniques constitutes a major constraint on hydrogen as a potential substitute for hydrocarbon fuels. For example, the Institute of Gas Technology has estimated that almost 60 trillion cubic feet of hydrogen would be necessary to provide the energy equivalent of present U.S. natural gas production, and the production of this amount of hydrogen would require more than 1 million megawatts of electric power, or more than three times the installed electrical generating capacity available in the United States.[80]

A far more realistic, short-range use of hydrogen would be for electrical power storage at power generating plants. Since the demand for electricity tends to fluctuate widely, during periods of low demand, electricity could be used to produce hydrogen through the electrolysis of water, and then the stored hydrogen could be used in fuel cells to meet peak demands for power. Such a system would permit generating plants to operate continuously at full capacity, thereby maximizing the efficiency of electric power generation and reducing costs.

Future commercial applications of hydrogen as an alternative energy supply will ultimately depend on the success in increasing the efficiency of fuel cells in converting hydrogen to electricity and increasing the efficiency of techniques for the electrolysis of water. On the latter, the EEC's experiments with the Mark 2 process offer considerable hope for progress. Moreover, once fusion reactors become commercially available, the high temperatures generated in such reactors may permit even further improvement in the efficiency of the electrolytic process.

NOTES

1. A recent evaluation of the potential for the development of geothermal energy is available in U.S. Geological Survey, *Assessment of Geothermal Resources of the U.S.: 1975*, circular no. 726, study edited by D.E. White and D.L. Williams (Washington, D.C., 1975). For other surveys of geothermal energy, see J.C. Denton, *Geothermal Energy: A Special Report by Walter J. Hickel* (Fairbanks: University of Alaska, 1972); P. Kruger and C. Otte, eds., *Geothermal Energy* (Stanford: Stanford University Press, 1972); and Federal Council of Science and Technology, Committee on Energy Research and Development Goals, *Assessment of Geothermal Energy Resources* (Washington, D.C., 1972).

2. Richard G. Bowen and Edward A. Groh, "Geothermal: Earth's Primordial Energy," *Technology Review*, October-November 1971, p. 45.

3. United Nations Symposium on the Development and Utilization of Geothermal Resources, Pisa, Italy, September 1970 (quoted in ibid., p. 48).

4. U.S. Congress, House, Committee on Science and Astronautics, *Energy Research and Development: Hearings before the Subcommittee on Science, Research, and Development* (Washington, D.C.: Government Printing Office, 1972), p. 343.

5. U.S. Congress, Senate, Committee on Interior and Insular Affairs, *Energy Research and Development: Problems and Prospects*, report prepared by Harry Perry (Washington, D.C.: Government Printing Office, 1973), p. 158.

6. Ibid.

7. Bowen and Groh, op. cit., p. 45.

8. Ibid., p. 48.

9. Federal Energy Administration, *Project Independence Report* (Washington, D.C. 1974), p. 152.

10. White and Williams, op. cit.

11. Ibid.

12. Bowen and Groh, op. cit., p. 48. This more optimistic estimate is also presented in Perry, op. cit., p. 158.

13. National Petroleum Council, Committee on U.S. Energy Outlook, *U.S. Energy Outlook* (Washington, D.C.: 1972), p. 53.

14. *Project Independence Report*, op. cit., p. 150.

15. National Academy of Engineering, Task Force on Energy, *U.S. Energy Prospects: An Engineering Viewpoint* (Washington, D.C., 1974), p. 66.

16. Bowen and Groh, op. cit., pp. 45-46. Other cost estimates which support the conclusions of Bowen and Groh are available in Geoffrey Robson, "Geothermal Electricity Production," *Science* 184 (April 19, 1974): 371, 374; and *Project Independence Report*, op. cit., p. 151.

17. Bowen and Groh, op. cit.

18. Ibid.

19. An interesting case study of the environmental impact of geothermal energy production was prepared for the geothermal plant at Wairakei field in New Zealand, a 145-milliwatt$_e$ capacity plant which has been in operation since 1964 (Robert C. Axtmann, "Environmental Impact of a Geothermal Power Plant," *Science* 187 [March 7, 1975]: 795-803). For a more general discussion of environmental problems associated with geothermal energy production, see Wilson Clark, *Energy for Survival* (New York: Double-

day, Anchor Books, 1974), pp. 327-30. A more favorable evaluation is presented in Bowen and Groh, op. cit., pp. 46-47.

20. Axtmann, op. cit.

21. Perry, op. cit., p. 37.

22. U.S. Atomic Energy Commission, *The Nation's Energy Future*, report submitted by Dixy Lee Ray (Washington, D.C.: Government Printing Office, 1973), p. 29.

23. "The FY 1976 Nuclear Budget," *Nuclear News*, March 1975, p. 31.

24. Luther J. Carter, "Solar and Geothermal Energy: New Competition for the Atom," *Science* 186 (November 29, 1974): 811-13.

25. Hoyt C. Hottel and Jack B. Howard, *New Energy Technology* (Cambridge: Massachusetts Institute of Technology Press, 1971).

26. "The Sun Breaks Through as an Energy Source," *Business Week*, May 19, 1973, p. 68. See also Clark, op. cit., pp. 467-511.

27. Clark, op. cit., p. 470.

28. George O.G. Loff and Richard A. Tybout, "Solar House Heating," *Natural Resources Journal* 10 (1970); and George O.G. Loff and Richard A. Tybout, "Cost of House Heating with Solar Energy," *Solar Energy* 14 (1973): 253-78. The conclusions of these studies are discussed in Clark, op. cit., pp. 486-89.

29. Clark, op. cit., pp. 370-74.

30. Jerome Weingart, remarks at National Science Foundation Conference on Solar Heating and Cooling, Washington, D.C., March 1973 (cited in ibid., p. 490).

31. Walter E. Morrow, Jr., "Solar Energy: Its Time Is Near," *Technology Review* 76 (December 1973): 33.

32. Clark, op. cit., p. 502; and "The Sun Breaks Through as an Energy Source," op. cit.

33. National Science Foundation and National Aeronautics and Space Administration, Solar Energy Panel, *Solar Energy as a National Resource* (College Park: University of Maryland, 1972).

34. Perry, op. cit., p. 169.

35. Ibid., p. 36.

36. Morrow, op. cit., p. 40.

37. Aden B. Meinel and Marjorie P. Meinel, *Power for the People*, privately published (Tucson, 1970). The Meinel concept is discussed in detail in Clark, op. cit., pp. 408-17.

38. Clark, op. cit., p. 417.

39. Perry, op. cit., p. 168.

40. Hottel and Howard, op. cit., p. 42; and Clark, op. cit., p. 385.

41. Perry, op. cit., p. 166.

42. Clark, op. cit., p. 391.

43. "Looking at the Sun: A Source of Money?" Boston *Phoenix*, September 17, 1974, p. 21.

44. Peter Glaser, "Power from the Sun: Its Future," *Science* 162 (November 1968): 857-61.

45. Perry, op. cit., pp. 166-67.

46. Ibid., p. 166. Perry also cites National Aeronautics and Space Administration, *Large-Scale Terrestrial Solar Power Generation Cost: A Preliminary Assessment*, study prepared by A.E. Shakowski and Lloyd I. Shure, Technical Memorandum, no. X-2520 (Washington, D.C., 1972), which estimates that the costs of solar cell central station power for terrestrial application would be two to three times that of conventional electrical generation, even for optimistic technological projections and excluding land costs, profits, and taxes.

47. Clark, op. cit., p. 407.

48. Ibid., pp. 403-4.

49. Morrow, op. cit., pp. 41-43.

50. *Project Independence Report*, op. cit., p. 142.

51. Clark, op. cit., p. 561.

52. William Heronemus's proposals are discussed in ibid., pp. 547-51.

53. "Back to the Windmill to Generate Power," *Business Week*, May 11, 1974, pp. 140-42; and Nicholas Wade, "Windmills: The Resurrection of an Ancient Energy Technology," *Science* 184 (June 7, 1974): 1,055-58.

54. James H. Anderson, Jr., "Economic Power and Water from Solar Energy" (Paper presented at American Society of Mechanical Engineers Winter Annual Meeting, New York, November 26-30, 1972).

55. Clark, op. cit., p. 429.

56. Anderson, op. cit.

57. Clark, op. cit., p. 433.

58. Melvin Calvin, "Solar Energy by Photosynthesis," *Science* 184 (April 19, 1974): 375-81.

59. *U.S. Energy Outlook*, op. cit.

60. George Szego, *The Energy Plantation: A Cost-Effective Means of Providing All the U.S. Energy and Power Needs by Utilizing Solar Energy* (Warrenton, Va.: Inter Technology Corporation, 1972), cited in Clark, op. cit., pp. 445-46.

61. Clark, op. cit., pp. 450-52, presents an excellent critique of large-scale "solar bioconversion" processes involving cultivation of "energy crops."

62. "Garbage Power," *Time*, March 18, 1974, p. 31.

63. "The Quest for U.S. Energy Sufficiency: National Mission for the 1970s," *Coal Age* 79 (April 1974): 109.

64. Clark, op. cit., p. 452.

65. Carter, op. cit.

66. Clark, op. cit., p. 383.

67. "Electricity Vs. Gasoline," *Petroleum Press Service*, September 1972, pp. 331-32.

68. Ibid., p. 332.

69. Ibid., p. 331. For a discussion and comparison of the leading electric battery types under development, see Hottel and Howard, op. cit., pp. 89-93, 312-17.

70. "Electricity Vs. Gasoline," op. cit.

71. Hoyt C. Hottel and Jack B. Howard, "An Agenda for Energy," *Technology Review*, January 1972, p. 48. For a more recent evaluation of progress in fuel cell research, see A.D.S. Tantraum, "Fuel Cells: Past, Present and Future," *Energy Policy*, March 1974, pp. 55-56. Among the corporations that have undertaken fuel cell research and subsequently abandoned efforts in this field are Union Carbide Corporation, Allis-Chalmers Manufacturing Company, Monsanto Company, Texas Instruments, and General Electric Company.

72. New York *Times*, December 20, 1973, pp. 61, 63.

73. *Wall Street Journal*, December 20, 1973, p. 28.

74. Allen L. Hammond, William D. Metz, and Thomas H. Maugh II, *Energy and the Future* (Washington, D.C.: American Association for the Advancement of Science, 1973), pp. 109-15.

75. Clark, op. cit., p. 219.

76. "The FY 1976 Nuclear Budget," *Nuclear News*, March 1975, p. 31.

77. "Hydrogen as a Fuel," *Petroleum Press Service*, July 1972, p. 254.

78. Ibid.

79. Ibid.

80. Hammond, Metz, and Maugh, op. cit., p. 122.

6

GENERAL CONSIDERATIONS IN THE FORMULATION AND IMPLEMENTATION OF EFFECTIVE ENERGY POLICIES

Before analyzing specific energy strategies that might be adopted given different assumptions regarding the availability and cost of crude oil imports, several general points should be stressed concerning the choices and constraints necessarily involved in the formulation and implementation of effective energy policies. While these comments will generally be framed in the context of U.S. policy, they are equally applicable in each of the other major consuming regions. The variations in specific energy strategies will be examined in great detail in later chapters.

The first point has almost been raised to the status of a platitude in recent literature on energy policy: Energy resources constitute an interacting, interdependent system, and effective policy formulation demands a comprehensive understanding of the roles of specific energy sources within this system. Energy policies that are formulated for one energy source without giving adequate consideration to its impact on the overall energy system have been responsible for many of the problems associated with the current energy "crisis." Numerous examples exist. Two specific illustrations of the counterproductive effects of fragmented energy policy formulation are the regulation of natural gas prices by the FPC and the implementation of atmospheric emission standards for both power generating plants and motor vehicles. While the latter is certainly not undesirable in itself, its implementation in isolation from other aspects of national energy policy has generated serious dislocations in the country's energy supply/demand picture which more comprehensive policy formulation might have been able to avoid.[1]

Despite the tiresome repetition of this point in the literature on this subject, it must again be said that energy policy formulation has traditionally been, and remains today, a highly fragmented process that is only beginning to move toward a more comprehensive planning approach. The federal government alone has spawned at least 64 separate agencies involved in various aspects of energy policy formulation, and this number could probably be multiplied several times if government agencies at the state and local level were included. One hopes that the FEA will become increasingly effective in handling day-to-day matters in the energy area and the Energy Resources Council will supply the much-needed coordination and the policy-making level. Also, the newly created ERDA is charged with centralizing energy research and development.

It remains to be seen how effectively this federal energy structure will function.[2] The persistent discrepancy between the universally acknowledged need for more comprehensive energy policy making and the reality of a highly fragmented, ad hoc approach to policy making may justify considerable skepticism regarding the eventual success of these recent reorganization efforts. Democratic political systems encompassing widely divergent interest groups may prove to be fundamentally incapable of adopting comprehensive and fully consistent policies in an area as complex and as vital to the entire population as energy. In any event, the advocates of a more activist government role in the field of energy must accept the burden of demonstrating how this consistency can be achieved in a manner compatible with democratic political decision making.

As to the specifics of energy policy formulation, many serious difficulties must be resolved. Chief among these, perhaps, is the necessity of achieving a balance of emphasis between the demand and supply sides of the energy equation. Until recently, discussions of energy strategy tended to focus primarily on analyzing the potential for expanding energy supplies. At present, however, increased attention is being paid to the possibilities for altering existing patterns of energy consumption.

The blueprint that the FEA has prepared outlining energy demand and supply options for the United States out to 1985 suggests that U.S. energy demand growth and dependence on foreign oil supplies could be reduced substantially by setting standards and providing incentives for more efficient energy use. On the other hand, it also concludes that effective government action to increase domestic energy supplies could eliminate oil imports by 1985, assuming a crude oil price of $11 per barrel.[3]

Perhaps the most controversial study recommended a shift in priorities from the accelerated development of alternative energy sources to a more aggressive energy conservation program. Issued in 1974 by the Energy Policy Project of the Ford Foundation, this study, entitled *A Time to Choose* concluded that it was both desirable and feasible to reduce the rate of energy growth in the next decade to a long-term average of 2 percent per year. The study further suggested that after 1985, it would be possible to sustain economic growth without further increases in annual energy consumption. Much of this reduction in the growth of energy demand would be achieved through changes in construction methods to improve the energy efficiency of space conditioning in buildings, improved gasoline mileage in automobiles, and greater energy efficiency in industrial processes as a consequence of the introduction of new technology and more systematic efforts to utilize "waste" heat from industrial processes to supply an increasing share of energy needs. A variety of policy instruments were recommended to achieve these objectives, including the restructuring of energy pricing, government' regulation of automobile performance, and government programs to accelerate technological innovation.[4]

The Ford Foundation study precipitated considerable controversy, as indicated by the dissenting views appended to the study by members of the advisory board of the Energy Policy Project. Perhaps the most severe criticism came from William P. Tavoulareas, president of Mobil Oil Corporation, who questioned both the feasibility and the desirability of many of the recommendations of the study. In addition, he challenged the study's emphasis on measures to restrain demand growth without a balanced appraisal of what can and should be done to augment energy supply. Tavoulareas also expressed reservations regarding the expansion of the government's role in the sphere of energy which would be necessary to implement the recommendations of the study.[5] Ten academics soon responded with a more comprehensive critique of the Ford Foundation study in a collection of papers entitled *No Time to Confuse*.[6]

Regardless of the specific merits of either side of this debate, the controversy has served to focus attention on the options that exist on both the demand and the supply side of the energy question and has increased public awareness of the opportunities and constraints associated with each option. Perhaps even more important, the debate has raised the fundamental issue of the role of government intervention in the market system to achieve specific energy policy objectives. It is true that widespread government intervention has already been undertaken in virtually every area of energy supply and distribution, but persuasive evidence has accumulated that suggests that the contemporary energy crisis, rather than stemming from any imminent resource scarcity, is actually a manifestation of the distortions resulting from this previous intervention.[7] Before expanding the scope of government intervention even further, policymakers should undertake a more systematic effort to define the roles of the market mechanism and government intervention in the production and allocation of energy and to ensure that these roles are fully compatible. Perhaps one of the most constructive steps toward the resolution of the present energy crisis would be to abandon much of the uncoordinated, ad hoc interventionist measures adopted in the past.

No attempt will be made here to resolve these very difficult and complex questions. However, since the first five chapters of this study covered the constraints and opportunities involved in energy resource development, the following chapter will consider the other side of the energy equation—demand.

There are a wide variety of policy instruments available for effecting shifts in aggregate and sectoral energy consumption. Direct reductions in aggregate energy consumption levels may be accomplished through alterations in the price structure for specific fuels, variations in fiscal policy or direct subsidies to provide incentives for reductions in energy consumption, or the imposition of rationing and other forms of quantitative controls on energy consumption. The most promising approach which could have a significant impact on long-term growth rates in energy consumption involves the implementation of policies designed to promote the accelerated development and commercial application of energy-efficient technology in both producing and consuming sectors. A major attraction of this approach is that it would minimize the demand on energy resources without requiring major adjustments in lifestyles or living standards. A third option which also has been proposed within this category focuses on the reallocation of fuels among the various energy-consuming markets to satisfy existing or anticipated demand more efficiently.

Current projections of the growth in energy consumption in the United States suggest a growth rate of somewhere between 2 and 3.5 percent over the next decade. If the current trend toward high-cost energy supplies is sustained, growth rates will probably remain at the lower end of the projected range, but even with an annual growth rate of 2.5 percent, energy consumption would double in slightly over 28 years. In the context of specific energy markets, the most rapid growth is projected for electric utilities, while transportation and commercial markets will also substantially increase energy consumption. Demographic trends reinforce the tendency toward increased growth in energy consumption, since the share of the U.S. population within the 20-to-35-year-old age group will increase substantially over the next 15 years as a consequence of high birth rates during the 1950s, and this group has traditionally had the highest per capita consumption of energy. The continuing migration from urban centers to suburban areas will further increase energy consumption.

NOTES

1. For one analysis of this example, see Federal Energy Administration, *Project Independence Report*, Appendix AVI, "The Clean Fuels Deficit: A Clean Air Act Problem" (Washington, D.C., 1972), pp. 305-19.

2. Robert Gillette, "Energy Reorganization: Progress in the Offing," *Science*, April 26, 1974, pp. 443-45.

3. *Project Independence Report*, op. cit., p. 14.

4. Ford Foundation, Energy Policy Project, *A Time to Choose: America's Energy Future* (Cambridge, Mass.: Ballinger, 1974), pp. 325-43.

5. William P. Tavoulareas, "Advisory Board Comments," in ibid., pp. 400-408.

6. M.A. Adelman et al., *No Time to Confuse* (San Francisco: Institute for Contemporary Affairs, 1975).

7. For a representative selection of studies supporting this conclusion, see Paul W. MacAvoy, "The Regulation-Induced Shortage of Natural Gas," in *Regulation of the Natural*

Gas Industry, ed. M. Keith C. Brown (Baltimore: Resources for the Future, 1972); Richard B. Mancke, *The Failure of U.S. Energy Policy* (New York: Columbia University Press, 1974); Richard B. Mancke, *Performance of the Federal Energy Office* (Washington, D.C.: American Enterprise Institute, 1975); Roger LeRoy Miller, *The Economics of Energy* (New York: Morrow, 1974); and Paul W. MacAvoy, Bruce E. Stangle, and Jonathan B. Tepper, "The Federal Energy Office as Regulator of the Energy Crisis," *Technology Review* 77 (May 1975): 39-45. Perhaps the most systematic criticism of government policy making in the energy field is provided by Edward J. Mitchell, *U.S. Energy Policy: A Primer* (Washington, D.C.: American Enterprise Institute, 1974).

IMPROVING ENERGY CONVERSION EFFICIENCY

The growth in energy consumption will be manifested in an increasing demand on energy resources unless a major effort is initiated to develop and apply new technology capable of improving energy conversion efficiencies. In the United States, the average thermal efficiency of energy conversion processes is approximately 33 percent, and even in the most sophisticated power generating plants, conversion efficiencies do not exceed 44 percent.[1] This means that roughly two-thirds of the potential energy available in our energy resources cannot be exploited with existing technology. Even moderate increases in conversion efficiencies would represent a significant addition to the overall domestic reserves of exploitable energy. Most of the energy currently lost in conversion processes appears as waste heat, which presents a major disposal problem since it results in thermal pollution of both the atmosphere and water. Research and development programs are already seeking methods by which the energy in waste heat can usefully be harnessed for a variety of purposes, including space heating and industrial process heat.[2] Such programs are an essential component of the effort to maximize the energy yield of existing resources and correspondingly reduce the urgency of imposing substantial, and potentially highly disruptive, curtailments on energy consumption.

Perhaps the most critical area for the accelerated improvement of energy conservation efficiencies, and in particular waste heat utilization, is the electric power generating sector. In 1975, electric utilities constituted the largest consumer of primary fuels of any energy sector in the United States, and their share of primary fuel consumption will probably increase during the rest of this century.[3] Moreover, vigorous expansion of electric power generation offers considerable potential for maximizing the role of domestic coal and uranium resources in supplying the national energy demand while simultaneously reducing our dependence on crude oil imports and dwindling natural gas reserves. The strategy of relying on electric power generation has been widely criticized, however, because existing generating plants have relatively low conversion efficiencies. With current technology, for example, it would be more efficient in terms of energy conversion to employ fuel oil or natural gas for space heating than to rely on electric heating systems.* This objection would largely be eliminated if technological innovations were introduced to substantially improve the energy conversion efficiencies of generating plants. In addition, recent developments in heat pump technology make this a highly attractive device for lowering the energy requirements (by as much as two-thirds) in an all-electric home.[4]

Considerable optimism has been expressed regarding the potential of stationary gas turbines employed as part of a combined-cycle generating plant. Gas turbines are already being employed commercially for peak shaving† and intermediate load service, but their cost and performance characteristics have generally not been satisfactory.[5] However, substantial progress has been made in the metallurgical field over the past decade, and this has made possible continued improvement of both compression ratios and turbine inlet temperatures. As a result, although steam turbines have apparently reached a plateau of thermal efficiency of a maximum of 40 percent, continued improvements in gas turbine technology will permit substantial increases in the thermal efficiency of these turbines.[6] The federal energy research and development program proposed by Ray for fiscal years 1975/79 included an allocation for the construction of a 100-milliwatt combined-cycle demonstration power plant by 1979.[7] One study of combined-cycle power plants concluded that a third-generation plant using synthetic gas from a third-generation coal gasifier in the 1990s will be capable of an overall thermodynamic efficiency of power production from coal of 50.4 percent.[8]

An alternative approach for improving the conversion efficiency of power generating plants involves the development of magnetohydrodynamic (MHD) techniques for base load power generation. MHD techniques essentially involve forcing electricity-conducting gas at a very high speed and temperature through a

---

*Wilson Clark, *Energy for Survival* (New York: Doubleday, Anchor Books, 1974), pp. 186-87. Clark points out that fuel oil may in fact be a less efficient source of energy than electricity for space heating if the costs of fuel oil transportation are taken into consideration.

†"Peak shaving" refers to the use of specific electric power generating units for the exclusive purpose of meeting peaks in the demand for electricity.

duct in the presence of a magnetic field and then extracting the current from the gas with electrodes.[9] Although the successful development of MHD techniques promises thermal efficiencies of over 50 percent, the commercial application of these techniques has been persistently frustrated by the need to sustain extremely high gas temperatures (4,000 to 5,000 degrees Fahrenheit) and by the inability to develop metal components capable of withstanding the adverse conditions in the MHD unit over a long period of time. In addition, high concentrations of nitric oxide associated with MHD operations must be substantially reduced or eliminated in order to comply with atmospheric emission standards. As a result of these problems, MHD development has been confined to small-scale research, and, at least until recently, there has been considerable pessimism regarding the possibility of commercial applications of MHD technology in the foreseeable future.[10]

Despite this widespread pessimism, a General Electric research team announced in 1974 that it had broken the MHD "efficiency barrier" of 20 percent in experiments with a closed-cycle MHD system. In a closed-cycle MHD system, an ionized inert gas is recycled continuously through the MHD generator, in contrast with the open-cycle MHD generator, in which the gas is purified after passing through the MHD generator and is then forced through a conventional gas or steam turbine. One advantage of the closed-cycle MHD system is that it requires operating temperatures of from 1,000 to 2,000 degrees Fahrenheit lower than the open-cycle system, thereby increasing reliability and reducing the need to develop new high-temperature materials. Much of the early MHD research concentrated on the open-cycle systems; only recently has attention shifted to the more promising closed-cycle system.

General Electric anticipates that if further experiments with the closed-cycle MHD system are successful, it will be able to construct a 100-milliwatt demonstration system by 1980 and that overall plant efficiencies for MHD systems may approach 60 percent.[11] Proponents of broader support for MHD research programs also point to the much more active research program maintained by the Soviet government in this field. However, in considering additional support for MHD research, it should be noted that the improved thermal efficiencies promised by MHD technology will eventually be attained through improvements in existing gas turbine technology, and unless MHD technology offers additional advantages, research funds might be more profitably spent in gas turbine development. The operating budget of the federal research and development program on MHD technology increased from $2.8 million in fiscal year 1974 to an estimated $7.6 million in fiscal year 1975, and the ERDA requested that Congress increase this budget to $13.8 million in fiscal year 1976.[12]

Other areas of research and development may improve the efficiency of electric power plants by developing new technologies for the storage, transmission, and distribution of electricity. As a result of the widely varying demand for electrical power in a specific area over any given period of time, electric generating equipment in the United States has an average load factor of approximately 50 percent, and the average load factor on transmission systems is even lower.[13] Until now, the absence of any widely applicable method of electrical energy storage has made this inefficient use of generating equipment unavoidable and has raised the cost of electricity considerably. However, active research programs are currently being undertaken on a variety of storage methods, including hydrogen fuel cells, compressed air storage, and bulk storage batteries.[14] In addition, research is being pursued to develop the technology necessary for higher voltage transmission of electricity, which would minimize the energy losses currently associated with this phase of the electricity supply system (approximately 10 percent of the total amount of electricity generated).[15] Among the methods being explored in this area are superconducting cryogenic cables, direct current transmission, and high-voltage underground transmission lines.[16] Thus, at every stage of the electricity supply system, research and development programs are attempting to develop more efficient technologies for power generation and distribution. In view of the increasingly central role of electric power generation in overall energy supplies, these programs deserve a high priority in any energy strategy.

FUEL SUBSTITUTION

Strategies designed to minimize dependence on high-priced and potentially unreliable crude oil imports will not only seek to improve energy conversion efficiencies for domestically available resources; they must also encourage the reallocation of fuel supplies to diminish crude oil consumption wherever efficient substitutes are available. Approximately 40 percent of the crude oil consumed in the United States—primarily for transportation and lubrication—has no readily available substitute; the rest may be replaced by one or more conventional energy sources without major technological problems.[17]

For example, approximately 25 percent of the boilers in fossil fuel steam generating plants are of the multiple fuel type. Half of these are currently burning oil or gas and could be shifted to coal fuel within a matter of weeks, assuming the availability of adequate coal supplies. Such conversion, however, requires EPA clearance, and this lengthens the time required for conversion considerably. A staff study made by the Office of Emergency Preparedness estimated that the 55 percent share of fossil fuel steam generating capacity currently supplied with coal could be raised to 65 percent within a year and, assuming entirely favorable conditions, could be raised as high as 76.9 percent by 1985.[18] Thus, significant potential exists for reducing the demand for crude oil and increasing the contribution of abundant domestic energy sources such as coal and uranium. Accelerated commercial applications of coal conversion processes to produce synthetic gas and crude oil could substantially increase the flexibility of domestic coal resources in satisfying energy demand and reduce the atmospheric emissions associated with the combustion of unprocessed coal.[19] While substitutes for crude oil are not readily available in large areas of the transportation sector, in which roughly one-half of the petroleum in the United States is consumed, continued improvements in the technology of electrified urban mass transit systems and systematic policies designed to encourage reliance on more efficient forms of long-distance transportation should permit at least some reduction in the growth of crude oil demand in this sector.[20]

RESTRAINTS ON CONSUMPTION GROWTH RATES

In addition to reallocating fuel supplies to maximize the contribution of domestic resources and reducing demand on domestic energy resources through the introduction of more efficient energy conversion, energy policies that would significantly modify the projected growth rate in energy consumption without threatening the continuing improvement of living standards can also be implemented. Another study submitted by the Office of Emergency Preparedness suggested that conservation policies might reduce the projected energy demand in 1980 by as much as 7.3 million barrels per day of oil equivalent (roughly two-thirds of projected imports) simply by concentrating in the following areas: (1) improving insulation in buildings, (2) introducing more efficient air conditioning equipment and systems, (3) developing more efficient transportation patterns, and (4) accelerating the introduction of more efficient industrial processes and equipment. These policies could reduce the growth in energy consumption by as much as 25 percent by 1985.[21] The National Academy of Engineering's recent report *U.S. Energy Prospects* concluded that a systematic program of conservation measures complemented by an increasing use of energy-efficient technology could reduce estimated 1985 energy consumption in the United States by 8 to 9 million barrels per day of oil equivalent.[22]

Early studies on energy policy frequently cited the "truism" that energy consumption was characterized by minimal price elasticity; that is, relatively large changes in the price of a particular fuel would result in very modest, if any, changes in the demand for that fuel. More recent studies have challenged this conclusion and suggest that energy consumption is characterized by a rather substantial price elasticity, particularly over the long term.[23] Thus, the dramatic increase in the prices of a broad variety of fuels that occurred during 1971-75 can be expected to provide strong incentives for the adoption of more efficient equipment and processes.

These incentives could be reinforced by the introduction of fiscal measures, such as a tax on automobile weight and horsepower, or by the implementation of new regulatory measures, such as a revision of building codes requiring more efficient insulation in all new buildings. However, since one of the assumptions underlying these interventionist measures involves the alleged inelasticity of demand for energy, the desirability of such measures should be reexamined now that this assumption no longer appears to be justified. Efforts by the government to increase energy conservation beyond the level that would be achieved through market incentives may result in "overkill" and a more wasteful allocation of economic resources.

One of the most prevalent errors encountered in analyses of energy conservation involves the tendency to focus exclusively on the technical efficiency of energy use in specific processes, thereby seeking to minimize the amount of energy consumed per unit of output without considering the possible effects this might have on other inputs. Thus, reduction of the energy input beyond a certain level may result in a substantial increase in another input, such as raw materials or labor. The proper approach would be to seek to minimize the total costs of all inputs in a particular process, and the market price mechanism provides an ideal method for attaining this objective.[24]

Unless specific imperfections in the market process can be identified, recommendations that the government intervene to reduce energy consumption beyond the levels that would prevail on the unhampered market appear to be motivated by the implicit, and somewhat paternalistic, assumption that consumers overvalue energy uses. Moreover, mandatory restrictions on energy consumption will divert energy from uses that are more highly valued by consumers to uses that are less highly valued. Thus, from the viewpoint of consumer satisfaction, the government measures will yield a less socially desirable situation than would have prevailed in an unhampered market.

Although critics of the high levels of U.S. energy consumption have often focused on the proliferation of electric household gadgetry, this is not the area in which the major energy savings will be achieved. In 1968, for example, 15 million electric toothbrushes and 16 million blenders in the United States consumed as much energy as would normally be consumed in one hour of travel by all the automobiles on the road in the United States.[25]

The two major areas for energy conservation are industry and space heating. In 1972, the industrial sector accounted for 28 percent of energy consumption, and the steel industry alone accounted for 5 percent of total energy consumption, in the United States. New steel production processes already in limited use could achieve as much as a 25 percent energy savings in this one industry over the next 25 years.[26] A process recently developed for the production of aluminum (traditionally the most energy-intensive industry) reduces electrical consumption by 30 percent. DuPont has been one of several companies to implement an energy conservation program for its plants which it claims has reduced its annual energy costs by 7 to 15 percent. Seventy percent of these savings were possible without any additional capital investment.[27] Total energy systems that maximize energy utilization in industrial plants are a relatively new concept and deserve broader application. In a period of inexpensive energy supplies, industrial plants were designed to minimize capital costs even at the expense of higher energy consumption. Dramatic increases in the cost of energy will certainly favor capital expénditure associated with design modifications in new industrial plants to minimize long-term energy consumption. Another method for energy conservation in this sector would be to encourage recycling. For instance, processing recycled aluminum requires one-twelfth of the energy required to produce aluminum from ore.[28]

A related conservation measure in the industrial sector would be to abandon the current declining block rate method used by electric utilities in calculating prices. Under this system, larger consumers of electricity pay less per kilowatt-hour than smaller consumers, thus reducing the price incentive for energy conservation measures. While this pricing system was previously justified on the basis of the substantial economies of scale associated with electricity generation, recent studies suggest that this justification may no longer be valid.[29]

Although it is difficult to distinguish between the impact of rising fuel prices and the impact of the concurrent economic recession, the substantial reductions in the growth rate of electricity consumption in 1974 and 1975 at least suggest that the short-term price elasticity of electricity consumption may be far greater than had previously been believed. Price increases will presumably have a far greater impact on electricity consumption over a longer period of time as consumers begin to make capital investments to replace existing energy consumption systems. Thus, consumers who are currently "locked in" to consumption of electricity by previous investments in a specific energy consumption system may switch to a different system utilizing another, less expensive energy source when existing capital equipment requires replacement. Industrial consumers are believed to be particularly sensitive to changes in the price of electricity.[30]

Roughly 20 percent of U.S. energy consumption is devoted to space heating (and cooling) of buildings, and there are major opportunities for energy conservation in this area through a more effective use of existing components. One study suggested that energy consumption in office buildings and other commercial structures could be reduced by 15 to 20 percent simply by introducing relatively minor design modifications prior to construction.[31] Space temperature control thermostats that use an on/off mechanism rather than a high/low mechanism lower efficiency by as much as 50 to 60 percent.[32] Furnaces that are not regularly cleaned require 5 to 10 percent more fuel to supply the same amount of heat.[33] A relatively modest additional investment of $280 in insulation for a 1,500-square-foot home could reduce thermal losses by

50 percent.[34] These are only some of the possibilities for achieving a substantial reduction in the growth of energy consumption for the space heating and cooling market.[35]

Another market with considerable potential for energy conservation is the transportation sector. This sector assumes particular importance in the context of a strategy for the reduction of crude oil imports, since approximately 50 percent of the crude oil consumed in the United States is used in some form of transportation. Moreover, the energy efficiency of various transport modes has tended to decrease over time as a result of the greater priority assigned to speed and convenience as well as, more recently, pollution control. Measured in terms of the standard net propulsion efficiency (NPE = number of payload unit-miles per gallon of fuel), total transportation movement in the United States has an NPE of approximately 40.[36] In comparison, high-yield transportation systems such as railroads, passenger buses, pipelines, and waterways have NPEs ranging from 100 to 300.[37] The relatively low performance of overall transportation movement is directly attributable to the increasing reliance on transport modes with very low NPEs—automobiles (30 to 40), trucks (50), and airplanes (20 to 30). Thus, major energy savings could be accomplished simply by reorienting long-distance freight transportation from trucks to railroads and long-distance passenger transportation from automobiles and airplanes to railroads and passenger buses. More efficient transportation technologies offer a long-term possibility of further energy savings, although several new transportation modes—such as the proposed supersonic transport—would actually be counter-productive in terms of energy consumption.[38]

On a much broader scale, long-term energy conservation will require a systematic reevaluation of government policies that have indirectly promoted higher consumption of energy. The rapid growth of sprawling suburbs, which has made automobiles a necessity in many parts of the country, has been at least partially encouraged by fiscal incentives and federal mortgage insurance policies which promote single-family home ownership. Low-density suburbs consume twice as much energy per inhabitant as cities and increase the difficulties involved in expanding mass transit systems. The Federal Highway Trust has been a major factor in the increasing reliance on automobiles and trucks for long-distance transportation. Serious consideration should be given to a reversal of these policies, and many proponents of energy conservation favor implementation of new fiscal incentives to promote energy conservation. For example, tax laws could be designed to discourage the production of elaborately packaged, disposable commodities and instead reward durability and recycling.[39]

NOTES

1. U.S. Congress, Senate, Committee on Interior and Insular Affairs, *Energy Research and Development: Problems and Prospects*, report prepared by Harry Perry (Washington, D.C.: Government Printing Office, 1973), p. 76.

2. For an interesting discussion of the status of research on "total energy" systems which harness the energy in waste heat, see Wilson Clark, *Energy for Survival* (New York: Doubleday, Anchor Books, 1974), pp. 233-44. A study by the Office of Emergency Preparedness has emphasized the importance of such "total energy" systems in the context of energy conservation programs (Office of Emergency Preparedness, *The Potential for Energy Conservation: A Staff Study* [Washington, D.C.: Government Printing Office, 1972], p. 35).

3. National Petroleum Council, Committee on U.S. Energy Outlook, *U.S. Energy Outlook* (Washington, D.C.: 1972), p. 20. An evaluation of the energy conservation potential in the electric power generating sector is provided in Federal Energy Administration, *Project Independence Report*, appendix (Washington, D.C., 1974), pp. 182-94.

4. Clark, op. cit., pp. 245-50. For an evaluation of the problems that remain before heat pumps can become more widely commercially available, see "Heat Pump Interest Grows Stronger," *Electrical World*, May 1, 1974, pp. 64-65.

5. Perry, op. cit., p. 102.

6. Hoyt C. Hottel and Jack B. Howard, *New Energy Technology* (Cambridge: Massachusetts Institute of Technology Press, 1971), p. 47.

7. U.S. Atomic Energy Commission, *The Nation's Energy Future*, report submitted by Dixy Lee Ray (Washington, D.C.: Government Printing Office, 1973), p. 16.

8. This study was cited in Hottel and Howard, op. cit., p. 47. For a more detailed analysis of combined-cycle power plants, see Allen L. Hammond, William D. Metz, and Thomas H. Maugh II, *Energy and the Future* (Washington, D.C.: American Association for the Advancement of Science, 1973), pp. 17-24.

9. Hottel and Howard, op. cit., p. 283.

10. Ibid., p. 47; and Perry, op. cit., pp. 103-4. For an analysis of MHD technology, see Hammond, Metz, and Maugh, op. cit., pp. 25-28.

11. *Technology Review*, January 1975, pp. 57-58; and "Closed Cycle MHD Potential Impressive," *Electrical World*, March 15, 1974, pp. 94-95.

12. "The FY 1976 Nuclear Budget," *Nuclear News*, March 1975, p. 29.

13. Perry, op. cit., p. 171.

14. A survey of various storage methods, including the most immediately promising method, pumped storage, is provided in Arthur L. Robinson, "Energy Storage (I): Using Electricity More Efficiently," *Science* 184 (May 17, 1974): 785-87.

15. *U.S. Energy Outlook*, op. cit., p. 71.

16. Perry, op. cit., pp. 138-39; and Hammond, Metz, and Maugh, op. cit., pp. 101-08. For a survey of recent research developments in the field of electrical transmission, see Peter R. Howard, "Electrical Transmission of Energy: Current Trends," *Energy Policy* 1 (September 1973): 154-60.

17. David C. White, "Energy, the Economy and the Environment," *Technology Review*, October-November 1971, pp. 20-21.

18. Office of Emergency Preparedness, *The Potential for Energy Conservation: Substitution for Scarce Fuels* (Washington, D.C.: Government Printing Office, 1973), pp. 9, 53-54.

19. Lawrence Lessing, "Capturing Clean Gas and Oil from Coal," *Fortune*, November 1973, p. 129; and *U.S. Energy Outlook*, op. cit., pp. 13, 72.

20. For one analysis of modifications in transportation systems that could result in increased energy efficiency, see Richard A. Rice, "Toward More Transportation with Less Energy," *Technology Review* 76 (February 1974): 45-53.

21. *The Potential for Energy Conservation: A Staff Study*, op. cit., p. ii. The conclusions of two reports by the Office of Emergency Preparedness concerning the potential for energy conservation are summarized in "The Conservation of Energy," *Petroleum Press Service*, July 1973, pp. 255-59.

22. National Academy of Engineering, Task Force on Energy, *U.S. Energy Prospects: An Engineering Viewpoint* (Washington, D.C., 1974), pp. 29-30.

23. H.S. Houthakker and P.K. Verleger, "Dynamic Demand Analyses of Selected Energy Resources" (Paper delivered to American Economic Association, December 1973). For the price elasticity of gasoline consumption, see H.S. Houthakker, P.K. Verleger, and D.P. Sheehan, "Dynamic Models of the Demand for Gasoline and Residual Electricity," *Journal of Agricultural Economics* 56 (May 1974): 412-18.

24. This criticism of many energy conservation studies is most clearly presented in Armen A. Alchian, "An Introduction to Confusion," in M.A. Adelman et al., *No Time to Confuse* (San Francisco: Institute for Contemporary Affairs, 1975), pp. 10-14.

25. New York *Times*, January 3, 1974, p. 35.

26. The share of the industrial sector in energy consumption is provided in *Project Independence Report*, op. cit., appendix, p. 16, while the estimates on energy conservation in the steel industry are available in Perry, op. cit., pp. 140-41.

27. *Newsweek*, January 22, 1973, p. 40.

28. Perry, op. cit., pp. 140-41. For more detailed analyses of the potential for energy conservation in the industrial sector, see *Project Independence Report*, op. cit., appendix, pp. 154-81; and Charles A. Berg, "Conservation in Industry," *Science* 184 (April 19, 1974): 264-70.

29. This conclusion is outlined in Jerome F. Hass, Edward J. Mitchell, and Bernell K. Stone, *Financing the Energy Industry* (Cambridge, Mass.: Ballinger, 1974), pp. 88-91. In addition, Ernst Habicht, director of energy programs for the Environmental Defense Fund, urged abandonment of this pricing practice in an article in the New York *Times*, December 26, 1973, p. 39. See also *Business Week*, April 21, 1973, p. 60; and Paul L. Joskow and Paul MacAvoy, "Regulation and the Financial Condition of the Electric Power Companies in the 1970s," *American Economic Review*, May 1975, pp. 295-301.

30. The price elasticity of electricity consumption is analyzed in Houthakker and Verleger, op. cit.

31. *The Potential for Energy Conservation: A Staff Study*, op. cit., p. 21.

32. Hottel and Howard, op. cit., pp. 321-23.

33. Ibid.

34. *Business Week*, April 21, 1973, pp. 59-60.

35. For a more detailed analysis of the energy conservation potential in the space heating and cooling market, see *Project Independence Report*, op. cit., pp. 123-53.

36. Richard A. Rice, "System Energy and Future Transportation," *Technology Review*, January 1972, p. 31.

37. Ibid., p. 37.

38. Ibid., p. 32. See also *The Potential for Energy Conservation: A Staff Study*, op. cit., p. 14; and Perry, op. cit., p. 140. A more detailed analysis of the energy conservation potential in the transportation sector is available in *Project Independence Report*, op. cit.,

appendix, pp. 90-122. For an examination of the role of the automobile in gasoline consumption, see Gerald Leach, "The Impact of the Motor Car on Oil Reserves," *Energy Policy* 1 (December 1973): 195-207.

39. A brief survey of some government policies that have indirectly promoted higher energy consumption was provided in a column by Anthony Lewis in the New York *Times*, January 3, 1974, p. 35.

One short-term constraint that every energy strategy must acknowledge involves the lengthy lead times required for alterations in existing energy systems, as a result of either the introduction of new technology or the redistribution of energy resources. Energy-producing and -consuming systems are generally characterized by long lifetimes—industrial generating plants have an operational life of 30 to 50 years, while homes and offices are built to last 50 years or more. Even the relatively short lifespan of the individual automobile is counterbalanced by the fact that it requires an extensive infrastructure (comprising highways, gasoline distribution networks, an automobile manufacturing industry, and a repair service network) that has a much longer operational life.[1] Thus, the construction of energy-producing and -consuming systems undertaken over the next five years will have a relatively minor short-term impact but a much more significant long-term impact.

The problem of lengthy lead times is further aggravated by the time-consuming research and development programs that must precede the commercial application of new technology. While "crash" research and development programs financed by massive funds may substantially reduce the length of the research and development phase, there is usually a lead time that cannot be shortened without introducing an unacceptable risk of failure. Most research and development programs begin with basic laboratory research and the construction of bench-scale models of the technology under investigation. If experiments at this stage prove successful, the technology is gradually scaled up to commercial size through the construction of pilot plants, demonstration plants, and finally full-scale prototypes. Testing of the technology is undertaken at each stage before the next stage is initiated.

Funding for a "crash" research and development program would permit the construction of larger-scale models more quickly, but the major advantage of such a program would become evident when there were several competing technologies that required testing. Research and development programs with limited funding would have to choose one of the alternative technologies at an early stage for subsequent scaling up, whereas a "crash" program would have sufficient funds to scale up and test all the promising technologies simultaneously. In the former case, if the particular technology chosen for scaling up were to develop insurmountable problems at a later stage, choosing an alternative technology and repeating the scaling-up process could cause major delays. Thus, the advantage of the "crash" program is that it reduces the risk of failure associated with attaining a given objective within a specified time, but constraints nevertheless remain on the minimum time required to develop a particular technology to the point of commercial application.[2]

The Manhattan Project is usually cited as the most successful example of a "crash" research and development program. Within a three-year period, scientists pursued simultaneous research on four different methods for the production of fissionable material and on two distinct designs for the nuclear weapon itself. The success of this program may perhaps be usefully contrasted with the research and development program launched following World War II to promote the commercial application of nuclear energy. Although this research program began in the early 1950s and for a considerable period of time has received as much as 80 to 85 percent of federal research and development expenditures, it has still had only a minimal impact on commercial energy supplies. The delays encountered in this program provide some indication of the lead times that can be expected in the commercial development of future alternative technologies unless extremely costly "crash" research and development programs along the lines of the Manhattan Project are approved. Moreover, the lengthy lead times associated with any fundamental alteration of existing energy systems make it imperative to formulate long-term energy strategies designed to meet anticipated needs over the next 30 to 40 years.

Long-term energy strategies will not be constrained by the imminent depletion of energy resources. Virtually all estimates of energy resource inventories agree that sufficient quantities of conventional fuels exist to supply even the most liberal projections of the growth in consumption until the period in the foreseeable future in which new energy technologies will be capable of providing society with unlimited sources of energy.

It is important to recognize that the "proved reserve" estimates cited earlier provide relatively little insight into the ultimate size of the resource base. Proved reserves in the extractive industries correspond to the inventories maintained in other businesses, and, just like in other businesses, it is generally unprofitable to develop proved reserves beyond certain levels which are at least partially determined by current rates of production.[3] Even the broader estimates of "potentially recoverable" reserves may often be misleading, since they are calculated on the assumption that present technology and present price levels will be maintained. Obviously, if prices were to rise or major innovations in extraction technology were to occur, the size of "potentially recoverable" reserves would increase significantly.

More important, economic analysis indicates that the ultimate size of the resource base is unknown, unknowable, and in fact uninteresting; the only relevant consideration should be the cost of extracting each incremental unit of the resource.[4] In this context, M.A. Adelman has calculated that the production cost, as distinguished from the market price, of crude oil from existing fields in the Arabian Peninsula will still be in the vicinity of 10 to 20 cents per barrel, (in 1968 prices) as late as 1985. Any shortage in the availability of crude oil before 1985 will therefore be due not to the depletion of the earth's remaining crude oil resource but to political intervention in the market mechanism. Comparable conclusions may be reached regarding the earth's coal resource.[5]

Instead, the major constraint on long-term energy strategies will be the availability of adequate capital resources necessary to finance increasingly capital-intensive forms of energy production. The constraint, therefore, will be not resource scarcity but capital scarcity. Effective energy strategies must anticipate and adapt to this fundamental transformation in the nature of energy production.

By any account, the capital investment requirements needed to meet projected energy consumption in the United States and other primary consuming regions will be enormous. Most estimates suggest that approximately $500 to $600 billion in capital investments will be required to supply the U.S. market alone by 1985. (Various estimates of capital investment requirements are available, and the estimates appear to escalate as each year passes. However, most of these estimates are based on assumptions of a sustained high growth rate in energy demand, and reduced growth in energy demand due to higher energy prices may help to counterbalance the inflationary escalation of construction costs.*) If a determined effort is made to reduce crude oil imports through accelerated commercial application of new energy technologies, capital investment requirements could be even higher. The adverse impact on private capital

---

*The Committee on U.S. Energy Outlook of the National Petroleum Council estimated in 1972 that the capital investment required for exploration, development, and processing of energy supplies (including electricity generation and transmission facilities) by 1985 would reach $450 to $550 billion (in 1970 dollars) (National Petroleum Council, Committee on U.S. Energy Outlook, *U.S. Energy Outlook* [Washington, D.C., 1972], p. 296). A more recent estimate indicates that under a high growth/cost scenario (assuming a 4.2 percent growth rate of energy consumption), capital investment requirements for the period 1971-85 will be as high as $679 billion (in 1970 dollars), or almost 30 percent of total business capital outlays projected during that period (Jerome Hass, Edward J. Mitchell, and Bernell K. Stone, *Financing the Energy Industry* [Cambridge, Mass.: Ballinger, 1974]).

investment produced by continuing uncertainty over the nature of long-term government energy policy cannot be overemphasized. Uncertainty regarding future government crude oil import policy has been a factor in recent delays in the construction of adequate refinery capacity in the United States, which in turn has seriously aggravated the present energy crisis. Private investors will naturally hesitate to invest in highly capital-intensive energy production systems without a reasonable assurance that sudden shifts in government energy policies will be avoided. For this reason, it is essential to formulate a comprehensive, long-term energy strategy that will minimize the uncertainties for private capital investment.

In addition to the uncertainties that have considerably diminished the incentive for private capital investment in energy supply systems, much has been written about the so-called gap between capital investment requirements and the availability of financing on the private capital markets. In the unhampered market, adjustments in the interest rate would serve as an equilibrating mechanism to eliminate this gap. Rapid growth in the demand for financing would raise the interest rate, and the higher financing costs would in turn raise the price of energy. This would precipitate a further reduction in the growth rate for energy demand and thereby diminish the need for additional capital investment. Any failure of the equilibrating mechanism must be attributable to some imperfection in the market process, and in an era of widespread government price regulation, such imperfections are often the direct result of government intervention.

Short-term and medium-term energy strategies must reconcile a series of contradictory objectives: (1) ensuring adequate supplies of low-cost energy, (2) minimizing the adverse impact on the environment, and (3) reducing dependence on foreign energy sources. In the short term, it is essential to establish clearly defined priorities that will enable choices to be made among these objectives in the formulation of energy policy. Efforts to deny the contradictory nature of these objectives in the context of existing technologies will simply result in the elaboration of conflicting energy policies which will further aggravate current energy supply problems. The ability to satisfy all these objectives can only be developed gradually in the long term, provided that research and development programs for new energy technology are explicitly designed now to develop alternative energy sources that are compatible with these three objectives.

In elaborating a realistic energy strategy, it is necessary to abandon the tendency to focus on any one energy source as a panacea for future supplies. The multiplicity of energy markets and the differing requirements of each one suggest that no single energy source will be capable of providing such a solution in the foreseeable future. Instead, policy-makers should seriously evaluate even the relatively limited contribution that specific energy sources may be able to make in order to promote a flexible and efficient energy mix capable of satisfying the growing and diversified demand.

One final prerequisite for the formulation of effective energy strategies involves the necessity of developing an adequate data base regarding the energy systems in the economy in order to permit accurate projections of long-term trends and to anticipate potential bottlenecks in energy supply. Government policies are only as effective as the data upon which they are based. Until recently, there was not even a systematic attempt by the federal government to integrate the data its agencies accumulated. Mechanisms must be established to ensure the systematic collection of data regarding every phase of energy operations and to evaluate the implications of this data for policy formulation.[6]

In order to evaluate specific energy strategy options for the United States and other major consuming regions, three scenarios involving differing assumptions regarding the availability and cost of crude oil imports will be considered in the next chapter. While the discussion of each scenario focuses on the options available to the U.S. government, Chapter 10 will analyze the variations in strategies that might be adopted in the other major energy-consuming regions— Western Europe and Japan.

These scenarios assume that the current high prices of crude oil imports will be maintained. The first scenario further assumes that sufficient quantities of crude oil at current prices will be available to meet the increasing demand in the major consuming regions. The second scenario considers the alternative possibility that available supplies of crude oil imports will gradually tighten if exporting countries are successful in the implementation of production controls designed to maintain the present high level of crude oil prices and/or to extend the life of their depleting resources. The final scenario examines the possibility that another, more widespread, politically motivated embargo by the Arab members of OPEC will be imposed and sustained over a long period of time.

None of these scenarios considers the possibility that the price of crude oil imports will decline substantially over the next decade since our primary concern is to evaluate the options available in the major consuming regions when confronted with high-priced crude oil imports. Nevertheless, there is no certainty that the prices of crude oil imports will remain at their current high levels, and imported crude price is a crucial parameter in energy policy formulation. Of the three scenarios, the first seems to be the most likely, although there is a definite possibility that the long-term supply constraints on crude oil imports assumed in the second scenario might emerge over the next few years. In the political arena, there is little ground for the optimistic view that an enduring lessening of tensions in the Middle East can be accomplished. Even though important steps have been taken toward dealing with the manifold aspects of dependence on high-priced Arab oil by the non-Communist world, there is a continuing need to consider the policy and planning problems of the third scenario.

NOTES

1. David C. White, "Energy, the Economy and the Environment," *Technology Review*, October-November 1971, p. 22.

2. U.S. Congress, Senate, Committee on Interior and Insular Affairs, *Energy Research and Development: Problems and Prospects*, report prepared by Harry Perry (Washington, D.C.: Government Printing Office, 1973), p. 104.

3. For an economic analysis of the concept of "proved" reserves, see Morris A. Adelman, *The World Petroleum Market* (Baltimore: Johns Hopkins University Press, 1972), pp. 24-30.

4. Edward J. Mitchell, *U.S. Energy Policy: A Primer* (Washington, D.C.: American Enterprise Institute, 1974), p. 6.

5. Adelman, op. cit., pp. 69-73, 77.

6. Perry, op. cit., pp. 123-24.

9

SCENARIO I: HIGH-PRICED CRUDE OIL IMPORTS

The first scenario assumes that the high prices of crude oil imports that have already been achieved will either be maintained at roughly existing levels or else will continue to rise as a result of market demand and producing-country government action. However, this scenario further assumes that there will be no restriction on supplies of crude oil imports at these price levels and therefore that the embargo on the United States by the Arab producing governments will not be repeated. In the blueprint prepared by the FEA, the federal government was given an assessment of various supply and conservation options to serve as the basis for the much more difficult task of setting energy policy goals and programs for the United States over the next ten years.[1]

The U.S. government response to the escalating price of crude oil imports and the Arab oil embargo has been somewhat erratic, largely due to its continued failure to reach a consensus regarding the relative priorities that should be given to the objectives of minimizing dependence on crude oil imports and minimizing energy costs. At least in the short term, these two objectives appear to be incompatible, and difficult choices must be made between them if effective energy policies are to emerge.

Prior to the embargo, the government had announced several measures designed to increase the availability of domestic supplies of energy. These measures included (1) removal of the mandatory oil import quota system and its replacement by a system of license fees to provide incentives for the construction of domestic refineries, (2) modification of emission control standards to permit a greater use of coal, and (3) expansion of the federal leasing program for offshore oil and gas exploration.[2] In addition, the government implemented a two-tiered price system for domestic crude oil which removed price controls on "new" oil (oil produced in excess of 1973 levels) as well as on oil produced from high-cost "stripper" wells. In 1975, this two-tiered system meant that approximately 40 percent of domestic crude oil production was sold at unregulated prices averaging $13 per barrel, while the remaining 60 percent was subjected to price controls lowering the average price to $5.25 per barrel.

During the embargo itself, the government imposed a variety of conservation measures supplemented by a mandatory allocation system for refineries. One recent study of the impact of these measures concluded that, due to overreaction by the government, these measures actually served to aggravate the supply shortage. In fact, this study concluded that the selective boycott against the United States was unsuccessful and that the most prominent manifestations of shortage, such as queuing up at gasoline stations, were the direct result of misdirected regulatory measures.[3]

By late 1975, there appears to have been a significant shift from earlier policy pronouncements which indicated a desire to provide price incentives for increased domestic energy production by easing price controls on crude oil and natural gas.[4] Popular dissatisfaction with the high price of energy and the growing sensitivity of politicians to the potential impact of further prices increases on the forthcoming national elections were major factors in the recent adoption of legislation that mandates an immediate reduction in the composite price of domestic crude oil by 70 cents per barrel and thus authorizes, subject to congressional approval, gradual increases in the composite price over a 40-month period.[5] Even if the increases are approved, the composite price would still be substantially below the price that would have occurred under an extension of the present price control program, and the domestic price of crude oil would remain substantially below the levels prevailing in the world market. Industry critics of this legislation argue that it will reduce capital investment in domestic exploration and production by 20 to 25 percent and virtually assure increasing crude oil imports in the next decade.[6]

In addition to its price control features, this legislation establishes gradually rising mandatory fuel economy standards for automobiles and requires the testing and labeling of electrical appliances for energy efficiency. Neither measure is expected to result in a significant reduction in crude oil imports, however. This legislation also authorizes the establishment of crude oil stockpiles to protect against the possibility of future embargoes.[7]

In contrast with government policy in maintaining price controls on domestic crude oil production, there were indications by the end of 1975 that Congress might eventually approve natural gas deregulation. Ironically, at the beginning of 1975 many believed not only that federal price controls would be maintained on interstate shipments of natural gas but that these controls might be extended to include intrastate sales as well. However, in subsequent congressional debate, the Senate defeated efforts to extend price controls and approved a measure authorizing immediate new gas deregulation and gradual deregulation for offshore gas production. Supporters of deregulation were hopeful that similar legislation would be approved by the House of Representatives. However, the House eventually adopted a bill which would maintain existing price regulations for 20-30 major producers and even extend these controls to intrastate sales. As a limited compromise, the bill does exempt "new" gas produced by small independent companies from price regulation.[8]

These policy initiatives in maintaining price controls and very limited conservation measures have been supplemented by an aggressive expansion of federal research and development expenditures for alternative energy sources, as well as a gradual reorientation of research and development programs to reflect a more diversified approach. The 1973 AEC proposed budget for a $10 billion research and development program covering fiscal years 1975/79 focused on five distinct task areas: (1) to conserve energy and energy resources, (2) to increase domestic production of oil and gas, (3) to substitute coal for oil and gas on a massive scale, (4) to validate the nuclear option, and (5) to exploit untapped energy sources to the maximum extent possible (solar, geothermal, fusion, and so on).

The average annual federal energy research and development expenditure of $2 billion recommended over this five-year period represented a more than tripling of the $640.2 million spent in fiscal year 1973. While federal research and development programs have traditionally concentrated on nuclear energy (often comprising as much as 90 percent of total expenditures), this new program recommended greater support for other research and development programs as well. In particular, federal support for coal-associated research would increase by 356 percent over fiscal year 1973 levels. Despite this diversification of support, nuclear energy research and development programs (including fusion research) would continue to receive approximately 65 percent of total federal energy research and development expenditures.

The budget report recommended close cooperation between private industry and government in attaining national energy research and development objectives and outlined various policies to maximize industry participation in the five-year research and development program. In general, the private sector would participate most actively in the achievement of short-term objectives, while the government would become increasingly involved in long-term energy research and development programs which require large-scale financing with little prospect of immediate return on investment. The proposed energy research and development strategy of the government would be based on three priorities (in order of importance): (1) national energy self-sufficiency, (2) the protection of environmental quality, and (3) the availability of low-cost energy supplies. The first two priorities were selected as the basis for the funding of government programs because they are considered to be in the national interest but are not entirely compatible with private profit incentives which determine industry research and development programs. On the other hand, the private profit incentive was considered the most effective mechanism for ensuring reductions in energy cost through competitive market forces, and therefore this objective would be primarily the responsibility of private industry.[9]

Although the proposed budget submitted by the AEC was never officially adopted by the government, it remains an influential document in the formulation of research and development expenditure programs, and it clearly reflected the commitment by the U.S. government to expand its efforts in this field. In comparison with an average annual growth of 7.8 percent in federal expenditures on energy research and development programs between 1969 and 1970, these expenditures rose by 29.9 percent between fiscal year 1973 and fiscal year 1974, and this trend accelerated with an expansion of 74 percent between fiscal year 1974 and fiscal year 1975 expenditures.[10] Despite this significant growth in energy research and development expenditures, the allocations thus far do not match the ambitious levels recommended in the AEC budgetary proposal. In fiscal year 1975, the government authorized expenditures of $998.8 million for energy research and development programs, in contrast with the AEC recommendation of $1,572 million.[11]

The growth in federal energy research and development expenditures has been accompanied by a reorganization of the administrative structures supervising government programs in this field. In 1974, the ERDA was established to coordinate programs in the field of energy. The ERDA will incorporate research and development programs that had been administered by a variety of government agencies, including the AEC (now disbanded), the Office of Coal Research, the Bureau of Mines, the National Science Foundation, and the EPA.[12]

An extensive report entitled *A National Plan for Energy Research, Development and Demonstration*, issued by the ERDA in June 1975, confirms earlier indications that the federal government's energy research and development strategy would gradually move away from its traditional concentration on nuclear energy programs and adopt a more diversified approach. While nuclear energy continues to receive approximately 60 percent of total federal energy research and development expenditures, major increases in funding for solar energy and geothermal energy programs are envisioned. The priority previously given to FBR development now appears to be considerably diminished, and the ERDA no longer believes that the FBR will reach commercial application before the year 2000. The program also places greater emphasis on the short-term objectives of increasing recovery capabilities from domestic crude oil fields and expanding the flexibility of coal reserves in domestic energy supplies through research in such fields as coal gasification and liquefaction. The ERDA hopes that these short-term programs will permit a reduction in crude oil imports from 6 million barrels per day in 1974 to 3.5 million barrels per day in 1985 and will ultimately permit the elimination of crude oil imports by 1995.[13]

Despite these indications of a more balanced approach in energy research and development, the congressional Office of Technology Assessment (OTA) issued a highly critical evaluation of the ERDA report following a comprehensive review of the document by six panels of experts assembled under OTA auspices. The OTA analysis criticized the ERDA's overemphasis on complex, costly technologies and its relative neglect of the potential of energy conservation and small-scale technical research which might have more immediate commercial application. For example, in contrast with the ERDA's acknowledgement of the importance of conservation and short-term solutions to growing crude oil imports, the agency's proposed budget for fiscal year 1976 allocates only 2 percent of its expenditures to conservation programs and 5 percent to short-term research programs.[14] However, many of the deficiencies criticized by the OTA analysis can be attributed largely to the fact that the ERDA report was prepared under very tight time constraints and that the agency consequently had been forced to rely heavily on research programs that had already been formulated by other government agencies. As the ERDA staff has more time to translate its new policy priorities into specific research programs, it is anticipated that major shifts in budgetary allocations will be made.

Another major policy initiative announced in 1975 involved the proposal for a $100 billion energy independence program. This program would establish a new government corporation, the EIA, to provide financial assistance to stimulate $600 billion in private-sector investment in energy over a ten-year period. The emphasis of such a program would be on the development of technologies capable of commercial application in the next decade. The proposed legislation for this program also included measures to minimize delays associated with federal regulatory proceedings that affect EIA projects. The ultimate objective of the program is to eliminate crude oil imports by 1985.[15]

The announcement of this proposal by President Ford in October 1975 soon generated considerable controversy in Congress. The ensuing debate has focused attention on the desirability of subsidizing private investment in high-cost alternative energy sources and guaranteeing minimum price levels for the output of commercial plants built under this program. While providing major incentive to accelerate private investment in this field, such a program would also in effect commit the nation to high-cost energy sources even if world crude oil prices were to decline substantially.

Critics point out that although such a program is presented as a response to the high prices of crude oil imports, it merely guarantees that the consumer will have to pay these high prices indefinitely. The rationale for this program would thus seem to depend on the uncertain proposition that initially high-cost alternative energy sources will decrease in cost as producers benefit from the learning curve associated with new technologies, or on such noneconomic objectives as the desire to minimize dependence on potentially insecure foreign energy sources. In any event, by the end of 1975, congressional criticism of the proposed legislation had raised strong doubts regarding its eventual enact-ment.[16] Once again, the objective of low-cost energy supplies appeared to be prevailing over the objective of maximizing national self-sufficiency in energy.

Before evaluating additional policy options that would be available in formulating a national energy strategy within this scenario, brief consideration must be given to the alterations in energy consumption that might be anticipated simply as a result of rising market prices for crude oil and other energy sources. In general, the lengthy lead times involved in the introduction of new energy-producing and -consuming systems as well as the lifespan of existing systems suggest that the general price elasticity of energy consumption will increase proportionally with the length of time involved. Moderate flexibility may be anticipated in shifts from one fuel to another in specific markets as a response to growing price differentials. Such a trend will be likely, for instance, among electric utilities equipped with multiple fuel boilers which are able to switch from crude oil to coal in very short periods of time with minimal additional investment. However, these shifts in fuel consumption will generally have to occur gradually as a result of short-term supply contraints among alternative fuels. In addition, the absence of readily available substitutes for a substantial portion of crude oil consumption (most notably in the transportation sector) will seriously limit the impact of such shifts on overall crude oil consumption.

Perhaps the most promising short-term impact of high prices on oil consumption will simply be a modest reduction in overall consumption levels, as both industrial and individual users restrain nonessential consumption of energy. Modifications in the heating and lighting of buildings serve as an obvious example of the largely voluntary adjustments that might be expected in response to higher-cost energy supplies, and while their impact on energy consumption may not be dramatic, they provide a margin of adjustment that may have been underestimated. There have been indications of a trend in this direction from the time of the Arab embargo crisis.[17] At this time it is impossible to gauge the future of such a trend or the degree to which energy consuming habits will be permanently modified. Such modifications will depend largely on a continuing and growing spread of "energy consciousness" within the public and an increased awareness of the numerous ways in which energy consumption may be reduced without seriously affecting customary lifestyles. The adjustments do have their limits, however, and while the individual automobile owner may, for example, try to reduce the number of separate trips he makes in a car, residential patterns in many parts of the United States have made heavy reliance on the automobile unavoidable. To a considerable extent, we are limited in the short term by the constraints imposed on us by existing energy-producing and -consuming systems.

Over the longer term, however, market incentives will probably perform a far more significant role in accelerating the development of both energy-efficient

technology and alternative energy sources while restraining additional investment in energy-wasteful technology. Detroit plans to expand its production of
smaller, lighter automobiles, and research will inevitably increase for the
development of new engine designs, more efficient mass transit systems, and so
on. Industrial processes permitting significant reductions in energy consumption
will become more economically attractive. Similarly, additional expenditures on
insulation of buildings will be offset by long-run savings in energy consumption.
On the other hand, new modes of transportation with extremely low NPEs, such
as the supersonic transport, will appear increasingly unattractive.

It should be emphasized, however, that both the short-term adjustments in
energy consumption and the long-run introduction of new energy-producing and
-consuming systems discussed above assume that the higher price of crude oil
imports will be passed along to the consumer. In recent years there has been an
increasing tendency among the major consuming regions to impose price
controls on a variety of petroleum products. If such controls are employed to
shield the consumer from the consequences of price increases in energy supplies,
continuing dislocations in these supplies may be expected, and market incentives
for adjustments to new supply conditions will be correspondingly reduced.

The problem is further complicated by the political sensitivity of non-
market measures to restrict energy consumption which imposes a major
constraint on government action to moderate projected increases in energy
demand. This constraint is particularly important in the first scenario, since the
extent of the energy crisis would be less acutely perceived by the public than in
the other two scenarios. Unless a pervasive sense of crisis exists, measures such as
rationing or outright prohibition of certain forms of energy consumption would
be extremely difficult to justify politically, particularly if they are imposed over
a long period of time.

Certain forms of government action which would have a more long-term
impact in modifying projected increases in energy demand are more politically
feasible in this scenario. For example, in an area that is particularly relevant for
crude oil consumption, the federal government might provide additional funding
for the accelerated development of urban mass transit systems and implement a
variety of policies designed to promote more efficient long-distance transportation patterns. In particular, transportation policies could provide a variety of
incentives to encourage a greater reliance on railroads for both long-distance
freight hauling and passenger transportation. The railroads have confronted
serious problems in recent years, and a comprehensive effort would be needed to
expand the role of railroads in the national transportation system. Reevaluation
of transportation policies would be necessary to coordinate more systematically
national energy and transportation needs. Such measures in the transportation
sector would receive widespread political support as a result of their simultaneous contribution to environmental protection. Moreover, the adverse impact of
rising crude oil prices on the national balance of payments would presumably

make large federal subsidies for the development of mass transit systems more readily justifiable.

Outside the transportation sector, government policy might also increase federal funding for research and development programs to develop more efficient energy technology in a variety of areas. One area in which these programs could have a significant effect is in the field of electric power generation. The establishment of the Electric Power Research Institute, which is funded by utility companies, could accelerate the development of several technologies that are already near commercial application. Government at all levels could also contribute to reductions in projected consumption in several ways—for example, by implementing stricter insulation standards in building codes.

On the supply side, market incentives provided by large increases in the price of crude oil will produce numerous alterations in the pattern and overall size of energy supplies. In the short term, previously noncompetitive conventional energy sources will occupy an increasingly important role in the supply of energy. Exploration and production operations will steadily expand to exploit geographically remote reserves of crude oil. The high costs of production normally associated with such reserves will no longer constitute an obstacle to their commercial development. In particular, offshore exploration and production will receive additional impetus. Production from existing reserves will be prolonged by the introduction of costly secondary and tertiary recovery techniques. Coal, which has been steadily declining in the energy supplies of all the major consuming regions, could reemerge as a serious competitor of crude oil.

Rising crude oil prices will also inevitably increase the short-term economic feasibility of nonconventional alternative energy sources that have reached advanced stages of technological development. Processes that have already been tested at the pilot-plant level—particularly coal conversion processes and oil shale extraction—can be introduced commercially in the near future, although a considerable amount of time will be required before these new technologies will contribute a substantial share of U.S. energy requirements. Greater incentives for the expansion of research and development programs will indirectly accelerate the technological development of long-term renewable energy sources such as solar energy, nuclear fusion, and hydrogen fuels.

Although careful consideration should be given to the effectiveness of market incentives in generating additional private research and development investment before resorting to government intervention, incentives in this area can be significantly reinforced by a variety of government measures, including fiscal measures and direct funding of energy research and development programs, as exemplified by the budget proposed by the AEC for fiscal years 1975-79.[18] Financial support of research and development programs is perhaps one of the most politically attractive government measures to affect the energy supply/

demand equation since it appeals to the electorate on three distinct levels: ensuring the availability of adequate energy supplies, protecting national security, and improving environmental quality. These measures, however, are utlimately limited by the government's ability to generate additional fiscal revenues and, at least in part, by the willingness of the public to shoulder an additional tax burden with the prospect of only long-run returns.

The government might also supplement market incentives by encouraging greater development of energy resources located on federal lands. A major share of remaining domestic energy resources are believed to be located on these lands and have thus far been only marginally developed as a result of highly restrictive leasing policies. The NPC estimates that 50 percent of remaining domestic crude oil and natural gas potential, 40 percent of coal reserves, 50 percent of uranium reserves, 60 percent of geothermal reservoirs, and 80 percent of oil shale deposits are located on federal lands.[19] Federal leasing policies will clearly represent a major determinant of the pace of development for domestic energy resources.

With the important possible exception of Middle Eastern crude oil exports, price increases for crude oil will provide widespread incentives for the expanded production of all forms of energy over present projections. One further qualification should be added to this generalization: While deregulation of domestic natural gas prices and rising crude oil prices will constitute important incentives for intensified domestic exploration for natural gas, there is disagreement regarding the probable size of undiscovered natural gas reserves in the United States. This represents a major unknown factor in projections concerning the future availability of domestic energy supplies.

Once again, the projections of increased energy supplies in this scenario depend critically on the assumption that price controls that would distort or effectively eliminate market price incentives will not be imposed. In addition, minimum lead times of three to five years are usually required for substantial increases in the supply of any energy source, and five to ten years or more may be necessary before adjustments to changing price levels are fully accomplished.

Assuming relatively unhampered movement of prices and minimum lead times, one serious contraint on short-term expansion of domestic energy supplies will undoubtedly be environmental legislation. Local and national opposition to offshore drilling and siting of petroleum-associated facilities (pipelines, refineries, and so on) has restrained the growth of domestic exploration and production activities. Legislative restrictions on strip-mining operations combined with rapid implementation of stack gas emission standards will render large domestic reserves of coal unusable with existing technology. Environmental issues have played an important role in lengthening lead times for the construction of nuclear generating facilities. Safety issues as well as concern over thermal pollution and the satisfactory disposal of radioactive wastes constitute persistent obstacles to an accelerated expansion of nuclear generating capacity in the United States. Oil shale extraction promises additional environmental opposition which will undoubtedly restrain both mining and waste disposal operations.

In the context of this limited scenario, it is unlikely that significant modifications in existing environmental legislation will materialize. It is therefore necessary to consider the effect that environmental restraints will have on both short- and long-term national energy strategies. Most immediately these restraints on the development of potential short-term alternative energy sources, particularly nonconventional oil sources such as oil shale and coal, will tend to increase and prolong reliance on high-priced crude oil imports. Over the long term, concern over environmental protection may produce a major reorientation of federal energy research and development objectives, placing a much higher priority on development of environmentally "clean" alternative energy sources. Presumably, this would substantially increase federal research and development expenditures on such non-nuclear alternatives as geothermal power, solar energy, and hydrogen fuels, as well as nuclear fusion. Depending on the size of the total federal energy budget, such a reorientation of objectives could further restrain the development of syncrude supplies (from oil shale and coal) as a medium-term alternative to conventional crude oil imports. Concern for maximum environmental protection would also stimulate larger research programs for in situ extraction processes for both oil shale and coal, although these alternative processes will probably require a lengthier and more costly development than more advanced surface extraction processes.

SCENARIO II:
LIMITED HIGH-PRICED CRUDE OIL IMPORTS

The second scenario maintains the assumption of continued high prices for crude oil imports and includes the additional assumption that oil-producing countries will impose some form of limited export controls on their crude oil production. This scenario therefore assumes that insufficient supplies of crude oil will be available for import to meet projected increases in energy consumption, even at current high prices.

Originally, such a situation was considered to be a likely consequence of the massive revenues that observers had predicted would be received by the Middle Eastern producing countries. With limited capabilities of absorbing this revenue through investment in their domestic economies, many felt that certain Middle Eastern producing governments (particularly Saudi Arabia) might have less incentive to increase production at the rapid rate required to meet anticipated demand. According to these observers, petroleum-exporting governments would have considerable incentives on purely economic grounds to restrict further increases in production and prolong the producing life of their depleting natural resources. Even before the Arab-Israeli conflict of October

1973, both Kuwait and Libya had already adopted restraints on production. More recently, Abu Dhabi did likewise.

As mentioned previously, events in the period following the Arab oil embargo suggest that the lack of incentives to expand production as a result of "surplus" revenues are not as strong as many had predicted. Petroleum demand has weakened, as a result of both widespread recession and higher crude oil prices, and the imports of most petroleum-exporting countries have risen dramatically. As a result, the growth of "surplus" revenues by the exporting governments has been much slower than was anticipated two years ago, and many of these governments are in fact experiencing serious liquidity problems.[20]

Nevertheless, it is becoming increasingly apparent that the petroleum-exporting governments are finding it necessary to restrict production in an effort to maintain the present high price levels for crude oil. The weakening of the demand for crude oil in the industrialized nations has given rise to a situation of surplus producing capacity. If the exporting governments (in particular Saudi Arabia) were to expand production to capacity levels, the excess supply would substantially weaken existing prices. Thus far, the leading exporting governments have resorted to informal restrictions on the growth of production* but OPEC may eventually attempt to impose a more formal system of production controls among its members.† Thus, the assumption of production restraints underlying this scenario may be fulfilled as a consequence of a desire by the petroleum-exporting governments to conserve a depleting resource and/or a desire to maintain the existing price structure. In either case, this scenario assumes that such production restraints would be imposed primarily for economic reasons (although, of course, political factors would inevitably play some role) and that they would have a more gradual impact on the supply situation than the sudden imposition of politically motivated embargoes would.

The prospects of growing and relatively short-term shortages in crude oil supplies from abroad in this scenario would considerably increase the flexibility of government energy policy in three major areas. First, a variety of sustained conservation measures designed to achieve a more rapid reduction in projected aggregate energy demand would become more politically feasible. The banning of certain nonessential uses of energy—for example, advertising and decorative or display lighting—would be possible over

---

*For example, the production of crude oil in Saudi Arabia for the ten-month period of January-September 1975 declined 17.5 percent in comparison with the same period in 1974.[21]

†OPEC attempted to implement a formal system of production proration among its member nations in the period 1965-67 but eventually abandoned its efforts as a result of difficulties in enforcing compliance.[22]

relatively long periods. Fiscal measures might also be widely introduced to reinforce market incentives and reduce the consumption of petroleum products and other forms of energy. Such measures might include additional gasoline taxes and graduated automobile taxes in proportion to engine size and automobile weight. The potentially regressive aspects of this form of taxation could be substantially reduced or eliminated through accompanying corrective fiscal measures.

A second area of increased flexibility would emerge in the field of environmental protection. Confronted with a growing gap between energy supply and demand, modifications in existing or proposed environmental legislation would almost certainly be implemented to assure adequate supplies of energy. The initial emphasis would be on measures to accelerate the short-term expansion of domestic production of coal, crude oil, and natural gas. Less immediate measures would probably also be undertaken to accelerate the commercial development of oil shale and coal gasification and liquefaction processes, as well as of nuclear energy. Federal leasing policies could be substantially altered to ensure maximum development of domestic energy resources, and AEC licensing modifications could reduce the lead time required for the construction of nuclear generating plants. Delays in the implementation of emission control standards as well as increased reliance on surface mining of coal would substantially improve the contribution of coal to domestic energy supplies.

The third area of increased government flexibility would involve the expansion of federal energy research and development programs for the development of both alternative energy sources and more efficient technologies for energy consumption. Short-term constraints on energy supply would probably increase the priority assigned to alternative technologies and processes in an advanced state of development so that they could be introduced commercially in a relatively short period of time. In particular, research and development programs for improved mining technology and processes for the production of syncrude from oil shale and coal would be substantially expanded. Both the current generation of nuclear fission reactors and the FBR development program would continue to receive a large share of overall federal budgetary support.

The tendency in this scenario would therefore be an increased use of environmentally objectionable fuels and more diversification of domestic energy supplies. Medium-term research and development objectives might also be expected to shift in the direction of more environmentally objectionable alternative energy sources as a consequence of their greater technological feasibility at the current stage of development. This would reduce the lead times necessary for their commercial application on a significant scale.

It should be noted that both this and the third scenario envision a far more active role for government in the areas of supply and demand of energy. Many economists have correctly pointed out that the price mechanism naturally performs an equilibrating function between energy supply and demand and that the most efficient solution to restriction on the supply of energy would simply be to permit the price of energy to rise correspondingly until a new equilibrium position is attained. While this argument may be correct, it neglects the fact that the government will be subjected to intense political pressure from a public that is no longer willing to accept sudden and great price increases in essential commodities and that will therefore call for the implementation of price controls.

To the extent that the government responds to such pressure, the equilibrating functions of the price mechanism will be hampered, and the government will find it necessary to expand its intervention in the market beyond simple price controls. Additional measures will be required, either to reduce energy demand through mandatory conservation measures or to increase the supply of alternative energy sources through various forms of subsidy. Economists generally argue that rather than resolving the allocational dilemmas raised by price controls, these additional measures will merely generate additional distortions in the allocation of energy supplies.

SCENARIO III:
TOTAL EMBARGO ON CRUDE OIL IMPORTS

The third scenario assumes that a sudden, widespread embargo on crude oil exports to the United States is placed by the producing countries and is sustained over a long period of time. This scenario is considered to be the most unlikely. Such an embargo would have to be politically motivated, and in order to be effective it would require substantial political agreement within a widely varying group of petroleum-exporting nations. Moreover, there is little if any historical evidence to suggest that a political embargo on any commodity in international trade can be sustained over a long period of time.

The embargo imposed on the United States in October 1973 by the Arab producing governments affected a relatively small portion of total U.S. crude oil supplies, although, had it been sustained over a longer period of time, it might have produced increasingly widespread dislocations in the domestic economy. This third scenario assumes that some future embargo may arise that would affect a much larger share of total crude oil imports. As indicated previously, crude oil imports from the Persian Gulf and Africa rose to 60 percent of U.S. crude oil imports in 1974, in comparison with the 46 percent share held by these regions in early 1973 (before the embargo), and this trend is expected to intensify.[23] Thus, if supply trends and capabilities are projected a decade or more into the future, the Middle East producing countries would provide a much larger share of U.S. crude oil supplies, and concerted action within this restricted group of countries might then have a much more serious effect. The policy initiatives adopted by the U.S. government in the period following the oil embargo have done little to remedy this trend and, in some cases, may even accelerate it. As a result, while the assumptions of this scenario may have greater immediate relevance for the other two major consuming regions—Western Europe and Japan—which depend upon Middle Eastern crude oil imports for a much larger share of their total energy supplies, the scenario may become increasingly relevant to U.S. policy makers over the next decade.

The crisis atmosphere that would inevitably accompany the sudden embargo envisioned in this scenario would increase the ability of governments to intervene actively on several levels in response to the dislocation in energy supplies. Far-reaching restrictions on energy consumption would probably be imposed, particularly if price controls on petroleum products were to prevent prices from reflecting the full extent of the scarcity. As in the October 1973 embargo, however, the governments would have at least four to six weeks to establish the necessary allocation systems and administrative machinery, since a certain amount of crude oil will be in transit at any one time and will supply consuming areas for a brief interim period (this may change if producing governments establish their own tanker fleets to move their crude oil exports). In addition, if the United States had previously expanded its strategic stockpiles of crude oil, an additional cushion would be available to permit the implementation of comprehensive conservation measures.*

The imposition of a widespread embargo on U.S. crude oil imports would undoubtedly also have a significant impact on medium- and long-term energy strategies. If severe enough, such an embargo could prompt a massive mobilization of funds and technical expertise for a broad "crash" research and development program to develop domestic energy sources. Under these conditions, the potential capital bottleneck in the development of alternative energy resources would either be eliminated or substantially reduced.

Nevertheless, even a "crash" research and development program confronts the irreducible lead time required to conduct the necessary preliminary research, construct pilot plants, evaluate results, and so on. The existing availability of skilled research and engineering personnel would eventually constitute an effective restraint on the potential size of research and development programs. Once a particular process or technology is finally available for commercial

---

*One little-noticed consequence of price controls is that they significantly reduce the incentive for private companies to maintain large stockpiles as a buffer against supply disruptions. If prices were permitted to rise to reflect the full extent of the scarcity, private companies could anticipate a large return on their investment in stockpiles, which are expensive to maintain. Thus, to the extent that price controls become a predictable policy instrument to be employed in periods of shortage, the government will find it necessary to assume a greater role in stockpiling crude oil.[24]

application, there will be an additional delay before it can make a significant contribution to overall energy supplies. An economy that presumably would already be experiencing severe dislocations as the result of an embargo on crude oil imports would be seriously limited in its ability to provide the inputs necessary for a dramatic expansion of highly capital-intensive energy-producing facilities. Constraints of nature would further aggravate these problems—for example, oil shale extraction capabilities are currently limited by the scarcity of large-scale water supplies in the vicinity of the major oil shale deposits. Expansion beyond these limits would require the construction of a major water supply infrastructure to transport water from other regions.

These limitations inherent even in "crash" research and development programs suggest that the medium-term energy strategy in this scenario would necessarily assign higher priority to more accessible, but environmentally objectionable, alternative energy sources. The urgency of developing sizable domestic resources in a short period of time will naturally focus attention on resources that already are, or soon could be, commercially available. Since only a limited amount of financial support could be absorbed by "crash" programs to develop these resources, it is likely that a diversified "crash" research and development program could be designed that would include accelerated development over a longer period (10 to 20 years) of environmentally attractive alternative energy sources that promise virtually unlimited availability—solar energy, nuclear fusion, and hydrogen fuels.

NOTES

1. Federal Energy Administration, *Project Independence Report* (Washington, D.C., 1974).

2. For a detailed summary of these measures, see "Complete Texts of New U.S. Action on Energy," *Petroleum Intelligence Weekly*, supplement, April 23, 1973, pp. 1-11.

3. Paul W. MacAvoy, Bruce E. Stangle, and Jonathan B. Tepper, "The Federal Energy Office as Regulator of the Energy Crisis," *Technology Review* 77 (May 1975): 39-45. See also Robert B. Stobaugh, "The Oil Companies in the Crisis," *Daedalus* 104 (fall 1975): 179-202.

4. These earlier policy initiatives were outlined in President Ford's State of the Union message of January 15, 1975, and are summarized "Ford's Energy Program," *Petroleum Economist* 42 (February 1975): 49-50.

5. New York *Times,* December 28, 1975, section 4, p. 1.

6. See the advertisement entitled "Flawed Energy Bill" sponsored by Mobil Oil Corporation in the New York *Times*, November 25, 1975, p. 34.

7. New York *Times*, December 28, 1975, section 4, p. 1.

8. "The Natural Gas Saga," *Petroleum Economist* 43 (March 1976): 84-86.

9. U.S. Atomic Energy Commission, *The Nation's Energy Future*, report submitted by Dixy Lee Ray (Washington, D.C.: Government Printing Office, 1973).

10. *Nuclear Industry* 22 (January 1975), p. 35.

11. Ibid.; and Ray, op. cit.

12. J. Herbert Hollomon et al., *Energy Research and Development* (Cambridge, Mass.: Ballinger, 1975), pp. 63-65.

13. Energy Research and Development Administration, *A National Plan for Energy Research, Development and Demonstration: Creating Energy Choices for the Future*, 2 vols. (Washington, D.C.: 1975).

14. The OTA report is summarized in Philip M. Boffey, "Energy Research: A Harsh Critique Says Federal Effort May Backfire," *Science*, November 7, 1975, pp. 535-37.

15. *Nuclear Industry*, October 1975, pp. 3-5.

16. Ibid.

17. For example, see "Energy Conservation Is Becoming a Habit," New York *Times*, October 20, 1975, pp. 1, 20, which concludes that despite general inaction by the government in the area of energy conservation, the public has adopted many practices to promote conservation in response to higher energy prices.

18. Ray, op. cit.

19. National Petroleum Council, Committee on U.S. Energy Outlook, *U.S. Energy Outlook* (Washington, D.C., 1972), pp. 10-11. For a highly critical review of federal resource management as applied to federal lands, see the Ford Foundation Energy Policy Project, *A Time to Choose: America's Energy Future* (Cambridge, Mass.: Ballinger, 1974), pp. 269-303.

20. *Petroleum Economist*, March 1975, p. 84; and *Petroleum Intelligence Weekly*, June 2, 1975, p. 7.

21. *Petroleum Intelligence Weekly*, November 10, 1975, p. 1.

22. For an analysis of these efforts, see Zuhayr Mikdashi, *The Community of Oil Exporting Countries* (London: George Allen and Unwin, 1972), pp. 111-36. See also George W. Stocking, *Middle East Oil: A Study in Political and Economic Controversy* (Nashville: Vanderbilt University Press, 1970).

23. *Petroleum Intelligence Weekly*, May 5, 1975.

24. Edward J. Mitchell, *U.S. Energy Policy: A Primer* (Washington, D.C.: American Enterprise Institute, 1974), pp. 43-44.

10

**ENERGY STRATEGY
OPTIONS IN OTHER
CONSUMING REGIONS**

WESTERN EUROPE

Both Western Europe and Japan differ markedly from the United States in the extent of the current dependence on imports to supply their energy needs. Western Europe (including the United Kingdom) currently relies on imports—mostly of oil—to supply approximately 60 percent of its total energy requirement.[1] Recent projections of energy demand for Western Europe indicate an annual growth rate in the range of 3 to 5 percent.*As for all projections of energy demand, it is extremely difficult to anticipate what impact price increases for crude oil imports will have on future trends. In any event, most forecast growth rates are considerably below those the area has experienced over recent years. Table 10.1 offers a comparison of several energy consumption forecasts for Western Europe made in 1973-74. On the supply side, moreover, it is believed that there will be growing volumes of North Sea crude oil and natural gas as well as increased nuclear power generation and a probable slowing or reversal in the downward trend of local coal production. The net result will be a decline in the dependence of Western Europe on imported energy supplies to something on the order of 40 percent of total energy consumption in 1985.[2]

---

*Recent projections by the OECD (which includes the United States, Canada, and Japan, as well as the leading Western European nations) indicate that the average annual growth rate for energy demand in its member nations would range between 3.8 and 4.3 percent, depending on differing assumptions regarding crude oil prices. These projections compare with the 4.9 percent rate anticipated prior to 1973 (*Nuclear News* 18 [February 1975]: 32).

TABLE 10.1

Energy Consumption Forecasts for Western Europe

Source / Year published	Shell[f,g] 1971	Shell[h] 1973	Shell[i] 1973	OECD-EEC[d] 1972	Banque Jordan[j] 1972	Odell[d] 1973	Odell[a,e] 1974
Forecast for 1975							
Coal (percentage)	20	21	—	22(19)	—	17(14)	—
Oil (percentage)	63	63	—	64(2)	—	56(6)	—
Gas (percentage)	12	12	—	10(9)	—	24(20)	—
$(10^9 \text{ m}^3$ per year)	180	170	185(60)	142(128)	—	350(290)	—
Primary electricity[b] (percentage)	5	4	—	4	—	3	—
Total $(10^9 \text{ m}^3$ per year)	1500	1410	—	1420(485)	—	1460(625)	—
Forecast for 1980							
Coal (percentage)	13	—	—	12(9)	—	11(9)	16(2)
Oil (percentage)	66(6)	—	—	€6(2)	—	55(22)	43(26)
Gas (percentage)	14	—	—	12(10)	—	27(22)	30(26)
$(10^9 \text{ m}^3$ per year)	265	—	260(200)	225(188)	—	520(425)	475(410)
Primary electricity[b] (percentage)	7	—	—	10	—	7	9
Total $(10^9 \text{ m}^3$ per year)	1890	—	—	1880(580)	—	1920(1150)	1580(1175)

(continued)

(Table 10.1 continued)

Source Year published	Shell[f,g] 1971	Shell[h] 1973	Shell[i] 1973	OECD-EEC[d] 1972	Banque Jordan[j] 1972	Odell[d] 1973	Odell[a,e] 1974
Forecast for 1985							
Coal (percentage)	9	—	11	11(8)	11(10)	10(8)	15(11)
Oil (percentage)	67(17)	—	60(10)	63(7)	60(3)	47(23)	36(27)
Gas (percentage)	15	—	14(9.5)	14(11)	10.5(7)	31(22)	34(27)
(10^9 m$_0^3$ per year)	340	—	340(230)	320(250)	265(180)	735(520)	665(530)
Primary electricity[b] (percentage)	9	—	14.5[c]	12	18	12	15
Total (10^9 m$_0^3$ per year)	2260	—	2430(1150)	2290(870)	2500(950)	2370(1540)	1960(1580)
Forecast for 2000							
Coal (percentage)	5	—	—	—	—	—	14(11)
Oil (percentage)	55	—	—	—	—	—	40(33)
Gas (percentage)	20	—	—	—	—	—	32(25)
(10^9 m$_0^3$ per year)	830	—	—	—	—	—	930(730)
Primary electricity[b] (percentage)	20	—	—	—	—	—	14
Total (10^9 m$_0^3$ per year)	4160	—	—	—	—	—	2910(2415)

(Table 10.1 continued)

[a]Odell's 1974 estimates are given for 1998, not for 2000.

[b]Primary electricity is hydroelectricity and nuclear electricity; the former contributes only a few percentage points.

[c]Considered as "maximum foreseeable growth."

[d]P.R. Odell, "Indigenous oil and gas developments and Western Europe's energy policy options," *Energy Policy* 1, no. 1 (June 1973): 47-64.

[e]P.R. Odell, "European alternatives to oil imported from OPEC countries: Oil and gas as indigenous resources," presented at the John F. Kennedy Institution Colloquium, May 1974, Eindhoven, The Netherlands.

[f]Shell 1971, H. Hoog in *Elektriciteit in onze toekomstige energievoorziening*, publication 12 in the "Future Shape of Technology" series of the Future Shape of Technology Foundation, The Hague, the Netherlands, 1972.

[g]N. Beale (Shell Planning Division), "The Energy Balance in the Year 2000," *Europe 2000: Perspectives for an Acceptable Future,* Fondation Europeene de la Culture, 1972.

[h]C.P. Coppack (Shell International Gas Ltd. London), "Natural gas," in *Energy in the 1980s, A Royal Society Discussion* (London: The Royal Society, 1974), pp. 463-83.

[i]A. Hols (Shell Internationale Petroleum Mij V.V. Den Haag), "The future Energy Supplies to the Netherlands," *Verhandelingen Koninklijk Nederlandsch Geologisch-Mijnbouwkundig Genootschap* 29 (1973), pp. 9-18.

[j]Bulletin d'Information, Banque Jordan, July 1972. Source: OECD.

Note: Numbers in parentheses give estimated supply from indigenous Western European sources.

Source: Bert de Vries and Jan Kommandeur, "Gas for Western Europe: How Much for How Long?" *Energy Policy* 3 (March 1975): 26-27.

In the aftermath of the Arab oil embargo of 1973, Western Europe has experienced a continuing drop in the level of crude oil imports from the peak reached in the first half of 1973. Total European crude oil imports declined by 9 percent from 1973 to 1974, and EEC estimates indicate that a further 20 percent drop occurred in the first half of 1975, in comparison with the first half of 1974.[3] The EEC also projected that aggregate energy demand by its member nations in 1975 would remain roughly equivalent to 1974 levels.[4]

A draft program on long-term energy strategy for Europe released by the EEC in 1974 asserted the feasibility of reducing the projected demand for oil in 1985 by almost 50 percent through greatly increased reliance on natural gas, coal, and nuclear power. Under this program, natural gas would maintain its present high growth rate, increasing its share in energy supply from 9 percent in 1975 to 25 percent in 1985. The downward trend in the share of coal in total energy consumption would continue, but various policies would be implemented to moderate this decline so that coal would still represent approximately 17 percent of total energy demand in 1985 as compared with 26 percent in 1973. This strategy is particularly ambitious in the field of nuclear power generation, anticipating that it will contribute 50 percent of total electricity generation in 1985, in comparison with about 6 percent at the present time. Some skepticism has been expressed both within the EEC and from outside observers regarding the possibility of attaining these objectives.* Nevertheless, they are useful in providing a general idea of the anticipated future pattern of European energy consumption.[6]

Even if these projections were to prove accurate, Western Europe would remain in a more vulnerable position than the United States regarding alterations in the availability and/or price of crude oil imports, particularly in view of its extreme dependence on imports from the Middle East. For this reason, the energy strategies adopted by the Western European countries should place a much greater emphasis on close cooperation to achieve both restraints in the growth of energy demand and research and development programs to develop energy-efficient technology and to increase the domestic availability of alternative energy sources.

Events following the October 1973 Arab crude oil production cutbacks and selective embargo graphically demonstrated the pervasive disagreement within the EEC over appropriate energy strategies and the assertion of nationalistic interests in the formulation of energy policies. The policies adopted by the EEC to attain the objectives set forth in the draft program for a long-term energy strategy for Western Europe should provide an important indication of the extent to which the member nations can cooperate effectively on energy policy. At a time when considerable benefits could be derived from closer Western European cooperation in the context of a comprehensive energy strategy, there remains doubt that such cooperation will be achieved, especially over the long run. Local resources of crude oil and natural gas—including the present contribution and great potential of the North Sea—are realistically viewed as purely national assets by the governments concerned.[7]

A recent development of great potential importance, which grew out of the Washington Energy Conference of February 1974, was the establishment, under the auspices of the OECD, of the International Energy Agency (IEA). At present, 16 OECD member nations (Austria, Belgium, Canada, Denmark, West Germany, Ireland, Italy, Japan, Luxembourg, the Netherlands, Spain, Sweden, Switzerland, Turkey, the United Kingdom, and the United States) are participating. Notable nonparticipants are France and Norway. According to an OECD statement, the main aims of the new agency are the following:

---

*For example, one of the directors of Gaz de France, the French national gas company, criticized the EEC projections for natural gas consumption as being too optimistic. The director maintained that indigenous Western European reserves were inadequate to supply 25 percent of Western Europe's energy consumption by 1985, as anticipated by the EEC, and that such a target could be met only by relying on substantial imports of natural gas, thus raising many of the same problems associated with reliance on imported energy sources, which the EEC's strategy was initially designed to resolve.[5]

- development of a common level of energy self-sufficiency in oil supplies, common demand restraint measures, and measures for the allocation of available oil in times of emergency
- development of an information system covering the international oil market
- development and implementation of a long-term cooperation program to reduce dependence on imported oil
- promotion of cooperative relations with oil-producing countries and with other oil-consuming countries[8]

In the period directly following its formation, the IEA proceeded to address three fundamental areas for improved cooperation in the field of energy: the establishment of a minimum "safeguard" price floor for crude oil imports to provide incentives for expanded investment in alternative energy sources; the development of comprehensive programs to promote energy conservation; and the expansion of international research and development programs to accelerate the commercial introduction of alternative energy technologies. France has consistently criticized as both unnecessary and confrontational the crude oil price floor proposal and related measures to ensure the sharing of crude oil imports in the eventuality of another embargo. Instead, France has favored the negotiation of bilateral government-to-government supply arrangements between oil-exporting and -importing countries as well as efforts to promote a dialogue between oil-producing and -consuming countries to discuss possible reforms in the structure of international trade.

Even within the IEA, considerable disagreement emerged over the proposed "safeguard" crude oil price floor as member nations attempted to arrive at a consensus on a specific price. Members with significant potential domestic energy reserves such as the United Kingdom and the United States favored a relatively high price floor to protect future production from these reserves, while countries lacking such domestic reserves sought a lower price floor. Compromise became easier as members were persuaded that crude oil prices would not decline substantially in the immediate future and therefore that virtually any price floor agreed upon would probably not need to be enforced over the next few years.[9] Finally, at the end of 1975, the IEA announced that its members had agreed to a $7-per-barrel price floor for crude oil imports, but it remained vague regarding the specific methods by which its member nations would enforce such a price floor. Moreover, the success of this policy is considered to be contingent upon the ability of member nations to guarantee the access of energy-poor members to the energy resources of the other IEA members.[10] French participation will also be essential for the success of any price support measure, and such participation was considered to be more likely at the end of 1975 than it had been before.[11]

On the issue of energy conservation, the IEA refrained from formulating specific targets and instead focused its efforts on establishing a framework for the annual review of conservation efforts by its member nations as well as discussion of the potential for future international cooperation in this field. In late 1975, however, the IEA expressed concern over the lack of progress in energy conservation by its member nations, attributing much of the reduction in energy demand in 1974 to economic recession and a warm winter. The IEA announced that its governing board had unanimously agreed on the need for an intensification of conservation programs in anticipation of economic recovery.[12]

The Agreement on an International Energy Program, which provided for the establishment of the IEA, also mentioned consideration of cooperation in energy research and development. However, IEA efforts in this field have been hampered by the differing policies of its member nations with regard to "intellectual property." As a result, the IEA has concentrated on the formulation of principles that can serve as a basis for structuring international research consortia and for determining ownership rights to the resulting intellectual property. In addition, tentative approval has been given to three specific programs for research collaboration under IEA auspices: hydrogen production, waste-heat utilization, and bioconversion techniques for producing fuel from organic wastes.[13]

Within the EEC itself, despite the existence of numerous joint research projects for long-term development of alternative energy sources (including nuclear fusion, solar energy, hydrogen production, and disposal of radioactive wastes), regional cooperation has proved difficult in fields with direct commercial value. For example, the EEC's nuclear agency Euratom recently cut back its operations, and morale among the staff has deteriorated as the agency continues to operate on the basis of makeshift annual programs.[14] Many of the larger countries in the EEC prefer to concentrate on strengthening their own national nuclear energy research and development programs. In another setback for greater regional cooperation, EEC members failed throughout 1973 and 1974 to reach a consensus on the relative merits of two uranium enrichment processes which were intended to serve as the basis for an expanded regional enrichment capacity.[15]

Efforts by the European nations, and especially France, to promote dialogue between the oil-producing and -consuming nations culminated in the convocation of a ministerial Conference on International Economic Cooperation in Paris in December 1975. In the aftermath of an earlier, generally unsuccessful conference held in Paris in April 1975, the objective of this dialogue shifted from the narrow effort by consuming nations to negotiate a long-term agreement on world crude oil prices and supply patterns to a broader attempt to establish a comprehensive new framework for the international economic system. This latter objective had been sought by a number of the oil-exporting countries (particularly Algeria) at the earlier April meeting and had initially encountered considerable resistance from the United States, which had sought to separate the issues of raw materials and economic development. Eventually, the U.S. position was modified, and agreement was reached on a new conference in which much of the actual work will be assigned to four commissions: energy, raw materials, development, and finance. In addition to the United States, Japan, and the EEC member countries, the conference will involve 24 other participants, including 19 developing nations.[16]

The elaboration of a viable long-term energy strategy for Western Europe critically depends upon the accuracy of current projections regarding the size of North Sea crude oil and natural gas reserves, as well as the rate of their development. Most industry representatives have been extremely conservative in their estimates of ultimate reserves located in the Norwegian and British sectors of the North Sea. Their estimates are usually in the range of 45 to 50 billion barrels, although at least one industry geologist has optimistically predicted reserves in the range of 55 to 67 billion barrels.[17] The conservativeness of these estimates has been consistently challenged by Peter Odell, director of the Economic Geography Institute at Erasmus University in Rotterdam. Odell estimates that ultimate reserves will be around 78 billion barrels.[18] Significantly, an official British government report, *Development of the Oil and Gas Resources of the UK*, revised downward the government's earlier estimates of the production rate for crude oil from the British sector of the North Sea over the next five years (100 to 126 million tons is the production rate currently anticipated for 1980) but revised slightly upward its estimates of ultimate recoverable reserves in areas that have already been licensed.[19]

Since less than 20 percent of the known geological structures have as yet been studied, future production estimates represent considerable guesswork. Nevertheless, major discoveries already made during exploratory drilling indicate that some of the more optimistic projections may not be entirely unrealistic. One factor that is even more difficult to anticipate involves the regulatory policies that might be adopted by the governments bordering the North Sea. Norway has already decided to restrict development of the offshore Ekofisk Field, and other governments are considering a variety of policies that would have a significant impact on offshore exploration and production operations.[20]

The single most important domestically available alternative to crude oil and natural gas in Europe over the short term is substantial domestic reserves of coal. Estimates of Western Europe's coal resources compiled by the U.S. Geological Survey indicate that total coal resources determined by mapping and exploration amount to 620 billion tons, while estimated total resources (including probable additional resources in unmapped and unexplored areas) amount to 830 billion tons. Since coal production in Western Europe yielded only 315 million tons in 1971, these resource estimates represent a considerable reserve of fossil fuel energy potentially available to European nations.[21]

In fact, however, the energy supply pattern for Western Europe since World War II has been characterized by the gradual displacement of coal by crude oil and natural gas. This process was substantially restrained by the extensive subsidies that most European governments provided to their domestic coal industries in an attempt to protect the position of domestic energy resources against competition from low-cost foreign imports. Ironically, most of these governments have decided in recent years to gradually phase out high-cost domestic production of coal and to rely on greater imports of other fossil fuels and expansion of nuclear power production.[22] These prices must now be fundamentally evaluated in the context of current price trends for Middle Eastern crude oil imports.

Three factors have persistently inhibited profitable expansion of Western European coal production: (1) most known coal deposits are located in deep, thin veins which are difficult and costly to mine; (2) despite recent efforts to promote large-scale mechanization and automation of mining operations, most European coal mining still relies on a relatively large underground labor force, resulting in high wage costs; and (3) as a consequence of these first two factors, Western European coal mining is characterized by extremely low productivity levels in comparison to both U.S. levels and to levels that might be achieved through more extensive utilization of advanced mining technology.[23]

In order to expand the contribution of coal to domestic energy supplies, Western European governments will have to initiate intensive research and development programs to develop more efficient mining technology and, simultaneously, adopt a variety of measures designed to accelerate commercial application of existing technology. Subsidies to the mining industry have substantially reduced the incentive to undertake the capital investment required for purchase of mining machinery, and governments have further expressed concern over the employment consequences of the adoption of more capital-intensive production techniques. To ease the transition, governments will have to reorient their policies to provide the financial support and administrative assistance necessary for a major shift of labor from the coal sectors of the economy.

Thus far, most discussions of Western European energy policies have deemphasized the potential role of coal as a domestic alternative to high-priced crude oil imports.[24] The reorientation of U.S. energy priorities to favor a sustained expansion of domestic coal production might have an indirect impact on European energy policy formulation. Very little attention has been devoted to research and development programs for coal conversion processes in Western Europe, although there would be significant potential for application of these processes in this region.[25] In particular, in situ gasification techniques might eventually increase the profitability of coal utilization in European domestic energy supplies.

Most Western European governments view nuclear power generation as the most promising medium-term alternative to crude oil imports, and in the past few years the commercial application of nuclear power has received a high priority in European energy policies. Current projections indicate that the nuclear generating capacity of 15,200 milliwatts already installed in Western Europe will expand to 93,900 milliwatts in 1980 and reach 178,300 milliwatts in 1985.[26] Although the United Kingdom and West Germany have led the other European nations in commercial utilization of nuclear energy, prolonged delays in the selection of a reactor model for the present phase in the expansion of nuclear generating capacity in the United Kingdom have reduced the British lead in this area. Even after a reactor model had been selected, the British government adopted a highly cautious approach to the funding of future commercial nuclear reactor development. Apparently, the government is reluctant to become "locked in" to a particular reactor design at this time, and it is postponing any major expansion program until the early 1980s, when it hopes that the relative merits of alternative reactor designs will be more readily apparent.[27] West Germany, on the other hand, is aggressively funding commercial nuclear reactor development, and it is expected to maintain its present lead in this field.[28] However, growing public concern over reactor safety and thermal pollution may have an impact on future construction programs.

France has also steadily expanded its program for the commercial use of nuclear energy, and in 1973 the French minister of industry and scientific development indicated that it might be possible to eliminate the need for oil products in electric power generation by the early 1980s, when he estimated that fully half of France's electric generating capacity might be supplied by nuclear energy.[29] During 1975, however, there was widespread debate in government circles over the decision that had previously been made to increase nuclear generating capacity to supply 25 percent of France's energy needs by 1985. Although the proponents of accelerated expansion of nuclear generating capacity have apparently won this debate, the government appears to be more cautious regarding future commitments to a particular nuclear reactor design, and a more diversified approach to research and development, encompassing non-nuclear alternative energy sources, may result.[30] Significantly, this controversy largely revolved around the environmental and safety issues associated with nuclear reactors, and it is likely that these issues will continue to emerge as obstacles in reactor development programs in Europe.

In view of current trends, most of the commercial nuclear plants installed in Western Europe over the next 15 years will probably be LWRs. Great Britain had pioneered in the development of the AGR, but persistent problems in the commercial application of this model have prompted increasing interest in other reactor models as a basis for future expansion of nuclear generating capacity. In July 1974, the British government finally selected the SGHWR as the model for future expansion of nuclear generating capacity. The SGHWR is a hybrid reactor containing characteristics of both the Canadian CANDU model and the U.S. BWR model. It employs heavy water as a moderator and ordinary light water as the coolant. An SGHWR prototype has been in operation at Winfreth, England, since 1967. The initial SGHWR program will involve the construction of 4,000 milliwatts of nuclear generating capacity over the next four years, with each reactor in the 600-to-660-milliwatt range.[31]

As a result of the increasing reliance on LWRs in Western Europe, these countries have depended on enrichment facilities operated by the AEC to provide the enriched uranium fuel. In early 1973, the AEC announced that European customers would have to pay higher prices and accept stiff new contract terms for future supplies of enriched uranium fuels.[32] In response to this development, the EEC began to explore the feasibility of programs to ensure European self-sufficiency in uranium enrichment facilities. A major conflict emerged between proponents of the diffusion process of uranium enrichment (led by France) and the newly developed centrifuge process (led by Great Britain and West Germany). Efforts to achieve a coordinated development program in this area eventually broke down, and as a consequence two separate research and development programs now appear to be inevitable, with the likelihood of considerable excess enrichment capacity in Western Europe by the 1980s.[33]

The difficulties experienced in reducing European dependence on both foreign uranium supplies and enrichment facilities will probably result in the assignment of a high priority to FBR development in European research and development programs. Several FBRs are scheduled for commercial operation in Western Europe by the late 1970s and early 1980s. These include the Phénix 1000 in France and the SNR 1 and 2 in West Germany. Depending on the success of these early models, FBRs may begin to have a significant impact on electric power generation as early as 1990.[34]

The European nations have also exhibited considerable interest in the high-temperature reactor (HTR), particularly as a source of nuclear process heat for such diverse applications as coal gasification, hydrogen production, steel making, and long-distance heat transport through chemical energy.[35] Much of the work in this area is being undertaken under licensing arrangements with Gulf General Atomics.[36]

In general, Western Europe finds itself in a more vulnerable position than the United States regarding energy imports, but its ability to respond to potential alterations in the availability or price of crude oil imports is considerably restricted by a relatively smaller domestic energy resource base and a persistent inability to develop comprehensive energy policies on a regional level which would maximize economies of scale. Instead, recent constraints on crude oil imports have generated growing conflicts within the EEC which have frustrated efforts to reconcile differing national priorities in energy policy formulation.

In the area of research and development, the European governments have tended to concentrate heavily on the commercial application of nuclear reactor technology. In general, however, the research and development programs in alternative energy technologies have not received a high priority in response to rising crude oil prices, and there has been relative neglect of promising non-nuclear sources of energy. Although funding for research and developments programs has been expanded and new initiatives have been announced in the area of cooperative international research ventures in the aftermath of the 1973 oil embargo, it is still too early to evaluate the long-term implications of these new efforts. [37]

JAPAN

Japan is the major energy-consuming region most vulnerable to variations in the availability and price of crude oil imports. In the decade ending in fiscal year 1972, Japanese energy consumption grew at unprecedented rates as a consequence of Japan's high economic growth rate. During this period, the average annual growth rate for energy reached 11.9 percent—more than double the world energy growth rate during the same period. In response to rapidly rising crude oil prices and slower domestic economic growth, the annual growth rate for energy demand in Japan is expected to continue at a much more modest level, averaging somewhere between 5.7 and 7.8 percent, in the 1973-85 period, depending on the assumptions adopted. [38]

Of even greater concern than the high growth rate for energy consumption is the fact that an increasing share of energy consumption is being supplied from nonindigenous sources. Japan's import-dependence ratio for primary fuel supplies has climbed steadily from a modest 18.8 percent in 1955 to 82.3 percent in 1970, and this percentage is expected to rise to 90 percent within the next few years. [39]

The increasing dependence on imported energy supplies is largely the result of the rapid growth of crude oil's share of total energy consumption (crude oil consumption increased at roughly twice the rate of aggregate energy consumption over this period). Indigenous crude oil and natural gas production accounted for only 1 percent of the total consumption of these two fossil fuels in fiscal year 1972, and this share will continue to decline over the next decade unless major offshore crude oil deposits are discovered and developed. In fiscal year 1972, imported oil contributed roughly 75 percent of Japan's total energy consumption. [40] Moreover, 81 percent of Japan's crude oil supplies during 1972 originated in the Middle East. [41] Japan's dependence on imported oil is projected to grow, since the country unfortunately lacks any substantial domestic energy resources. Table 10.2 indicates one projection of the contribution of various energy sources to Japan's energy supply over the next decade.

TABLE 10.2

Japan's Primary Energy Supply Forecast

	1965 (actual)	1970	1975	1980	1985	Supply shares of primary energy (percentage)				
						1965	1970	1975	1980	1985
Electricity (10^9 kilowatt-hours)	77	85	157	314	530	11.3	6.7	8.3	11.5	14.7
Hydroelectricity (10^9 kilowatt-hours)	77	80	95	104	136	11.3	6.3	5.0	3.8	3.8
Nuclear (10^9 kilowatt-hours)	–	5	62	210	394	–	0.4	3.3	7.7	10.9
Coal (10^6 kilowatt-hours)	73	92	83	97	110	27.3	20.7	13.3	10.9	9.3
Domestic (10^6 tons)	55	41	20	20	20	19.1	8.1	2.9	2.0	1.5
Imported (10^6 tons)	18	51	63	77	90	8.2	12.6	10.4	8.9	7.8
Petroleum (crude oil equivalent, 10^9 liters)	102	234	379	524	671	58.4	70.8	76.3	73.7	71.3
(for generating)	(14)	(44)	(66)	(69)	(57)	(7.5)	(13.2)	(13.3)	(9.7)	(6.1)
Natural gas (10^9 square meters)	2	2	2	2	2	1.2	0.9	0.4	0.3	0.2
Liquefied natural gas (10^6 tons)	–	1	6	18	30	–	0.4	1.7	3.6	4.5
Total (10^{13} kilocalories)	166	310	467	668	885	100.0	100.0	100.0	100.0	100.0

Source: Masao Sakisaka, "World Energy Problems and Japan's International Role," *Energy Policy* 1 (September 1973): 104.

In the context of this dependence on external energy supply, the short- and medium-term response of the Japanese government to variations in the avilability and/or price of crude oil imports would probably involve some combination of the following three elements: (1) the implementation of policies to restrict aggregate energy demand, (2) a shift in exploration and production strategy to the systematic development of conventional energy resources in the Pacific Basin, and (3) the accelerated commercial development of nuclear generating plants. Policies to restrict energy demand would probably not have much impact as they would in the United States or Western Europe, since the Japanese have traditionally been rather frugal consumers of energy and there is much less nonessential consumption which might be eliminated in the short term without serious impact on the economy.

While Japan itself suffers from a serious shortage of indigenous energy supplies, the Pacific Basin has in recent years emerged as a significant source for a variety of conventional fossil fuel reserves. Very little systematic exploration of these reserves has been undertaken, but early indications are that they would constitute a viable (although generally high-cost) alternative to Middle Eastern crude oil imports. Indonesia has already emerged as a major producer and exporter of crude oil, and it will soon expand its role as an exporter of LNG as well. Major offshore crude oil reserves are known to exist in the area bounded by Japan, Korea, and the People's Republic of China as well as in the continental shelf off of Southeast Asia. Accelerated exploration and production from these reserves will be seriously hampered by jurisdictional disputes which have already emerged.[42]

Additional crude oil and natural gas supplies are located in Siberia, and Japanese interests may eventually participate in their development and utilization. Negotiations have been pursued with the Soviet Union since 1973 for an LNG supply contract involving imports to Japan for 10 million tons per year, and similar negotiations are in process for long-term crude oil supplies from western Siberia. Japan's attempts to secure energy supplies from the Soviet Union have encountered considerable diplomatic opposition from Communist China, which fears that such commercial development of the Soviet Union's Siberian resources will also strengthen its military capabilities in the region. Since Japan had already signed a crude oil supply contract with China for 1 million tons in 1973 and hopes to obtain additional supply contracts from China, Japanese officials have encouraged U.S. participation in the Siberian development projects in an effort to ease China's opposition to bilateral cooperation between Japan and the Soviet Union.[43]

Although substantial crude oil reserves are also located in Alaska and western Canada, most of the production from these areas will probably be required for domestic markets with very little available for export to Japan. However, one other potential source of crude oil for the Japanese market is the substantial reserves recently discovered in the western part of South America, particularly in Ecuador and Peru.

To supplement its inadequate domestic reserves of natural gas, Japan began importing LNG from Alaska in 1969. Japanese companies have also signed supply contracts with Indonesia and Abu Dhabi and are actively seeking contracts with other LNG-exporting countries. Escalating crude oil prices and increasingly restrictive antipollution legislation should serve to increase the demand for LNG in Japan. Preliminary estimates by the Japanese government indicate that Japan will be importing between 36 and 62 million tons of LNG in fiscal year 1985 to supply between 7 and 9 percent of Japan's total energy consumption.[44]

Japan's indigenous coal production experienced sharp decline during the latter part of the 1960s, despite increasing financial support provided by the government.[45] In fiscal year 1972, indigenous coal production dropped to 28 million tons, representing 5.3 percent of the country's total energy consumption, while coal imports reached 50 million tons, supplying 11.3 percent of total energy consumption. Domestic coal production is currently estimated to level off at 20 million tons, while coal imports are expected to rise steadily to approximately 121 million tons in fiscal year 1985.[46] Efforts to expand the domestic production of coal are constrained by poor geological conditions and restricted labor supply.

In 1972, 93 percent of Japan's coal imports was supplied by three countries—the United States, Canada, and Australia. Japan has also imported an average of 2.5 million tons of Soviet coal annually over the last five years, and it hopes to obtain as much as 10 million tons per year from Siberia.[47]

However, substantial additional coal reserves have also been identified in both the People's Republic of China and Indonesia.[48] While China would probably not be willing to export substantial quantities of coal for both economic and political reasons, the results of recent coal exploration programs in Indonesia suggest that it may soon be capable of sustaining substantial coal exports.

Thus far, nuclear generating plants account for a negligible share of Japan's total energy supplies (0.7 percent of the total in fiscal year 1972), and total generating capacity has reached only 1,823 milliwatt$_e$.[49] In 1971, the government announced a substantial upward revision of its target for nuclear power generation by 1985. According to the new projections, Japan will seek to install 60,000 milliwatts of nuclear generating capacity by 1985, representing roughly 11 percent of Japan's primary energy supply and replacing coal as the second major source of energy.[50]

In the intervening years, however, Japan has been experiencing intense local environmental opposition to proposals to construct new nuclear power plants, and the relative effectiveness of this opposition in delaying plant construction has increased doubt as to whether Japan will be able to meet its ambitious nuclear expansion targets.[51] In an effort to avoid further environmental opposition, the government has actively considered a variety of novel site location proposals, including underground reactors, sea surface reactors, and submarine reactors.[52]

While nuclear energy is conventionally classified as an "indigenous" energy source, it is important to note that Japan is at present totally dependent on foreign supplies of enriched uranium. Domestic reserves of uranium ore are extremely limited, but Japan has long-term supply contracts or joint ventures with five countries—the United States, Canada, the United Kingdom, Australia, and France/Nigeria.[53] Substantial uranium reserves exist in Australia, and it is likely that Japan will seek a more active role in developing these reserves.

Japan has relied on contracts with the AEC for uranium enrichment, but projected shortages in domestic enrichment capacity in the United States make it likely that Japan will seek alternative arrangements to diversify its supply of enriched uranium. In particular, Japan is considering proposals for joint ventures with foreign consortia in the construction of new enrichment plants. The Japanese Nuclear Fuel Corporation has also announced its intention to build a centrifuge plant capable of supplying one-third of Japan's enriched uranium needs by 1985.[54]

In addition to the expansion of nuclear generating capacity using existing LWR designs, Japan is pursuing active research and development programs in FBRs and nuclear fusion technology. The government is also sponsoring research on advanced thermal reactors (ATR) and HTGR designs to serve as a "bridge" between the present generation of LWRs and commercial breeder reactors. A 165-milliwatt$_e$ test ATR is expected to begin operation in 1975-76, while a 50-milliwatt$_e$ test HTGR will be built by the end of this decade. Construction of a 300-milliwatt$_e$ prototype FBR will begin in 1976-77.[55] Commercial development of breeder reactors is expected to receive a high priority due to the absence of adequate domestic uranium supplies.

In the longer run, Japanese research and development strategy will probably focus on the development of their thermonuclear fusion and of more advanced non-nuclear energy sources such as solar energy and geothermal energy. The extreme reliance on external sources of energy supply will tend to increase interest in any option that offers the possibility of a "limitless" supply of fuel and therefore minimizes dependence on energy imports.

The Agency for Industrial Science and Technology announced in 1973 the creation of a new agency to administer a 26-year energy research and development program known as the "Sunshine Project." The objective of this program, which involves annual expenditures of $160 million, is to develop "clean energy for the 21st century." While the desire to promote environmental protection was a major factor in the initiation of this program, many of the projects within it are designed to develop indigenous sources of energy more fully. Among the specific goals of the program are the development of commercial methods of electric power generation from solar energy and volcanic heat and the beginning of the commercial production of synthetic natural gas as well as hydrogen fuels.[56]

Under this program, Japan hopes to begin the operation of two 100-milliwatt power plants—one using solar energy and the other using geothermal energy—by 1985. A 300-milliwatt power plant operating on volcanic heat is anticipated to begin operation by 1990. In the field of coal gasification, a 1 million-cubic-meter-per-day syngas plant is tentatively projected for 1985, while a 10,000-barrel-per-day coal liquefaction plant is planned for 1990. Japan also hopes to begin commercial production of hydrogen through thermochemical water splitting by 1985 in preparation for a transition to a "hydrogen economy," scheduled to begin in 1995.[57] These are ambitious objectives, and it remains to be seen whether the Japanese government will provide the substantial financial support required to make the program a success.

Of all the major consuming regions, therefore, Japan is the most vulnerable to short-term variations in the availability or price of crude oil imports. It lacks a large degree of flexibility in altering its energy consumption patterns, through either price mechanisms or administrative controls, and it has only negligible indigenous supplies of energy. As a result, Japan's only medium-term alternative to large-scale Middle Eastern crude oil imports is to increase its reliance on the extensive conventional energy supplies available in the Pacific Basin. Such a strategy would probably be accompanied by a major reformulation of Japan's foreign economic and diplomatic policies to strengthen ties with the major potential exporters of energy supplies in this area. Japan will confront a major challenge in creatively responding to the growing nationalism of countries located in the Pacific Rim. This nationalism has generated a growing resentment of the extensive Japanese investment in the resource extraction industries located in these countries, and unless it is effectively countered, it could result in more pervasive restrictions on foreign investment in these areas.

On a more long-term basis, Japan's energy supply pattern will have a substantial impact on the direction and size of its energy research and development programs. Up until the supply disruptions accompanying the October 1973 Arab-Israeli conflict, Japan had given relatively little consideration to the vulnerability of its position. These disruptions (reinforced by memories of similar difficulties prior to World War II), however, have had a major psychological impact on Japan, and it seems inevitable that these recent events will focus much more systematic attention on the need to develop comprehensive, long-term energy policies. In particular, it will be necessary for Japan to effectively integrate its long-term energy strategy with its broader social and environmental policies. In recent years, the Japanese government has announced its intention to promote a restructuring of its industrial sector to permit more balanced regional development and to improve the quality of the environment. While the economic recession of 1973-75 significantly delayed implementation of these policies, more aggressive efforts in this area could have a substantial impact on the pattern of future energy consumption. By planning for a transition from the energy-intensive, resource-processing industries which provided the basis for economic growth in 1950-70, to less energy-intensive, advanced-technology industries over the next few decades, the government may be able to continue economic growth while restraining the growth in energy consumption to more acceptable levels.[58]

NOTES

1. "Safeguarding Europe's Supplies," *Petroleum Economist*, May 1974, p. 166.

2. This was the optimistic conclusion of an EEC study in 1974, reported in "Safeguarding Europe's Supplies," op. cit., pp. 166-69. For a more recent, and more pessimistic, projection of the effectiveness of EEC energy conservation efforts, see "EEC Energy Hopes Dimmed," *Petroleum Economist* 42 (November 1975): 404-07.

3. "Europe's Imports in Decline," *Petroleum Economist* 42 (November 1975): 421-23. See also *Petroleum Intelligence Weekly* 14 (November 24, 1975): 7-8.

4. *Petroleum Intelligence Weekly* 14 (September 8, 1975): p. 2.

5. "Safeguarding Europe's Supplies," op. cit.; and New York *Times*, May 31, 1974, pp. 41, 44.

6. "Gas Supply Problems Ahead," *Petroleum Economist* 41 (July 1974): 263-66. See also Bert de Vries and Jan Kommandeur, "Gas for Western Europe: How Much for How Long?" *Energy Policy* 3 (March 1975): 24-37.

7. For a critical evaluation of European efforts at cooperation in the energy field, see John Walsh, "European Community Energy: Regulation or Mainly Information," *Science* 184 (June 14, 1974): 1,158-61.

8. Fernand Spaak, "An Energy Policy for the European Community," *Energy Policy* 1 (June 1973): 35-37; and "Towards a European Policy," *Petroleum Press Service*, June 1972, pp. 198-99. A more recent review of IEA activities is available in "The International Energy Agency," *Petroleum Economist* 42 (May 1975): 173-74.

9. *Petroleum Intelligence Weekly* 14 (November 24, 1975): 1-2.

10. *Petroleum Intelligence Weekly* 14 (December 29, 1975): 3.

11. *Petroleum Intelligence Weekly* 14 (December 8, 1975): 4.

12. *Petroleum Intelligence Weekly* 14 (September 29, 1975): 5-6.

13. *Petroleum Intelligence Weekly* 14 (June 30, 1975): 8.

14. *Economist*, November 24, 1973, p. 68.

15. The prolonged controversy within the EEC over these two uranium enrichment processes was extensively covered in the *Economist* and *Financial Times* during 1973 and 1974.

16. *Petroleum Intelligence Weekly* 14 (December 8, 1975): 2.

17. These estimates were cited in papers submitted to "The Political Implications of North Sea Oil and Gas," conference cosponsored by the Royal Institute of International Affairs (United Kingdom) and the Norwegian Institute of International Affairs, Tonsberg, Norway, February 1975. The proceedings are reported in *Energy Policy* 3 (June 1975): 158-59.

18. Ibid. For more detailed presentations of Odell's critique, see Peter Odell, "The North Sea Oil Province: A Simulation Model of Development," *Energy Policy*, December

1974, pp. 316-29; and Peter Odell, "Indigenous Oil and Gas Developments and Western Europe's Energy Policy Options," *Energy Policy* 1 (June 1973): 47-64.

19. Cited in *Petroleum Economist* 42 (May 1975): 172.

20. Bjorn Aamo, "The Basic Objectives of Norwegian Oil Policy" (Paper delivered to "The Political Implications of North Sea Oil and Gas" conference, Tonsberg, Norway, February 1975), reported in *Energy Policy* 3 (June 1975): 159.

21. U.S. Geological Survey, *Coal Resources of the United States*, bulletin no. 1275, study prepared by Paul Averitt (Washington, D.C.: Government Printing Office, 1967).

22. Richard L. Gordon, *The Evolution of Energy Policy in Western Europe: The Reluctant Retreat from Coal* (New York: Praeger, 1970). See also "All European Coal Crisis," *Petroleum Press Service*, April 1972, pp. 127-31; and "Europe's Energy Deficit," *Petroleum Press Service*, December 1972, pp. 445-48.

23. "All European Coal Crisis," op. cit.

24. For one analysis of the new potential for coal in the aftermath of the large price increases for crude oil imports, see Richard Bailey, "The U.K. Coal Industry: Recent Past and Future," *Energy Policy*, June 1974, pp. 152-58.

25. For a brief survey of coal research and development programs undertaken by Germany, France, and the United Kingdom, see J. Herbert Hollomon et al., *Energy Research and Development* (Cambridge, Mass.: Ballinger, 1975), pp. 166-68, 188-190, 245-46. One study concludes that a major factor impeding coal gasification research and development programs in England is the continuing uncertainty over the future availability and price of natural gas from the North Sea (John Surrey and William Walker, "energy R & D: A U.K. Perspective," *Energy Policy* [June 1975]: 98-100).

26. A.J. Surrey, "The Future Growth of Nuclear Power: Part 1. Demand and Supply," *Energy Policy* 1 (September 1973): 114.

27. Surrey and Walker, op. cit., p. 102. For a warning regarding the risks associated with further delays in commercial reactor development in the United Kingdon, see R.L.R. Nicholson, "The Nuclear Power Paradox in the U.K.," *Energy Policy*, June 1973, pp. 38-46.

28. Ibid., pp. 91-93.

29. *Le Monde*, December 9-10, 1973, p. 3.

30. *Petroleum Intelligence Weekly*, May 5, 1975, p. 5; and *Petroleum Intelligence Weekly*, May 19, 1975, p. 5.

31. Surrey and Walker, op. cit., p. 102. For background on the selection of the new reactor design, see Nigel Hawkes, "Energy in Britain: Shopping for a New Reactor," *Science* 183 (January 11, 1974): 57-59.

32. *Economist*, October 27, 1973, p. 75.

33. William D. Metz, "Uranium Enrichment: U.S. 'One Ups' European Centrifuge Effort," *Science* 183 (March 29, 1974): 1,270-72.

34. A.J. Surrey, "The Future Growth of Nuclear Power: Part 2. Choices and Obstacles," *Energy Policy* 1 (December 1973): 208-10. For a recent survey of the French FBR program, see William D. Metz, "European Breeders (1): France Leads the Way," *Science* 190 (December 26, 1975): 1,279-81. See also Hollomon et al., op. cit., pp. 171-75. 201, 255-56.

35. Hollomon et al., op. cit., pp. 174-75, 201, 154-55.

36. Surrey and Walker, op. cit., p. 104.

37. This critical evaluation of European research and development efforts in the energy field is confirmed by Hollomon et al., op. cit., pp. 129-38.

38. Masao Sakisaka, "Japan's Energy Policy Under Review," *Energy Policy* 2 (December 1974): 346.

39. John Surrey, "Japan's Uncertain Energy Prospects: The Problem of Import Dependence," *Energy Policy* 2 (September 1974): 215. Surrey's article is one of the most

useful summaries of Japanese energy policy available in English, and much of the analysis in this chapter relies on data supplied by his article.

40. Sakisaka, op. cit., p. 347.

41. John Surrey, op. cit., p. 215.

42. Ibid., pp. 226-27.

43. Ibid., pp. 215, 218, 227-28. For an interesting analysis of the problems encountered by the Soviet Union in the development of its Siberian energy sources, see Leslie Dienes, "Geographical Problems of Allocation in the Soviet Fuel Supply," *Energy Policy*, June 1973, pp. 3-20.

44. John Surrey, op. cit., pp. 214-15.

45. Ibid., pp. 209-11.

46. Sakisaka, op. cit., p. 347.

47. John Surrey, op. cit., pp. 220-21.

48. For a survey of Communist China's energy resources, see Genevieve C. Dean, "Energy in the People's Republic of China," *Energy Policy* 2 (March 1974): 33-54.

49. Sakisaka, op. cit., p. 347; and John Surrey, op. cit., p. 213.

50. "Japan's Energy Prospects," *Petroleum Press Service*, June 1972, pp. 202-05; and Sakisaka, op. cit., p. 347.

51. John Surrey, op. cit., pp. 213-14.

52. Sakisaka, op. cit., p. 347.

53. Hollomon et al., op. cit., p. 210.

54. John Surrey, op. cit., p. 221.

55. Hollomon et al., op. cit., pp. 215-16.

56. *Petroleum Press Service*, September 1973, pp. 348-49. For a more recent report on Japanese energy policy, see "Policy-Making in Japan," *Petroleum Economist* 41 (October 1974): 369-71.

57. Hollomon et al., op. cit., p. 219.

58. John Surrey, op. cit., pp. 229-30.

11

EVALUATION OF
ENERGY STRATEGIES

Perhaps the most important lesson to be derived from this study of the parameters for energy policy formulation is that there are no easy solutions. As discussed earlier, the state of existing energy technology requires that policy-makers confront very difficult choices among three attractive, yet often contradictory, objectives: (1) ensuring adequate supplies of low-cost energy, (2) minimizing the adverse impact on the environment of energy production and consumption, and (3) reducing dependence on foreign energy sources. These choices can only be avoided at the expense of additional disruptions in the supply of energy. Moreover, these choices must be made with a long-term perspective, since the most desirable or easiest choice in the short term may have disastrous long-term implications. The only satisfactory method of reconciling these distinct objectives is to design research and development programs to develop energy technology over the long term that will be compatible with all three objectives. In the meantime, priorities will have to be established to permit choices among these objectives.

Another conclusion of this study is that intensified external pressure, in the form of either price increases for crude oil imports or supply restrictions, increases the flexibility of the governments of the principal consuming regions in three critical categories of policy formulation: (1) reduction of aggregate energy demand to supplement market price incentives, (2) modification of environmental policies, and (3) support for research and development programs for alternative energy sources and energy-efficient technology. The generalization must be modified in the case of Western Europe, where it appears that external pressures increase the flexibility of national governments while generating widespread tensions within the EEC. As a result, regional cooperation in energy policies may ironically become increasingly difficult under external pressure.

Moreover, in all three consuming regions, intensified external pressure may increase the potential flexibility of national governments in the formulation of energy policies, but it simultaneously increases the tendency for policy-makers to focus exclusively on short-term supply constraints without adequately considering the impact of their response to these constraints on long-term supply and demand trends.

Since the flexibility of government policy seems to increase in direct proportion to the degree of external pressure, probably the greatest difficulties would be encountered in situations in which the price and availability of crude oil imports were affected in a gradual manner. In such a case, the political unpopularity of measures designed to restrict energy consumption would still constitute a major constraint on government policy. The problem would therefore be to satisfy the steadily expanding energy demand in the context of rising energy prices and environmental constraints on the expansion of the production of the most readily available alternative energy sources. While the long-term price elasticity of energy demand and market incentives for the development of environmentally acceptable alternative energy sources will ultimately resolve the problem, certain short-term and medium-term difficulties could arise.

As external pressure intensifies, the economic feasibility of specific alternative energy sources recedes as an obstacle to their development, while technological feasibility progressively emerges as the primary consideration in the formulation of an energy research and development strategy. Both private industry and government agencies will be able to mobilize increasingly large capital resources to finance accelerated research and development programs, since the threat of disruptions in the pattern of crude oil imports will presumably increase the priority assigned to development of indigenous sources of energy, as a result of both profit incentives and security considerations. The need to ensure reliable sources of energy under such circumstances would stimulate the development of indigenous energy sources even if they were not fully economically competitive with alternative sources. On the other hand, although "crash" research and development programs have a limited capability for reducing the lead times necessary to develop a particular process or technology, technological feasibility will remain a major constraint on the development of alternative energy resources, particularly in the short term.

The lead times inherent in the development of alternative energy sources suggest that short-term strategies in response to supply restrictions must focus on policies to diminish aggregate energy demand while accepting increasing reliance on a variety of relatively accessible, although environmentally objectionable alternative energy sources. To the extent that such energy sources as offshore and Alaskan crude oil, shale oil, and coal remain inaccessible due to environmental restrictions, reductions in the supply of crude oil imports would result in major energy supply shortages (unless prices were permitted to rise freely to reflect the true extent of the shortages). The U.S. domestic energy resource base in particular is dominated by coal (90 percent of identifiable recoverable and submarginal energy resources), and environmental constraints have restricted both the production and consumption of this energy resource. Future restrictions on crude oil imports will produce pressure for the modification of environmental legislation to permit greater utilization of domestic coal reserves. This is one of the difficult choices an effective energy strategy will require.

If widespread supply restrictions were placed on crude oil imports, the crisis atmosphere generated would increase the likelihood of the accelerated development of environmentally desirable long-range energy sources, which would require massive capital investment. Unavoidable lead times would prevent short- or medium-term utilization of such "exotic" fuel sources as nuclear fusion, hydrogen, and solar energy for electric power generation, but "crash" research and development programs could make these sources commercially available in a much shorter time (10 to 25 years) than would otherwise have been possible. Thus, the flexibility in the development of alternative energy resources in response to sustained constraints on energy imports is particularly great over the long term.

A comparison of the three major energy-consuming regions reveals that the United States remains in the most secure position regarding crude oil imports. It is the least dependent on crude oil imports in the context of its total energy consumption, and its position is further strengthened by the domestic availability of massive, relatively accessible alternative energy reserves as well as by advanced research and development programs in all aspects of energy technology. But despite these assets, the United States also confronts several major obstacles in the formulation of an effective energy strategy. The U.S. public remains highly confused regarding the implications of current trends in energy supply and demand and unfortunately disposed to the cynical view that recent dislocations in energy supply have been the result of covert manipulation by the large petroleum companies in concert with the federal government.* This widespread atmosphere of suspicion will make effective policy formulation extremely difficult, and, in particular, it will inhibit the making of the unpleasant choices that must be made among incompatible objectives in energy

---

*An effective rebuttal of this interpretation of the energy crisis would require a separate book; unfortunately, none exists at the present time. Of all the criticisms of the oil companies' behavior, perhaps the most cogent are those advanced by the economist M.A. Adelman, although even his criticisms are directed primarily at the acquiescent response of the U.S. State Department to OPEC price initiatives in 1971-73.[1] More generally, it appears that the blame for most manifestations of the energy crisis must be assigned to government policies that have hampered the role of the price mechanism in reconciling supply and demand.[2]

supply. Such an atmosphere will also further hamper efforts to develop systematic and comprehensive energy strategies and instead will reinforce the current preoccupation with short-term energy problems.

Two additional constraints also affect efforts to formulate energy policies in the United States. An active ecology movement has emerged over the past several years which has consistently opposed a variety of measures to increase the contribution of indigenous resources to U.S. energy supplies. While such environmental restrictions may be desirable from an ecological viewpoint, it is essential that their consequences for the avilability of energy supplies be fully understood. Up until very recently, this had not occurred, and the result has aggravated current energy shortages in the United States. The ecology movement has a responsibility to consider the full impact of the legislation it supports and to propose alternative energy strategies that would minimize the adverse effect of this legislation.

A second constraint on the development of alternative energy strategies in the United States involves the difficulties in mobilizing the massive capital investment required for the commercial application of highly capital-intensive processes. The private sector needs incentives to undertake capital investment on the scale required in lengthy research and development programs. In addition, private industry must be reasonably confident that government energy policies will remain relatively stable so that normal commercial risks will not be further increased by risks of sudden changes in policy that might have serious consequences for private investment. Capital markets will also have to be significantly reoriented in order to provide unprecedented quantities of investment funds, and private corporations will have to rely on external financing to a much larger extent than in the past.

NOTES

1. M.A. Adelman, "Is the Oil Shortage Real? Oil Companies as OPEC Tax Collectors," *Foreign Policy,* no. 9, Winter 1972-73, pp. 69-107; and Morris A. Adelman, *The World Petroleum Market* (Baltimore: Johns Hopkins University Press, 1972). An example of a more critical evaluation of the role of U.S. oil companies is provided by Christopher T. Rand, *Making Democracy Safe for Oil* (Boston: Little Brown, 1975). For a favorable analysis of oil company actions, see Robert B. Stobaugh, "The Oil Companies in the Crisis," *Daedalus* 104 (fall 1975): 179-202.

2. For analyses supporting this contention, see the works cited in Chapter 6, footnote 7.

12

SUMMARY: CONSTRAINTS
AND OPPORTUNITIES
IN ALTERNATIVE
ENERGY STRATEGIES

Recent trends in energy supply and demand have reinforced the dependence of the three major energy-consuming regions—the United States, Western Europe, and Japan—on crude oil imports from the Middle East and Africa. A high growth rate in aggregate energy demand has been accompanied by continued reliance on fossil fuels as the primary energy source, and increasing constraints on the production and consumption of coal and natural gas have shifted a high proportion of the incremental growth in energy consumption to crude oil. The emergence of the United States as an important net importer of crude oil from the Eastern Hemisphere has required a significant reorientation of international crude oil markets.

The rapidly escalating cost of crude oil from the Middle East over the past several years combined with the Arab production cutbacks and the embargo imposed in October 1973 have catalyzed a widespread reevaluation of energy policies in the major consuming regions. Governments concerned about the adverse impact of high-cost crude oil imports on their balance of payments and the economic and political risks associated with dependence on potentially unreliable crude oil sources are in the process of formulating energy strategies designed to reduce the need for crude oil imports and make maximum use of indigenous energy resources.

These energy strategies stress the need to accelerate research and development programs for the commercial production of alternative energy sources. An evaluation of these alternatives dispels any pessimistic conclusions regarding the imminent depletion of the earth's energy resources and permits considerable optimism regarding the long-term availability of virtually inexhaustible sources of energy, such as nuclear fusion, solar energy, and hydrogen fuels. However, the real difficulties emerge in the effort to overcome short- and medium-term constraints in the accelerated development of alternative energy sources.

Thus, while physical resource scarcity will not emerge as a constraint in satisfying future energy demand, increasingly capital-intensive energy production systems may place strains on existing capital markets, and a major effort will be required to mobilize the necessary capital funds. Private investment in these fields will be particularly sensitive to the possibility of shifts in government energy policy. Realism and stability in this area are needed in order to maximize the willingness of the private sector to commit the large investments that must be made if the potential of alternative energy sources is to be achieved.

Policy-makers must also deal with the hard facts of irreducible technological lead times, both in the initial research and development stages and in the construction of large-scale commercial facilities. Even "crash" research and development programs with massive government funding will not be able to reduce lead times beyond a certain point without introducing unacceptable risks of failure. The major contribution of such "crash" programs would be to permit simultaneous research and development projects on several alternative processes in a specific field such as coal gasification. Once a specific technology has successfully completed the research and development phase, additional delays are inevitable before significant commercial production can be attained, and if government policies attempt to accelerate the commercial production of a variety of alternative energy sources at the same time, widespread shortages in necessary inputs of specialized materials and skilled engineering manpower can be anticipated. Furthermore, both energy-producing and energy-consuming systems are characterized by lengthy lifetimes which limit the impact of short-term energy policies and underline the need for sound long-term energy planning. Unless these constraints are realistically confronted in the early stages of the planning process, persistent delays will hamper the implementation of government policies.

A third constraint in commercial production from alternative energy sources concerns its adverse environmental impact. In each case, there are unique environmental advantages and disadvantages that complicate efforts to compare the merits of several processes, but the environmental constraints are particularly great for alternative energy technology that is in an advanced research and development stage.

As an example, coal constitutes the major short-term alternative to crude oil and natural gas in the United States, and it is also the most abundant indigenous fossil fuel resource over the long term. Environmental restrictions on atmospheric emissions of sulfur dioxide have been a major factor in encouraging the shift from underground mining of coal in the East to surface mining in the West, where most of the country's low-sulfur coal reserves are located. These restrictions have also been an important incentive in stimulating research and development programs on coal conversion processes that permit the precombustion removal of sulfur from the coal. However, policies currently being considered to restrict surface mining of coal would effectively prevent access to a large share of the nation's reserves of low-sulfur coal. Such measures will simultaneously reduce the economic feasibility of coal conversion processes that would have been able to compete with conventional energy resources by relying on inexpensive coal from surface mining operations in the West. This paradoxical outcome of policies designed to protect the environment illustrates the need for a more effective integration of environmental legislation in the framework of a comprehensive energy strategy.

Another example of environmental constraints on the accelerated development of alternative energy sources arises in the field of nuclear reactors. Growing concern over the possibility of the accidental release of radioactive emissions from nuclear reactors or during the handling of radioactive materials in the nuclear fuel cycle has already had a serious impact on the expansion of commercial nuclear power generation. Unless research and development programs in nuclear energy and other alternative sources devote adequate attention to the environmental impact of commercial production using these new technologies, public concern may significantly delay their application.

Apart from these constraints, there is an enormous amount of uncertainty in attempting to analyze the competitive economics of alternative energy resources and to assess the scale and timing of their contribution to the total energy supply mix. Perhaps the source of greatest uncertainty is the unpredictability of future crude oil prices and their impact not only on energy demand but throughout the economies of consuming countries. In addition, inflation has played havoc with the outlook for equipment prices; lead times in equipment procurement are very long; and there is pervasive doubt as to the future course of the world economy. It can be said, nevertheless, that at current prices, exploitation of many non-oil energy resources should be economically feasible and will in all likelihood, be pursued, in view of the advantages from the standpoint of national security.

In addition to an evaluation of the potential impact of the accelerated commercial production of alternative energy sources on future energy supplies, long-term energy strategies must also give adequate attention to the potential impact on aggregate consumption levels of policies designed to alter the existing pattern of energy consumption. Such policies could be oriented toward three basic objectives: (1) a reduction in the growth of aggregate energy consumption levels as a result of price incentives supplemented by appropriate fiscal measures and regulatory policies, (2) accelerated commercial production of energy-efficient technologies designed to raise the low 33 percent average thermal efficiency of existing energy technology, and (3) reallocation of fuels among markets to satisfy existing levels of energy demand more efficiently.

The field of electric power generation emerges as a crucial focus for research and development programs in energy-efficient technology, since electric power plants are responsible for a high and growing share of primary fuel demand. Moreover, there are realistic prospects of achieving major improvements in the efficiency of technologies associated with the production, storage, transmission, and distribution of electricity that will therefore have considerable impact on overall energy consumption. The transportation sector remains the most inflexible of the major energy-consuming markets, and it will continue to be critically dependent on oil products for the foreseeable future.

The formulation of energy strategies, particularly in the short and medium term, must confront the existence of serious contradictions among three desirable objectives: (1) the availability of adequate supplies of energy at affordable costs, (2) the preservation or improvement of environmental quality, and (3) independence from potentially unreliable crude oil imports. Unless these contradictions are openly acknowledged and a clear list of priorities is drawn up to permit choices to be made among these objectives, energy policies will not be able to resolve existing problems adequately. Over the long term, however, it should be possible to satisfy all three objectives, provided that research and development programs are explicitly designed to develop alternative energy sources that are compatible with the three objectives and provided that adequate funding is available for these programs.

An effective response to existing dislocations in energy supply and demand also depends on an understanding of the complex interactions among various energy sources that avoids a narrow focus on isolated fuels. Such a comprehensive understanding remains seriously inhibited by the highly fragmented nature of energy policy formulation, which spans dozens of overlapping government agencies in each country. In addition, policy-makers lack the detailed data base necessary to anticipate future trends in energy supplies and to evaluate the differing impacts of various policy options on future energy supply and demand trends.

In view of the crucial importance of the future price and availability of crude oil imports as a parameter for energy strategies, this study has examined the policy options available to the governments of the major consuming regions in three alternative scenarios with differing assumptions concerning crude oil imports. These scenarios reveal that the flexibility of consuming governments in energy policy formulation varies proportionally with the intensity of pressure on the price or availability of crude oil imports. This flexibility is manifested in several distinct areas: restrictions on energy consumption, modifications in environmental constraints, and support for accelerated research and development programs on alternative energy sources. Unfortunately, intensified pressure on crude oil imports also tends to focus attention on short-term supply constraints without permitting an adequate consideration of the long-term impact of energy policies. The intermediate scenario, which assumes gradual constraints on the availability of crude oil imports as a result of production cutbacks in the oil-exporting countries, presents the greatest policy dilemma, since the consuming governments would lack flexibility in restricting the rapid growth of energy consumption while simultaneously confronting serious constraints on the expansion of the production of indigenous energy sources.

As a result of irreducible lead times during the research and development phase and potential bottlenecks in engineering and construction capabilities, substantial expansion of commercial production from alternative energy sources may be virtually impossible over the short term, and energy policies within this time framework must therefore concentrate on restricting growth in energy consumption and accepting increased dependence on environmentally objectionable fossil fuels—particularly coal. As the pressure on crude oil imports intensifies, the economic feasibility of alternative energy sources progressively yields to technological feasibility as a constraint on the expansion of indigenous production of energy.

A comparison of the policy options available to the three major consuming regions confirms that the United States is in the least vulnerable position with regard to dependence on potentially unreliable crude oil imports. Crude oil imports from the Middle East still represent a relatively modest share of total energy consumption in comparison with either Western Europe or Japan, and the United States possesses the most diversified resource base for the indigenous production of energy among the three major consuming regions.

However, this wealth of resources offers only the potential for a satisfactory energy supply situation; whether or not this potential is ever realized depends on the ability of policy-makers to formulate a comprehensive long-term energy strategy that realistically confronts existing constraints on energy supplies. Thus far, the policy-making record in the leading energy-consuming nations does not inspire much optimism. Government measures that were often rationalized on the basis of the need to correct market "imperfections" have generally proved to be highly imperfect themselves and have often resulted in unforeseen adverse consequences. the challenge currently confronting the governments of the leading energy-consuming nations is twofold: to achieve a proper balance between the market mechanism and government intervention in attaining national energy policy objectives and to establish policy-making institutions capable of formulating comprehensive long-term energy strategies that are better integrated with broader socioeconomic and political concerns.

To conclude, it should be stressed once again that the two fundamental variables that will necessarily affect the formulation of long-term energy strategies are the availability and the price of crude oil imports. This study has considered the impact that rising prices or the restricted availability of crude oil imports might have on the energy strategies of the major consuming regions. The scenarios presented were based primarily on the extrapolation of recent trends in order to evaluate the consequences of growing pressures on energy imports.

As a consequence of its concern with evaluating policy flexibility in response to continued high crude oil prices and possible future supply constraints, this study might have underemphasized the persistent uncertainty regarding the validity of these two assumptions. This uncertainty has in fact played a major role in inhibiting private investment in the development of alternative energy sources. At the same time, it has also restrained the governments of the energy-consuming nations from implementing more aggressive policies designed to achieve energy self-sufficiency, since such policies run the significant risk of prematurely locking nations into high-cost energy sources.

Some well-qualified authorities on world crude oil prices have argued that the current high prices of crude oil from OPEC countries are largely a temporary phenomenon and that the price of crude oil imports can be expected to decline gradually over the next 10 to 15 years. If these projections are accurate, they will have serious implications for long-term energy strategy that have not been fully considered in this study. The success of long-range planning in the energy sector will critically depend on the accuracy of current projections regarding the price and availability of crude oil imports.

BOOKS

Abelson, Philip H. *Energy: Use, Conservation and Supply*. New York: American Association for the Advancement of Science, 1974.

Adelman, M.A. *The World Petroleum Market*. Baltimore: Johns Hopkins University Press, 1972.

―――― et al. *No Time to Confuse*. San Francisco: Institute for Contemporary Affairs, 1975.

Ayres, Robert, and Richard McKenna. *Alternatives to the Internal Combustion Engine*. Baltimore: Johns Hopkins University Press, 1972.

Berkowitz, David A., and Arthur M. Squires, eds. *Power Generation and Environmental Change*. Cambridge: MIT Press, 1971.

Beydoun, Z.R., and H.V. Dunnington. *The Petroleum Geology and Resources of the Middle East*. Beaconfield, England: Scientific Press, 1975.

Bohi, Douglas, and Milton Russell. *Policy Alternatives for Energy Security*. Baltimore: Johns Hopkins University Press, 1975.

Bramson, Gerard M. *Energy Taxes and Subsidies*. Cambridge, Mass.: Ballinger, 1974.

Burn, Duncan. *The Political Economy of Nuclear Energy*. London: Institute of Economic Affairs, 1967.

Campbell, Robert W. *The Economics of Soviet Oil and Gas*. Baltimore: Johns Hopkins University Press, 1968.

Clark, Wilson. *Energy for Survival*. New York: Doubleday, Anchor Books, 1974.

Cleland, S., Z. Mikdashi, and I. Seymour, eds. *Continuity and Change in the World Oil Industry*. Beirut: Middle East Research and Publishing Center, 1970.

Cochran, Thomas B. *The Liquid Metal Fast Breeder Reactor*. Baltimore: Resources for the Future, 1974.

Connery, Robert H., and Robert S. Gilmour, eds. *The National Energy Problem*. Lexington, Mass.: Lexington Books, 1974.

Darmstadter, Joel. *Energy in the World Economy*. Baltimore: Johns Hopkins University Press, 1971.

Denton, J.C., ed. *Geothermal Energy: A Special Report by Walter J. Hickel*. Fairbanks: University of Alaska, 1972.

Elliot, Iain F. *The Soviet Energy Balance*. New York: Praeger, 1975.

Erickson, Edward W., and Leonard Waverman, eds. *The Energy Question: An International Failure of Policy*. Toronto: University of Toronto Press, 1974.

Fabricant, Neil, and Robert M. Hallman. *Toward a Political Power Policy*. New York: Braziller, 1971.

Fisher, J.C. *Energy Crises in Perspective*. New York: Wiley, 1974.

Freeman, S. David. *Energy: The New Era*. New York: Walker and Co., 1974.

Ford Foundation, Energy Policy Project. *A Time to Choose: America's Energy Future*. Cambridge, Mass.: Ballinger, 1974.

Fuller, John G. *We Almost Lost Detroit*. New York: Reader's Digest Press, 1975.

Goeller, Harold E. et al. *World Energy Conference Survey of Energy Resources*. New York: U.S. National Committee of the World Energy Conference, 1974.

Gordon, Richard L. *The Evolution of Energy Policy in Western Europe: The Reluctant Retreat from Coal*. New York: Praeger, 1970.

Hammond, Allen L.; William D. Metz; and Thomas H. Maugh II. *Energy and the Future*. Washington D.C.: American Association for the Advancement of Science, 1973.

Hartshorn, J.E. *Politics and World Oil Economics*. New York: Praeger, 1967.

Hass, Jerome; Edward J. Mitchell; and Bernell K. Stone. *Financing the Energy Industry*. Cambridge, Mass.: Ballinger, 1974.

Holdren, John, and Philip Herrera. *Energy: A Crisis in Power*. San Francisco: Sierra Club, 1971.

Hollomon, J. Herbert et al. *Energy Research and Development*. Cambridge, Mass.: Ballinger, 1975.

Hottel, Hoyt C., and Jack B. Howard. *New Energy Technology*. Cambridge: MIT Press, 1971.

Klebanoff, Shoshana. *Middle East Oil and U.S. Foreign Policy*. New York: Praeger, 1974.

Kruger, P., and C. Otte, eds. *Geothermal Energy*. Stanford: Stanford University Press, 1972.

Landsberg, Hans H., and Sam H. Schurr. *Energy in the United States: Sources, Uses and Policy Issues*. New York: Random House, 1968.

Lovejoy, W.F., and P.T. Homan. *Economic Aspects of Oil Conservation Regulation*. Baltimore: Johns Hopkins University Press, 1967.

Lovins, Amory B. *World Energy Strategies*. Cambridge, Mass.: Ballinger, 1975.

MacAvoy, Paul W. *Economic Strategy for Developing Nuclear Breeder Reactors*. Cambridge: MIT Press, 1969.

Mallakh, Ragaei el, and Carl McGuire. *Energy and Development*. Boulder, Colo.: International Research Center for Energy and Economic Development, 1974.

Mancke, Richard B. *The Failure of U.S. Energy Policy*. New York: Columbia University Press, 1974.

————. *Performance of the Federal Energy Office*. Washington, D.C.: American Enterprise Institute, 1975.

Meinel, Aden B., and Marjorie P. Meinel. *Power for the People*. Tucson: Privately published, 1970.

Mikdashi, Zuhayr. *The Community of Oil Exporting Countries*. London: George Allen and Unwin, 1972.

Miller, Roger LeRoy. *The Economics of Energy*. New York: Morrow, 1974.

Mitchell, Edward J., ed. *Dialogue on World Oil*. Washington, D.C.: American Enterprise Institute, 1974.

————. *U.S. Energy Policy: A Primer*. Washington, D.C.: American Enterprise Institute, 1974.

National Academy of Sciences (Academy Forum). *Energy: Future Alternatives and Risks*. Cambridge, Mass.: Ballinger, 1975.

Nau, Henry R. *National Politics and International Technology: Nuclear Reactor Development in Western Europe*. Baltimore: Johns Hopkins University Press, 1974.

Penrose, Edith. *The Large International Firm in Developing Countries: The International Petroleum Industry*. London: Allen and Unwin, 1968.

Percival, John W.H. *Oil Wealth: Middle East Spending and Investment Patterns*. London: Financial Times, 1975.

Posner, Michael V. *Fuel Policy: A Study in Applied Economics*. London: Macmillan, 1973.

Rand, Christopher T. *Making Democracy Safe for Oil*. Boston: Little, Brown, 1975.

Ridgeway, James. *The Last Play: The Struggle to Monopolize the World's Energy Resources*. New York: Dutton, 1973.

Rifai, Taki. *The Pricing of Crude Oil*. New York: Praeger, 1974.

Schurr, Sam H. *Economic Growth and the Environment*. Baltimore: Johns Hopkins University Press, 1972.

—— et al. *Energy in the American Economy, 1850-1975*. Baltimore: Johns Hopkins University Press, 1960.

Stocking, George W. *Middle East Oil: A Study in Political and Economic Controversy*. Nashville: Vanderbilt University Press, 1970.

Tanzer, Michael. *The Energy Crisis: World Struggle for Power and Wealth*. New York: Monthly Review Press, 1975.

Taylor, Theodore B., and Mason Willrich. *Nuclear Theft: Risks and Safeguards*. Cambridge, Mass.: Ballinger, 1974.

Van Tassel, Alfred J., ed. *The Environmental Price of Energy*. Lexington, Mass.: Lexington Books, 1975.

Williams, Robert H., ed. *The Energy Conservation Papers*. Cambridge, Mass.: Ballinger, 1975.

Willrich, Mason. *Global Politics of Nuclear Energy*. New York: Praeger, 1971.

—— et al. *Energy and World Politics*. New York: Free Press, 1975.

——, ed. *International Safeguards and Nuclear Industry*. Baltimore: Johns Hopkins University Press, 1973.

Yager, Joseph B., and Eleanor B. Steinberg. *Energy and U.S. Foreign Policy*. Cambridge, Mass.: Ballinger, 1974.

Yannacone, Victor J., ed. *Energy Crisis: Danger and Opportunity*. St. Paul: West Publishing, 1974.

REPORTS, PAPERS, AND UNPUBLISHED STUDIES

Aamo, Bjorn. "The Basic Objectives of Norwegian Oil Policy." Paper delivered to "Political Implications of North Sea Oil and Gas" conference, Tonsberg, Norway, February 1975.

Anderson, James H., Jr. "Economic Power and Water from Solar Energy." Paper presented at American Society of Mechanical Engineers Winter Annual Meeting, New York, November 26-30, 1972.

Breyer, Stephen, and Paul MacAvoy. *Energy Regulation by the FPC*. Washington, D.C.: Brookings Institution, 1974.

British Petroleum. *Statistical Review of the World Oil Industry: 1974*. London, 1975.

Brookes, L.G. "Toward the All Electric Economy." Paper delivered at U.K. Institute of Petroleum Summer Meeting, Harrogate, England, June 5-8, 1973.

Brookings Institution. *Cooperative Approaches to World Energy Problems*. Washington, D.C., 1974.

Chandler, Geoffrey. "Energy: The Changed and Changing Scene." Keynote address delivered at U.K. Institute of Petroleum Summer Meeting, Harrogate, England, June 5-8, 1973.

Clegg, M.W. "New Sources of Oil: Oil Sands, Shales and Synthetics." Paper delivered at U.K. Institute of Petroleum Summer Meeting, Harrogate, England, June 5-8, 1973.

Collado, Emilio G. "The Energy Outlook and World Trade." Speech presented to 60th National Foreign Trade Convention, New York, November 13, 1973.

Committee for Economic Development, Research and Policy Committee. *Achieving Energy Independence*. New York, 1974.

Cox, Kenneth E., ed. *Hydrogen Energy*. Albuquerque: University of New Mexico, 1974.

Economist Intelligence Unit. *International Oil Symposium: Selected Papers*. London, 1973.

————. "Oil in the Middle East." In *Quarterly Economic Review*. Annual supplement. London, 1975.

Energy Research and Development Adminstration. *A National Plan for Energy Research, Development and Demonstration: Creating Energy Choices for the Future*. 2 vols. Report no. ERDA-48. Washington, D.C.: Government Printing Office, 1975.

Federal Council for Science and Technology, Committee on Energy Research and Development Goals. *Assessment of Geothermal Energy Resources*. Washington, D.C., 1972.

Federal Energy Administration. *Project Independence Report*. Washington, D.C., 1974.

Federal Energy Office, Office of Economic Data Analysis and Strategic Planning. *U.S. Energy Self-Sufficiency: An Assessment of Technological Potential*. Washington, D.C., 1974.

————, Office of Policy Analysis and Evaluation. *A Proposed Program for U.S. Energy Self-Sufficiency by 1980*. Washington, D.C., 1974.

Federal Power Commission, Bureau of Power. *The Potential for Conversion of Oil-Fired and Gas-Fired Electric Generating Units to Use of Coal*. Form no. 36. September 1973.

Garvin, Clifton. "Energy in Transition: How to Smooth the Passage." Speech presented to Explorers Club Dinner Symposium on the Energy Crisis, New York, November 28, 1973.

Hamilton, Adrian. "Outlook for Europe." Paper delivered at U.K. Institute of Petroleum Summer Meeting, Harrogate, England, June 5-8, 1973.

Holloway, Frederic A. "Synthetic Fuels: Why, Which Ones and When?" Paper presented to *Oil Daily* "Synthetic Energy: The Immediate Outlook" forum, Tulsa, May 2, 1973.

Horst, K.M., and R.S. Palmer. "Cost Targets for Commercial LMFBR's." Paper delivered to American Power Conference, Chicago, April 1974.

Houthakker, H.S., and P.K. Verleger. "Dynamic Demand Analyses of Selected Energy Resources." Paper delivered to American Economic Association, New York, December 1973.

Hunter, Robert E. *The Energy Crisis and U.S. Foreign Policy*. Foreign Policy Association Headline Series, no. 216. New York, 1973.

Institute of Fuel. *Energy for the Future*. London, 1973.

Institute of Gas Technology. *Clean Fuels from Coal*. Chicago, 1973.

Kuegemann, Victor E. *North America's Natural Resources Related to Energy and Construction*. Hamilton, Bermuda: TRI Ltd., 1973.

Leslie, D.C. "Nuclear Energy 1: An Effective Competitor." Paper delivered at U.K. Institute of Petroleum Summer Meeting, Harrogate, England, June 5-8, 1973.

————. "Nuclear Energy 2: From Fission to Fusion." Paper delivered at U.K. Institute of Petroleum Summer Meeting, Harrogate, England, June 5-8, 1973.

Lichtblau, John H. "Middle East Oil and the U.S. Energy Crisis." Paper presented to "Mounting Energy Crisis and the Middle East" seminar, School of Advanced International Studies, Washington, D.C., September 19, 1973.

MacDonald, Walter. "International Energy Market Trends through 1980." Paper presented to the American University of Beirut, "Third Oil Seminar," Beirut, Lebanon, April 23, 1969.

National Academy of Engineering, Task Force on Energy. *U.S. Energy Prospects: An Engineering Viewpoint*. Washington, D.C., 1974.

National Academy of Sciences. *Mineral Resources and the Environment*. Washington, D.C., 1975.

National Aeronautics and Space Administration. *Large-Scale Terrestrial Solar Power Generation Cost: A Preliminary Assessment*. Study prepared by A.E. Shakowski and Lloyd I. Shure. Technical Memorandum, no. X-2520. Washington, D.C., 1972.

National Council of Churches of Christ in the U.S.A., Committee of Inquiry. *The Plutonium Economy: A Statement of Concern*. New York, 1975.

National Petroleum Council. *Emergency Preparedness for Interruption of Petroleum Imports into the United States*. Washington, D.C., 1974.

————, Committee on U.S. Energy Outlook. *U.S. Energy Outlook*. Washington, D.C., 1972.

National Science Foundation. *Energy Research Needs*. Report prepared by Resources for the Future, in cooperation with Massachusetts Institute of Technology Environmental Laboratory. Washington, D.C., 1971.

————, Research Applied to National Needs. *Summary Report of the Cornell Workshop on Energy and the Environment*. Washington, D.C.: Government Printing Office, 1972.

National Science Foundation and National Aeronautics and Space Administration, Solar Energy Panel. *Assessment of Solar Energy as a National Resource*. Report no. NSF/RA/N-73-001, Washington D.C.: Government Printing Office, 1972.

Oak Ridge National Laboratory. *An Inventory of Energy Research*. Washington, D.C.: Government Printing Office, 1972.

Office of Emergency Preparedness. *The Potential for Energy Conservation: A Staff Study*. Washington, D.C.: Government Printing Office, 1972.

————. *The Potential for Energy Conservation: Substitution for Scarce Fuels*. Washington, D.C.: Government Printing Office, 1973.

Office of Science and Technology. *Patterns of Energy Consumption in the United States*. Prepared by Stanford Research Institute. Washington, D.C., 1972.

————, Energy Advisory Panel. *An Assessment of the New Options in Energy Research and Development*. Washington, D.C., 1973.

Organization for Economic Cooperation and Development. *Energy and Environment: Methods to Analyze the Long-Term Relationship*. Paris, 1974.

————. *Energy Policy: Problems and Objectives*. Paris, 1966.

————. *Energy Prospects to 1985: An Assessment of Long-Term Energy Developments and Related Policies*. 2 vols. Paris, 1974.

————. *Energy Research and Development: Problems and Perspectives*. Paris, 1975.

————. *Uranium: Resources, Production and Demand*. Paris, 1973.

————, Oil Committee. *Oil: The Present Situation and Future Prospects*. Paris, 1973.

Robinson, Colin. *A Policy for Fuel?* Institute of Economic Affairs Occasional Paper, no. 31. London, 1969.

————. *Competition for Fuel*. Institute of Economic Affairs Occasional Paper, no. 31, supplement. London, 1969.

Rothkopf, M.H., and H. de Vries. "Modelling Future Energy Supply." Paper delivered at U.K. Institute of Petroleum Summer Meeting, Harrogate, England, June 5-8, 1973.

Siegel, Howard M. "Coal Liquefaction: Research, Cost and Commercialization." Paper presented to first International Coal Research Conference, Washington D.C., October 27, 1973.

Stauffer, T.R.; R.S. Palmer; and H.L. Wyckoff. "An Assessment of the Economic Incentive for the Fast Breeder Reactor." Paper delivered to Seminar on Energy Policy, Harvard University, December 4, 1974.

Szego, George. *The Energy Plantation: A Cost-Effective Means of Providing All the U.S. Energy and Power Needs by Utilizing Solar Energy*. Warrenton, Va.: Inter Technology Corporation, 1972.

———. *The U.S. Energy Problem*. Warrenton, Va.: Inter Technology Corporation, 1973.

Teller, Edward. *Energy: A Plan for Action*. New York: Commission on Critical Choices for America, 1975.

Ubbeholde, A.R. "Alternative Sources of Energy." Paper delivered at U.K. Institute of Petroleum Summer Meeting, Harrogate, England, June 5-8, 1973.

U.S. Atomic Energy Commission. *The Nation's Energy Future*. Report no. WASH-1281. Report submitted by Dixy Lee Ray. Washington, D.C.: Government Printing Office, 1973.

———. *Reactor Safety Study: An Assessment of Accident Risks in U.S. Commercial Power Plants*. Draft. Report no. WASH-1400. Washington, D.C., 1974.

———. *Report of the Cornell Workshops on the Major Issues of a National Energy Research and Development Program*. Oak Ridge, Tenn., 1973.

———. *The Safety of Nuclear Power Reactors (Light Water-Cooled) and Related Facilities*. Report no. WASH-1250. Washington, D.C., 1973.

———, Advisory Task Force on Power Reactor Emergency Cooling. *Emergency Core Cooling*. Report submitted by William K. Ergen. Washington, D.C.: Atomic Energy Commission, 1967.

———, Forecasting Branch. *Nuclear Power: 1973-2000*. Report no. WASH-1139. Washington, D.C., 1972.

U.S. Congress, House, Committee on Science and Astronautics, Subcommittee on Energy. *Energy Research and Development: An Overview of our National Effort*. 93d Cong., 2d sess., May 1973.

———, House, Committee on Science and Astronautics, Subcommittee on Energy. *Geothermal Energy*. 93d Cong., 1st sess., September 1973.

———, House, Committee on Science and Astronautics, Subcommittee on Science, Research, and Development. *Energy Research and Development*. 92d Cong., 2d sess., 1972.

———, Joint Economic Committee, Subcommittee on Economic Progress. *The Energy Outlook for the 1980s*. Study prepared by W. N. Peach. 93d Cong., 2d sess. Washington, D.C.: Government Printing Office, 1973.

———, Senate, Committee on Commerce. *Energy Waste and Energy Efficiency in Industrial and Commercial Activities*. 93d Cong., 2d sess., May-June 1974.

———, Senate, Committee on Commerce. *Industry Efforts in Energy Conservation*. 93d Cong., 2d sess., 1974.

——, Senate, Committee on Interior and Insular Affairs. *Energy Research and Development: Problems and Prospects.* Report prepared by Harry Perry. 93d Cong., 1st sess. Washington, D.C.: Government Printing Office, 1973.

U.S. Department of Commerce. *An Assessment of U.S. Energy Options for Project Independence.* Report no. UCRL-51638. Prepared by Lawrence Livermore Laboratory. Springfield, Va., 1974.

U.S. Department of the Interior. *United States Energy through the Year 2000.* Study prepared by Walter Dupree and James A. West. Washington, D.C.: Government Printing Office, 1972.

U.S. Geological Survey. *Assessment of Geothermal Resources of the U.S.: 1975.* Circular no. 726. Study edited by D. E. White and D. L. Williams. Washington, D.C., 1975.

——. *Coal Resources of the United States.* Bulletin no. 1275. Study prepared by Paul Averitt. Washington, D.C.: Government Printing Office, 1967.

Winger, John G. et al. *Outlook for Energy in the United States to 1985.* New York: Chase Manhattan Bank, 1972.

ARTICLES

Adelman, Morris A. "American Import Policy and the World Oil Market." *Energy Policy* 1 (September 1973): 91-99.

——. "Foreign Oil: A Political-Economic Problem." *Technology Review* 76 (March-April 1974): 43-47.

——. "Is the Oil Shortage Real? Oil Companies as OPEC Tax Collectors." *Foreign Policy,* no. 9, winter 1972-73, pp. 69-107.

Akins, James E. "The Oil Crisis: This Time the Wolf Is Here." *Foreign Affairs* 51 (April 1973): 462-90.

"Alberta Looks to Oil Sands." *Petroleum Economist* 41 (August 1974): 288-91.

"All European Coal Crisis." *Petroleum Press Service,* April 1972, pp. 127-31.

Auer, P. L. "An Integrated National Energy Research and Development Program." *Science* 184 (April 19, 1974): 295-301.

Axtmann, Robert C. "Environmental Impact of a Geothermal Power Plant." *Science* 187 (March 7, 1975): 795-803.

"Back to the Windmill to Generate Power," *Business Week,* May 11, 1974, pp. 140-42.

Bailey, Richard. "The U.K. Coal Industry: Recent Past and Future." *Energy Policy,* June 1974, pp. 152-58.

Benedict, Manson. "Electric Power from Nuclear Fission." *Technology Review,* October-November 1971, pp. 32-41.

Berg, Charles A. "Conservation in Industry." *Science* 184 (April 19, 1974): 264-70.

Berg, R. R. et al. "Prognosis for Expanded U.S. Production of Crude Oil." *Science* 184 (April 19, 1974): 331-36.

Berkson, Harold, and Harry Perry. "Must Fossil Fuels Pollute?" *Technology Review,* December 1971, pp. 34-43.

"Blueprint for Europe." *Petroleum Press Service.* November 1972, pp. 403-05.

Boffey, Philip M. "Energy Research: A Harsh Critique Says Federal Effort May Backfire." *Science,* November 7, 1975, pp. 535-37.

"Bonn's Energy Program." *Petroleum Press Service.* October 1973, pp. 367-69.

"Boost for Nuclear Power." *Petroleum Press Service.* July 1971, pp. 247-48.

Bowen, Richard G., and Edward A. Groh. "Geothermal: Earth's Primordial Energy." *Technology Review,* October-November 1971, pp. 42-48.

Boyd, F. C. "Nuclear Power in Canada: A Different Approach." *Energy Policy,* June 1974, pp. 126-35.

"Britain's Energy Outlook." *Petroleum Economist* 41 (June 1974): 221-23.

"Britain's State Oil Proposals." *Petroleum Economist* 42 (May 1975): 163-65.

Bupp, Irvin C., and Jean Claude Derian. "The Breeder Reactor in the U.S.: A New Economic Analysis." *Technology Review,* July-August 1974, pp. 26-36.

Bylinsky, Gene. "KMS Industries Bets Its Life on Labor Fusion." *Fortune,* December 1974, pp. 149-56.

Calvin, Melvin. "Solar Energy by Photosynthesis." *Science* 184 (April 19, 1974): 375-81.

"Canada's Tar Sands Next." *Petroleum Press Service.* December 1972, pp. 451-53.

Carter, Luther J. "Solar and Geothermal Energy: New Competition for the Atom." *Science* 186 (November 29, 1974): 811-13.

Chapman, D. T. et al. "Electricity Demand Growth and the Energy Crisis." *Science* 178 (November 1972): 703-08.

"Closed Cycle MHD Potential Impressive." *Electrical World.* March 15, 1974, pp. 94-95.

"Coal: The Second Energy Crisis." *Business Week.* March 16, 1974, pp. 23-24.

Cochran, Thomas B.; J. Gustave Speth; and Arthur R. Tamplic. "Plutonium Recycle: The Fateful Step." *Bulletin of the Atomic Scientists,* November 1974, pp. 15-22.

Combs, James B. "The Geology and Geophysics of Geothermal Energy." *Technology Review* 77 (March/April 1975): 46-49.

"Complete Texts of New U.S. Action on Energy." *Petroleum Intelligence Weekly.* Supplements 1-3. April 23, 1973, pp. 1-32.

"Computer Study of Energy." *Petroleum Press Service.* January 1973, pp. 15-17.

"The Conservation of Energy." *Petroleum Press Service.* July 1973, pp. 255-59.

Cook, Earl. "The Flow of Energy in an Industrial Society." *Scientific American.* September 1971, pp. 135-44.

Davison, R. R., and W. D. Harris. "Methanol from Coal Can Be Competitive with Gasoline." *Oil and Gas Journal* 71 (December 17, 1973): 70-72.

Day, G. V. "The Prospects for Synthetic Fuels in the U.K." *Futures* 4 (December 1972): 331-43.

Dean, Genevieve C. "Energy in the People's Republic of China." *Energy Policy* 2 (March 1974): 33-54.

de Vries, Bert, and Jan Kommandeur. "Gas for Western Europe: How Much for How Long?" *Energy Policy* 3 (March 1975): 24-37.

Dienes, Leslie. "Geographical Problems of Allocation in the Soviet Fuel Supply." *Energy Policy,* June 1973, pp. 3-20.

Dunham, J. T.; C. Rampacek; and T. A. Henrie. "High-Sulfur Coal for Generating Electricity." *Science* 184 (April 19, 1974): 346-51.

Eastland, B. J., and William C. Cough. "Prospects of Fusion Power." *Scientific American.* February 1971, pp. 50-64.

"Economics of Nuclear Power." *Petroleum Press Service.* December 1971, pp. 461-63.

"EEC Energy Hopes Dimmed." *Petroleum Economist* 42 (November 1975): 404-07.

"Electricity Vs. Gasoline." *Petroleum Press Service.* September 1972, pp. 331-33.

Emmett, John L.; John Nuckolls; and Lowell Wood. "Fusion Power by Laser Implosion." *Scientific American* 230 (June 1974): 24-37.

"Energy Policy for Britain." *Petroleum Press Service.* October 1971, pp. 369-71.

"Europe's Energy Deficit." *Petroleum Press Service.* December 1972, pp. 445-48.

"Europe's Imports in Decline." *Petroleum Economist* 42 (November 1975): 421-23.

"Exports Fall as Revenues Soar." *Petroleum Economist* 42 (March 1975): 84-86.

Faltermayer, Edmund. "Clearing the Way for the New Age of Coal." *Fortune.* May 1974, pp. 215-19.

Farmanfarmaian, Khodadad et al. "How Can the World Afford OPEC Oil?" *Foreign Affairs* 53 (January 1975): 201-22.

"Ford's Energy Program." *Petroleum Economist* 42 (February 1975): 49-50.

"France Feels the Pinch." *Petroleum Economist* 41 (October 1974): 404-05.

"The FY 1976 Nuclear Budget." *Nuclear News.* March 1975, pp. 28-34.

"Gas Supply Problems Ahead." *Petroleum Economist* 41 (July 1974): 263-66.

Geiger, Robert E., and John D. Moody. "Petroleum Resources: How Much Oil and Where?" *Technology Review* 77 (March-April 1975): 39-45.

"Geothermal Growing as Power Source." *Electrical World.* June 1970.

Gillette, Robert. "Energy Reorganization: Progress in the Offing." *Science.* April 26, 1974, pp. 443-45.

————. "Laser Fusion: An Energy Option, But Weapons Simulation Is First." *Science* 188 (April 4, 1975): 30-34.

————. "Nuclear Safety (1): The Roots of Dissent." *Science.* September 1, 1972, pp. 771-76.

————. "Nuclear Safety (II): The Years of Delay." *Science.* September 8, 1972, pp. 867-71.

————. "Nuclear Safety (III). Critics Charge Conflict of Interest." *Science.* September 15, 1972, pp. 970-75.

————. "Nuclear Safety (IV): Barriers to Communication." *Science.* September 22, 1972, pp. 1,080-82.

————. "Nuclear Safety: AEC Report Makes the Best of It." *Science* 179 (January 26, 1973): 360-63.

————. "Nuclear Safety: Calculating the Odds of Disaster." *Science* 185 (September 6, 1974): 838-39.

————. "Oil and Gas Resources: Academy Call USGS Math 'Misleading.'" *Science* 187 (February 28, 1975): 723-27.

————. "Plutonium (1): Questions of Health in a New Industry." *Science* 185 (September 20, 1974): 1,030-31.

————. "Plutonium (II): Watching and Waiting for Adverse Effects." *Science* 185 (September 27, 1974).

Glaser, Peter. "Power from the Sun: Its Future." *Science* 162 (November 1968): 857-61.

Hafele, Wolf. "Energy Choices that Europe Faces: A European View of Energy." *Science* 184 (April 19, 1974): 360-67.

Hafele, Wolf, and Alan S. Manne. "Strategies for a Transition from Fossil to Nuclear Fuels." *Energy Policy* 3 (March 1975): 3-23.

Hambleton, M. W. "The Unsolved Problem of Nuclear Wastes." *Technology Review*. March-April 1972.

Hammond, A. L. "A Timetable for Expanded Energy Availability." *Science* 184 (April 19, 1974): 367-69.

Hammond, Ogden, and Martin B. Zimmerman. "The Economics of Coal-Based Synthetic Gas." *Technology Review* 78 (July-August 1975): 43-51.

Harleman, Donald R.F. "Heat: The Ultimate Waste." *Technology Review*. December 1971, pp. 44-51.

"Harnessing the Sun's Power." *Petroleum Press Service*. June 1972, pp. 212-13.

Hawkes, Nigel. "Energy in Britain: Shopping for a New Reactor." *Science* 183 (January 11, 1974): 57-59.

"Heat Pump Interest Grows Stronger." *Electrical World*. May 1, 1974, pp. 64-65.

Hogerton, John F. "U.S. Uranium Supply and Demand, Near Term and Long Range." *Nuclear News*, May 1975.

Hottel, Hoyt C., and Jack B. Howard. "An Agenda for Energy." *Technology Review*. January 1972, pp. 38-48.

Houthakker, H. S.; P. K. Verleger; and D. P. Sheean. "Dynamic Models of the Demand for Gasoline and Residual Electricity." *Journal of Agricultural Economics* 56 (May 1974): 412-18.

"How Much Oil Offshore?" *Petroleum Press Service*. September 1973, pp. 328-31.

"How Near Is Nuclear Fusion?" *Petroleum Press Service*. August 1973, pp. 295-97.

Howard, Peter R. "Electrical Transmission of Energy: Current Trends." *Energy Policy* 1 (September 1973): 154-60.

Hubbert, M. King. "The Energy Resources of the Earth." *Scientific American* 224 (September 1971): 61-70.

"Hydrogen as a Fuel." *Petroleum Press Service*. July 1972, pp. 253-55.

"In Energy Impasse, Conservation Keeps Popping Up." *Science* 187 (January 10, 1975): 42-45.

"Increasing Gas Turbine Outputs for Combined Gas/Steam Systems." *Technology Review*. December 1970.

"The International Energy Agency." *Petroleum Economist* 42 (May 1975): 173-74.

"Japan's Energy Prospects." *Petroleum Press Service.* June 1973, pp. 202-05.

"Japan's Nuclear Prospects." *Petroleum Press Service.* June 1971, pp. 209-11.

Joskow, Paul L., and Paul MacAvoy. "Regulation and the Financial Condition of the Electric Power Companies in the 1970s." *American Economic Review.* May 1975, pp. 295-301.

Katz, Milton. "Decision-Making in the Production of Power." *Scientific American* 224 (September 1971): 191-200.

Kinney, Gene T. "Project Independence: Is It Out of Reach for the U.S.?" *Oil and Gas Journal.* March 4, 1974, pp. 21-23.

Kulcinski, Gerald L. "Fusion Power: An Assessment of Its Potential Impact in the U.S.A." *Energy Policy,* June 1974.

Landsberg, Hans H. "Low-Cost, Abundant Energy: Paradise Lost?" *Science* 184 (April 9, 1974): 247-53.

Lantzke, Ulf. "The OECD and Its International Energy Agency." *Daedalus* 104 (fall 1975): 217-28.

Lapp, Ralph. "Nuclear Safety: The Public Debate." *New Scientist.* February 14, 1974, pp. 394-96.

"Large HTGR Enters Market." *Electrical World.* February 15, 1974, pp. 45-48.

Leach, Gerald. "The Impact of the Motor Car on Oil Reserves." *Energy Policy* 1 (December 1973): 195-207.

Lessing, Lawrence. "Capturing Clean Gas and Oil from Coal." *Fortune,* November 1973.

———. "New Ways to More Power with Less Pollution." *Fortune.* November 1970.

———. "Power from the Earth's Heat." *Fortune.* June 1969.

Levy, Walter J. "World Oil Cooperation or International Chaos." *Foreign Affairs* 52 (July 1974): 690-713.

Lidsky, Lawrence. "The Quest for Fusion Power." *Technology Review.* January 1972, pp. 10-21.

"Lignite Has Its Drawbacks—But It's Cheap." *Business Week.* March 16, 1974, pp. 102-6.

Loff, George O.G.; and Richard A. Tybout. "Cost of House Heating with Solar Energy." *Solar Energy* 14 (1973): 253-78.

———. "Solar House Heating." *Natural Resources Journal* 10 (1970).

"The Looming Oil Battle off the East Coast." *Business Week.* April 27, 1974, pp. 80-84.

Lovins, Amory B. "World Energy Strategies: Facts, Issues and Options." *Bulletin of the Atomic Scientists* 30 (May-June 1974): 14-32.

Lowe, William W. "Creating Power Plants." *Technology Review*. January 1972, pp. 25-30.

Mabro, Robert, and Elizabeth Monroe. "Arab Wealth from Oil: Problems of Its Investment." *International Affairs* 50 (January 1974): 15-27.

McAuley, R. "Enough Energy—If Resources are Allocated Right." *Business Week*. April 21, 1973, pp. 50-60.

MacAvoy, Paul W. "The Regulation-Induced Shortage of Natural Gas." In *Regulation of the Natural Gas Industry*, edited by M. Keith C. Brown. Baltimore: Resources for the Future, 1972.

MacAvoy, Paul W.; Bruce E. Stangle; and Jonathan B. Tepper. "The Federal Energy Office as Regulator of the Energy Crisis." *Technology Review* 77 (May 1975): 39-45.

MacAvoy, Paul W. et al. "The Economics of the Energy Crisis." *Technology Review* 76 (March-April 1974): 49-59.

Manne, Alan S., and Oliver S. Yu. "Breeder Benefits and Uranium Availability." *Nuclear News* 18 (January 1975): 46-52.

Massachusetts Institute of Technology Energy Laboratory, Policy Study Group. "Energy Self-Sufficiency: An Economic Evaluation." *Technology Review* 76 (May 1974): 22-58. 58.

Meadows, Dennis L.; Roger F. Naill; and John Stanley-Miller. "The Transition to Coal." *Technology Review* 78 (October/November 1975): 19-29.

"Methane from Coal." *Petroleum Press Service*. April 1971, pp. 141-42.

Metz, William D. "European Breeders (1): France Leads the Way." *Science* 190 (December 26, 1975): 1,279-81.

———. "Nuclear Fusion: The Next Big Step Will Be a Tokomak." *Science* 187 (February 7, 1975): 421-23.

———. "Uranium Enrichment: U.S. 'One Ups' European Centrifuge Effort." *Science* 183 (March 29, 1974): 1,270-72.

Mikdashi, Zuhayr. "The OPEC Process." *Daedalus* 184 (fall 1975): 203-17.

Morrow, Jr., Walter E. "Solar Energy: Its Time Is Near." *Technology Review* 76 (December 1973): 30-43.

"The Natural Gas Saga." *Petroleum Economist* 43 (March 1976): 84-86.

Nephew, Edmund A. "The Challenge and Promise of Coal." *Technology Review* 76 (December 1975): 20-29.

"The New Shape of the U.S. Oil Industry." *Business Week*. February 2, 1974, pp. 50-58.

"New U.S. Energy Policy." *Petroleum Press Service*. May 1973, pp. 164-66.

Nicholson, R.L.R. "The Nuclear Power Paradox in the U.K." *Energy Policy*. June 1973, pp. 38-46.

"Nine Million Barrels/Day from New Areas." *Petroleum Economist* 42 (February 1975).

Nordhaus, William D. "The Allocation of Energy Resources." *Brookings Papers on Economic Activity* 3 (1973): 529-76.

"Nuclear Reactor Safety." *Bulletin of the Atomic Scientists* 31 (September 1975): 15-42.

Odell, Peter. "Indigenous Oil and Gas Developments and Western Europe's Energy Policy Options." *Energy Policy* 1 (June 1973): 47-64.

——. "The North Sea Oil Province: A Simulation Model of Development." *Energy Policy*. December 1974, pp. 316-29.

"The Oil Crisis: In Perspective." *Daedalus* 104 (fall 1975).

"Oil in France's VIth Plan." *Petroleum Press Service*. August 1971, pp. 294-97.

"Oil Shale Economics Today." *World Petroleum*. May 1972, pp. 21-24.

Parker, Albert. "World Energy Resources: A Survey." *Energy Policy* 3 (March 1975).

Penrose, Edith. "The Development of Crisis." *Daedalus* 104 (fall 1975): 39-57.

Perry, Harry. "The Gasification of Coal." *Scientific American* 230 (March 1974): 19-25.

"Policy Proposals for Germany." *Petroleum Press Service*. July 1973, pp. 259-61.

"Policy-Making in Japan." *Petroleum Economist* 41 (October 1974): 369-71.

Pollack, Gerald A. "The Economic Consequences of the Energy Crisis." *Foreign Affairs* 52 (April 1974): 452-71.

Post, R.F., and F.L. Ribe. "Fusion Reactors as Future Energy Sources." *Science* 186 (November 1, 1974): 397-407.

Postma, Herman. "Engineering and Environmental Aspects of Fusion Power Reactors." *Nuclear News*. April 1971, pp. 57-62.

"Potential for Synthetic Oil." *Petroleum Press Service*. July 1973, pp. 249-51.

"Problems of Transition." *Petroleum Press Service*. July 1973, pp. 242-44.

"The Quest for U.S. Energy Sufficiency: National Mission for the 1970s." *Coal Age* 79 (April 1974).

"Reactor Core Cooling Hearings." *Energy Digest*. March 28, 1972, pp. 59-64.

"Reshaping Project Independence." *Petroleum Economist* 41 (October 1974): 405-8.

Rice, Richard A. "System Energy and Future Transportation." *Technology Review*. January 1972, pp. 31-37.

——. "Toward More Transportation with Less Energy." *Technology Review* 76 (February 1974): 45-53.

Robinson, Arthur L. "Energy Storage (I): Using Electricity More Efficiently." *Science* 184 (May 17, 1974): 785-87.

Robson, Geoffrey. "Geothermal Electricity Production." *Science* 184 (April 19, 1974): 371-74.

Rose, David J. "Controlled Nuclear Fusion: Status and Outlook." *Science*. May 21, 1971, pp. 797-808.

——. "Energy Policy in the U.S." *Scientific American* 230 (January 1974): 20-29.

——. "Nuclear Electric Power." *Science* 184 (April 19, 1974): 351-59.

"Safeguarding Europe's Supplies." *Petroleum Economist*. May 1974, pp. 166-69.

Sakisaka, Masao. "Japan's Energy Policy Under Review." *Energy Policy* 2 (December 1974): 346-49.

——. "World Energy Problems and Japan's International Role." *Energy Policy* 1 (September 1973): 100-06.

Schuler, George H.M. "The International Oil 'Debacle' since 1971." *Petroleum Intelligence Weekly*. Supplement. April 22, 1974, pp. 1-36.

Simonet, Henri. "Energy and the Future of Europe." *Foreign Affairs* 53 (April 1975): 450-63.

Sloeum, Marianna P. "Soviet Energy: An Internal Assessment." *Technology Review* 77 (October/November 1974): 16-33.

Smernoff, Barry J. "Energy Policy Interactions in the United States." *Energy Policy* 1 (September 1973): 136-53.

Smith, A. Robert. "ERDA: The New Glamour Agency." *Bulletin of the Atomic Scientists* 31 (January 1975): 29-31.

"South Africa Relies on Coal." *Petroleum Economist* 41 (July 1974): 257-59.

Spaak, Fernand. "An Energy Policy for the European Community." *Energy Policy* 1 (June 1973): 35-37.

Squires, Arthur M. "Capturing Sulfur During Combustion." *Technology Review*. December 1971, pp. 52-59.

———. "Clean Fuels from Coal Gasification." *Science* 184 (April 19, 1974): pp. 340-46.

Stauffer, T.R. "Oil Money and World Money: Conflict or Confluence?" *Science* 184 (April 19, 1974): 321-25.

Stevenson, Adlai E., III. "Nuclear Reactors: America Must Act." *Foreign Affairs* 50 (October 1974): 64-76.

Stobaugh, Robert B. "The Oil Companies in the Crisis." *Daedalus* 104 (fall 1975): 179-202.

Summers, Claude M. "The Conversion of Energy." *Scientific American*. September 1971, pp. 149-60.

Surrey, A.J. "The Future Growth of Nuclear Power: Part I. Demand and Supply." *Energy Policy* 1 (September 1973): 107-29.

———. "The Future Growth of Nuclear Power: Part II. Choices and Obstacles." *Energy Policy* 1 (December 1973): 208-24.

Surrey, John. "Japan's Uncertain Energy Prospects: The Problem of Import and Dependence." *Energy Policy* 2 (September 1974): 204-30.

Surrey, John, and William Walker. "Energy R & D: A U.K. Perspective." *Energy Policy* 3 (June 1975): 90-115.

"Sweden Opts for Low Energy Use." *Petroleum Economist* 42 (May 1975): 169-70.

Tantraum, A.D.S. "Fuel Cells: Past, Present and Future." *Energy Policy*. March 1974, pp. 55-66.

"Towards a European Policy." *Petroleum Press Service*. June 1972, pp. 198-99.

"Towards Pollution-Free Gasoline." *Petroleum Economist* 42 (November 1975): 425-27.

Tsurumi, Yoshi. "Japan." Symposium on "The Oil Crisis: In Perspective." *Daedalus* 104 (fall 1975): pp. 113-28.

Tugendhat, Christopher. "Financing the Future of Oil." *Banker* 122 (April 1972): 465-79.

Turner, Louis. "Politics of the Energy Crisis." *International Affairs* 50 (July 1974): 404-15.

"Turning Point for Japan." *Petroleum Press Service*. February 1973, pp. 48-51.

"Two-Thirds Left in the Ground." *Petroleum Press Service*. October 1971, pp. 367-69.

"U.K. Energy Perspective." *Petroleum Press Service*. February 1973, pp. 57-59.

"U.S. Coal-to-Gas Process Is Ready." *Oil and Gas Journal*. September 9, 1974, pp. 86-88.

"U.S. Eyes the Continental Shelf." *Petroleum Economist* 41 (August 1974): 299-301.

"Uranium Enrichment: Rumors of Israeli Progress with Lasers." *Science* 183 (March 22, 1974): 1,172-74.

Wade, Nicholas. "Windmills: The Resurrection of an Ancient Energy Technology." *Science* 184 (June 7, 1974): 1,055-58.

Walsh, John. "European Community Energy Policy: Regulation or Mainly Information." *Science* 184 (June 14, 1974): 1,158-61.

———. "Problems of Expanding Coal Production." *Science* 184 (April 19, 1974): 336-39.

West, Jim. "Drive Finally Building in U.S. to Develop Oil Shale." *Oil and Gas Journal*. February 25, 1974, pp. 15-19.

"West German Energy Outlook." *Petroleum Economist* 42 (June 1975): 207-09.

White, David C. "Energy, the Economy and the Environment." *Technology Review*. October-November 1971, pp. 18-31.

———. "The Energy-Environment-Economic Triangle." *Technology Review* 76 (December 1973): 10-19.

———. "The U.S. Energy Crisis: A Scientist's View." *Energy Policy* 1 (September 1973): 130-35.

Wilson, Carroll. "A Plan for Energy Independence." *Foreign Affairs* 51 (July 1973): 657-75.

Wilson, R. "The AEC and the Loss of Coolant Accident." *Nature*. 1973.

Wolf, M. "Solar Utilization by Physical Methods." *Science* 184 (April 19, 1974): 382-86.

"World Energy Patterns." *Petroleum Press Service*. April 1973, pp. 138-39.

"World Oil and Gas Resources." *Petroleum Economist* 42 (June 1975): 203-5.

"Worldwide Energy Outlook to 1985." *Oil and Gas Journal*. November 12, 1973, pp. 119-32.

Wright, Arthur W. "Contrasts in Soviet and American Energy Policies." *Energy Policy* 3 (March 1975): 38-46.

PERIODICALS

While I have attempted to individually identify any articles that were particularly useful in the preparation of this book, the following periodicals generally provide excellent coverage of developments in energy-related fields:

Chemical and Engineering News (Washington, D.C.)
Coal Age (New York)
Electrical World (New York)

Energy Policy (Guildford, England)
Middle East Economic Digest (London)
Middle East Economic Survey (Beirut)
Nuclear Industry (New York)
Nuclear News (New York)
Oil and Gas Journal (Tulsa, Okla.)
Petroleum Economist (formerly *Petroleum Press Service*) (London)
Petroleum Intelligence Weekly (New York)
Science (Washington, D.C.)
Technology Review (Cambridge, Mass.)

JOHN HAGEL III is currently enrolled in a joint MBA-JD program at Harvard Law School and Harvard Business School. After completing undergraduate studies at Wesleyan University, he received a B.Phil. in Modern Middle Eastern Studies at Oxford University. He has worked with the international Public Affairs department of Mobil Oil Corporation and has also worked in the Middle East as a consultant in the negotiation of government contracts.

RELATED TITLES
Published by
Praeger Special Studies

*THE UNITED STATES AND INTERNATIONAL OIL:
A Report for the Federal Energy Administration on
U.S. Firms and Government Policy
Robert B. Krueger

THE PRICING OF CRUDE OIL: Economic and
Strategic Guidelines for an International Energy
Policy (expanded and updated edition)
Taki Rifai

ARAB OIL: Impact on the Arab Countries and
Global Implications
edited by Naiem A. Sherbiny
and Mark A. Tessler

*THE ENERGY CRISIS AND U.S. FOREIGN POLICY
edited by Joseph S. Szyliowicz
and Bard E. O'Neill

ENERGY, INFLATION, AND INTERNATIONAL
ECONOMIC RELATIONS: Atlantic Institute Studies—II
Curt Gasteyger, Louis Camu,
and Jack N. Behrman

---

*Also available in paperback as a PSS Student Edition.